The Cross in the Closet

The Cross in the Closet

One man's abominable
quest to find Jesus
in the margins

Timothy Kurek

BlueHead
Publishing

Copyright © 2012 Timothy Kurek

Visit at timothykurek.com

Published in the United States by BlueHead Publishing, LLC.

BLUEHEAD PUBLISHING and colophon are registered trademarks of BlueHead Publishing, LLC

Visit at blueheadpublishing.com

Library of Congress Cataloging-in-Publication Data
Kurek, Timothy.
The cross in the closet: one man's abominable quest to find jesus in the margins / by Timothy Kurek
p. cm.
ISBN 978-0-9835677-4-5 (alk. paper)
LCCN 2012947790
1. Gay--Social aspects. 2. Gay. 3. Christian.

Printed in the United States of America on acid-free paper.

First Edition

Book & Cover Design by Dave Thompson

For Marissa.

For your inspiration to "write it down."

endorsements

"Tim Kurek has written a book that could be described as 'spiritual espionage.' As a young fundamentalist, he goes undercover—accepting all the attendant moral and personal ambiguities—and gathers 'intelligence' that few heterosexual people have ever had access to. He tells his story with skill and grace, revealing secrets that need to be heard from where he began (Liberty University) to wherever you are. A one-of-a-kind book with unforgettable moral impact."

—Brian D. McLaren, Author, Speaker: *A New Kind of Christianity*; *Why Did Jesus, Moses, the Buddha, and Mohammed Cross the Road?*

"It took great courage and serious commitment for Timothy Kurek to begin his year long journey into our world, the world of lesbian, gay, bisexual and transgender Americans. I'm delighted that readers of *The Cross in the Closet* will gain a whole new understanding of the stereotypes and untruths that cause my sisters and brothers so much suffering. I hope many will standby this straight ally and support the message found in his book, the message that says God truly does love us all. I encouraged him to take this journey and now that it's over I will stand by him still. I admire Timothy's courage and creativity, and his journey into our world will make a difference! You go, Tim!"

—Mel White, Author, *Stranger at the Gate*

"I hope Tim's voice echoes through the halls of every Mc-Mansion church until Christian hubris is humbled. Fundamentalist arrogance is today threatening a religion founded foremost on empathy and love. *The Cross in the Closet* serves as a blunt reminder and should be a wake up call to every closeted bigot that dares to thump a bible."

—Greg Barrett, Author, *The Gospel of Rutba: Christians, Muslims, and the Good Samaritan Story in Iraq*

"*The Cross in the Closet* is the book I've been waiting for. Now—at last—I have the book to give to every person I know (and there are many) struggling to understand how and why so-called Christians hate gay men and women and what to do about changing their minds. Kurek writes movingly and well. This is the best book I've read that opens the door to understanding what it is like to be labeled gay and trapped in a community that dismisses your very self before even hearing you out. Brilliant!"

—Frank Schaeffer, Author, *Crazy For God*

table of contents

about my title

I believe everyone has a calling in their life. A purpose. A cause. Something unique that gives the mundane, meaning. During my two decades in the conservative church every pastor of every church I attended spoke about finding that purpose. They referred to our callings as our cross to bear. The image conjured was a gruesome sight to behold: bloody flesh nailed to slick timber, stained red. Finding your cross isn't about finding happiness, they said. It's about our search for meaning.

I too believe we all have our crosses to bear...

I just never realized I would find my cross in the closet.

foreword

It has taken me a lifetime to come out of the closet. And I'm gay. I have witnessed first hand the positive and negative responses some have expressed toward my friend Tim for his "coming out" experiment—I for one think him to be a hero.

He is a hero because he sought to understand the thing he once loathed. How many of us are big enough to even consider that possibility, much less spend a year of our lives, our reputations and emotional capital living the role of our former foe—in an effort to understand.

The *Cross in the Closet* has great potential to help many followers of Jesus who are concerned by the thought of appearing to condone "the lifestyle" of the homosexual person. Many fear that it will put their gay friend's soul in eternal peril, or moreover, put their own soul in hell for not having stood for righteousness.

Jesus asked us to follow the greatest commands of all: To love; to love our God and to love our neighbor as we love ourselves. Jesus' story of the Good Samaritan makes it very clear what he would think of the religious and pious, who would have nothing to do with the enemy outcast left bleeding and dying by the road. Jesus gave us permission to love the outcast. His story compels us to care for the outsider—in point of fact, the one who did so was the hero of the story.

If you are struggling with the "gay thing" this book is for you. Look through the eyes of one who has learned to love those he hated—those "fags" who are God's beloved sons and daughters. They are the one's we will one day need to give an account for—an explanation for our decision to leave them bleeding and dying along side the road.

This could be your year of living and loving dangerously. Just like Timothy did. Just like Jesus did.

—James Alexander Langteaux, Author, *Gay Conversations with God*

author's note

If I have learned anything in my brief time on this planet, it is that people are imperfect. No one has it all figured out. In the same way people aren't perfect, books aren't perfect. This book isn't. It is messy and limited, as I am messy and limited. So before you begin this book, let me clarify a few points of imperfection, if for no other reason than so you might read past its flaws to the heart of the message I am sharing.

I am speaking about a very sensitive issue. I would even wager to say that it is the most heated social issue of our day. I want to make clear that I am not an expert in lesbian, gay, bisexual, or transgendered issues. I haven't spent years with my nose buried in books, studying every nuance of LGBT culture, history, or community. I am not a professor, a theologian, or an expert in anything other than my own personal journey...but I have learned a lot from my experiences. If you are looking for highly detailed answers to the intellectual questions you may have regarding LGBT issues, there are many people more qualified than me out there you could ask instead.

I frequently use terminology that is technically incorrect. To refer to the "gay community," for instance, is to relegate that populace to a monolithic entity. It is as technically incorrect as the "straight community." People are diverse and communities are diverse, so when I use that term, don't shutter. I also sometimes use the word gay instead of LGBT, for the same reason. The LGBT spectrum is as diverse as any other, including the "Christian community," so read this book with that diversity in mind.

I also want to stress that this is not a book about being gay. I am fundamentally unqualified to write that book. Instead this book is about the label of gay and how the consequences of that label shaped and changed my life.

What this book is really about is prejudice: specifically, *my* prejudice. In traditional orthodox Christianity, one repents before salvation becomes possible. To repent means to turn away. In order to repent of my past sins, I had to acknowledge what my sins ultimately were, and I have done my best not to hold back, not to try to whitewash who I used to be to make myself look better than I was. An author friend once told me to write what scares me; this book is a result of that sage advice.

I hope this book speaks to you. Thank you for picking it up and reading it. No matter what you believe, know that I love you.

Your friend,

Timothy Kurek

Part I: Genesis

"We don't see things as they are,
we see them as we are."

—Anais Nin

0 in the beginning

Spring 2009: Four months into the project

The protest sign in my hands feels awkward, surreal, as I stand in the vigil line. Rain drenches my sweatshirt and jeans, and the cold makes it difficult to feel my body. I am in lower Manhattan, protesting with a group of Soulforce activists outside the Vatican's embassy to the United Nations. The knot in my stomach is the result of nerves and intense culture shock, but still I stand here in the rain, holding my red, octagonal sign to my chest. The morale of the group is waning: my new friends stand silent like statues against the backdrop of the booming metropolis. Matthew, one of the leaders of the group, sings "We Shall Overcome," his pleasant tenor fighting the sense of hopelessness we all seem to feel as we look at the vacant building across the street. Chris and Bryan join in, and I feel all the more awkward because I can't. I do not know the words. I know the words to hymns and many contemporary praise songs, but not protest songs.

This particular protest is small, from what the others have told me; there are just under thirty of us here. But it seems intimate, passionate, a last stand against an ideal no one here supports. Not even me, anymore.

Until I got to New York City, I did not even know the Vatican has an embassy to the United Nations, but here I am. The gates are barred and locked like the doorway to a prison, but we can see inside. The letters on the lobby wall read *The Path to Peace*. This very morning, the Vatican vetoed a bill in the UN that would decriminalize homosexuality across the globe. Why?

So some countries can go on killing or imprisoning gay people just for their orientation? Until I found myself standing on this corner earlier this morning, I didn't know that people were still killed for being gay. My eyes are fixed on the lobby wall, on the word *peace*, and I am sure of one thing: I hate this building—because this building reminds me of me.

I'm out of place. Unbeknownst to everyone around me, I am heterosexual. I am a conservative fundamentalist Christian, undercover for a year, questioning everything I have been taught about the label of *gay*.

Matthew finishes the song and again reverent silence falls upon the group. And it is in this silence that I remember the last time I was at a Soulforce protest.

It was four years ago to the month. And back then, Soulforce was my enemy.

The birth of doubt: Four years earlier

I entered Liberty University—the evangelical equivalent of West Point—four years earlier, in 2004, and became what the students affectionately call a "Jerry's Kid." As a student, I was expected to follow a lengthy code of conduct called the *Liberty Way*; my parents were thrilled, encouraging me to become what the brochures had promised, a "Champion for Christ." And that was when I first encountered Soulforce—the lesbian, gay, queer, and transgendered (LBGT) civil rights group. The young Soulforce activists were an odd-looking bunch, all waiting to embark on their first freedom ride across the country. The campus at Liberty was to serve as their training ground, a gauntlet of dogma they would have to overcome in order to make the trip.

Jerry Falwell—president and founder of LU, and also a famous televangelist—warned us about Soulforce, briefing us on the "real threat": their amoral, degenerate leader, Mel White. He spoke of Mel's "agenda" as if it were some master plot to invade Christendom with machine guns and rocket launchers.

From the way Jerry described him, Mel might as well have been a gay Rambo. Jerry spoke more passionately about this man than almost any other I had heard him speak against, and his words felt more personally motivated. I was skeptical that this Mel White character was any worse than any other liberal activist I had watched on cable news.

I walked outside the arena where convocation (a mandatory biweekly chapel service) was held, that sunny spring morning, with my own agenda, and I found a small cluster of the young Soulforce activists about twenty strong. They seemed like normal college kids, but I knew better. I'd been taught to be wary of gays. They were all HIV-positive perverts, and liberal pedophiles. I saw my hall-mate, Patrick, already engaged in an intense debate with an activist, but it wasn't going well. He was losing. Badly.

"So you aren't supposed to love your neighbor as yourself?" The young man challenging my friend was tall and awkward looking, and his tone was even and delicate. It didn't take long to figure out that he was letting Patrick make all of the mistakes. A worthy adversary.

"Well," Patrick was saying. "I mean…Yes, but we are supposed to…That is to say, we are supposed to…"

Both sides of the crowd shook their heads disapprovingly. I decided to answer the young man's question.

"Yes, we are supposed to love our neighbor," I said, "but sometimes loving people means telling them how evil their decisions are." My voice caught the young man's attention and he smiled at me, welcoming me into the conversation. Patrick melted gratefully into the crowd and disappeared. Coward.

"But we can't judge the heart. We have to love and accept people for who they are, without motives." His voice was laced with something I couldn't put my finger on. It made me uneasy. I had learned early on in religious debates that it was my job to control the conversation, and I wanted him to answer *my* questions. I was not going to get pulled into a debate over queer rights.

"Why exactly are you guys here?" I said. "Picking fights doesn't seem to be the best way of communicating with someone who disagrees with you."

"We are fighting for the rights of our friends who attend this college even though they're gay. We're their voice because they can't speak up." He was trying to humanize those I didn't see as human, but it would not work. They were abominations, every last one of them, and I would not be bullied by a fag lover who was most likely a faggot himself.

"They should leave, then!" I said. "This is *our* campus, a *Christian* campus. They should've known better than to even apply." My face was flushed.

"That's not true. They should be able to come and learn here with just as much freedom as anyone else. It's wrong to exclude them just because they're gay."

I looked over my shoulder and noticed that another dozen or so students had walked up to listen to my conversation. The attention was empowering and addictive, even, like a drug.

"That's their choice, and it's mine to not want to be around them. And you're not even representing them, anyway—you're promoting that adulterous homo Mel White, and the break-down of the traditional moral family. You guys are wasting your time."

The oohs and ahs behind me began to fuel my pride. I was doing it! I was being a *Champion for Christ*! My parents would be so proud.

"What's your name, brother?" His tone was even softer this time.

"That's really none of your business, and we aren't brothers. You've chosen to be an enemy of God…and that makes you my enemy too." The words, once spoken, elicited a stranger mixture of feelings.

"I just want you to know something, whatever your name is: I love you and I'm sorry you have such negative feelings about me and my friends." And at that moment, something inside of me broke, and I felt sick to my stomach. "I really do," he said.

His empathy wasn't a lie. Knowing that I believed him bothered me. No, it more than bothered me. It *infuriated* me. I didn't want to have anything in common with him because he was my opposite. I was a child of God, and he wasn't. We played for very different teams.

"Repent, and trust in God to heal you of your sin," I said. "I'm not going to waste any more of my time." Knowing I couldn't say anything else, I walked away, only stopping to reluctantly shake the hands of a few fellow students who supported my botched attempt to be a Champion for Christ.

As I crossed the street and walked up a few steps towards my New Testament Survey course, I felt an intense burden. Was my anger justified, or was it purely hubris? Should I have acted so offensively? Shouldn't I have spoken with the same softness of voice that my enemy had? Was I even justified in thinking him an enemy? Something wasn't right, and I did not know what it was. I had gone out there to teach Soulforce a lesson, and instead I had been talked down like a child. I sympathized with Patrick.

For the next two months the scene outside the arena replayed in my mind, and no matter how much I thought about it, I could not put my finger on why I felt such anger. I had done exactly as I had always been instructed: I fought for the truth and for my values, without compromise. Why did I feel so guilty? A few months later, my parents got a divorce, and I was needed at home. I left and never went back to Liberty.

~~~

A lot has changed since that first encounter four years ago. The octagonal sign in my hand is proof enough of that. It reads *Stop*

Spiritual Violence. I wonder what I look like to the crowds of people passing by on their way to work in the morning rain. Several police officers are posted on either side of our group now, the hissing of their radios making me nervous. I am the stranger here, the awkward seeker disguised by a label that does not belong to me…But it is in that awkwardness that my perspective is being challenged. That voice inside of me that rose so violently during my first encounter with Soulforce is finally being silenced.

Just last night I was taught the principles of non-violent protests for the first time, and I cannot fathom how different my life would be if protests were a regular part of it. I feel naked and vulnerable, like the whole of Manhattan sees through me, judges me, judges all of us, for better or for worse. But even in the midst of this tension, New York is beautiful to me. I am shocked at how beautiful it is, even in the freezing rain.

For a kid raised in the heart of the Bible Belt, this experience is beyond alien. The growing presence of police standing around and in front of us becomes more unnerving by the minute. I am told that we might be arrested, depending on how far we take our protest, and the thought scares me. It scares me, but it doesn't seem to scare anyone else standing with me. They have all been arrested before for actions similar to this one, and it makes me wonder: Would I allow myself to be arrested for my beliefs? If I didn't, would that make me a phony?

Mel White's assistant, Lindsey Hawkins, stands next to me, bubbly as always. Her smile is infectious and I love it. I watch her eyes dart back and forth from the female detective several yards away to the cops in front of the embassy's courtyard. She has a crush on the lieutenant. If I were not in the closet, I probably would, too.

"You like her, don't you?" I whisper out of the corner of my mouth, smiling.

"Shut up! I do not!" Lindsey hits me on the shoulder.

"Non-violence, my ass!" I say, trying not to be too disruptive. She is a magnificent girl. Too bad she's gay.

Lindsey has become my Yoda over the past twenty-four hours, and every time she speaks I feel compelled to listen. For being so young, she commands a passion that I have never seen before—a passion for the cause of equal rights, and for her faith. It is yet another thing I admire but find disconcerting at the same time. Looking through the lens of my past, everything now seems amiss, and I cannot fully embrace it.

Matthew begins another protest song, probably because Lindsey and I are having a difficult time maintaining silence. She looks at me and I mime a kissing face in the direction of the lieutenant.

"I'm going to kill you!" She laughs as the rest of the protesters begin singing.

Fall 2006: The doubt grows

My religion began changing and deteriorating in the two years after leaving Liberty. I still played the part of the dutiful Pharisee, however, even as I began seeing holes in my own theology. Those holes made me feel like an apostate. How could I doubt what I had always *known* to be absolute truth? I hid my skepticism well, attending and even serving at several churches near my home—but I knew the charade would eventually have to end, and I would have to question everything I'd been taught. It was an overhaul I wasn't looking forward to...an overhaul that began when I accepted an invitation to a karaoke bar near downtown Nashville. It was an odd place to find answers.

I was a twenty-year-old bigot, pacing back and forth outside of the trashiest dive bar I had ever laid eyes on. Pacing with me was Josh, my best friend, matching my stride step for step.

"But, Tim, you have to come!" he said, urging me toward the door.

Over the past twenty-four hours, Josh had been building this place up as a quasi-magical venue. "A place of wonder and enchantment," he had called it. "You haven't seen karaoke until you've seen a three-hundred-pound bull-dyke singing 'Muskrat Love' to her partner!"

"Bull-dyke?" I asked. "*Partner*? You've got to be kidding me!"

"Oh…" He paused. "Did I forget to mention that we've nicknamed Tuesday night karaoke *Lesbaoke*?"

My inner Pharisee came barking to the surface, but I could not say no to Josh's enthusiasm and reluctantly agreed.

The little dive bar had once been ranked by a reputable music magazine as the thirteenth-dingiest bar in the country, but in truth, it was nothing short of beautiful. Walking in for the first time with Josh, I remember my eyes watering as they adjusted to the smoke and my nose to the smell of cheap beer. I felt wildly uncomfortable. It was a simple-looking establishment, an old house converted into a speakeasy during the Prohibition. The décor was characterized by the beer signs of a bygone era, and the aged neon lights in the front window glowed so dimly I wondered why anyone bothered even turning them on. The elderly bar stools wobbled, their weight shifting back and forth as people sat on them, drinking, ignorant of the stories these antique seats could tell. Unlike most bars, this one served only beer, and it was cheap. Behind the bar I only saw three taps, their light brown wooden handles labeled with masking tape, nozzles dripping the cool amber liquid that I had, at this point, only twice allowed myself to taste. In the middle of the front room a pool table stood, well used. Though it too looked to be on its last leg, two gentlemen played with Zen-like concentration, enjoying it as if it was a woman. A classy woman. A dame, even.

I looked back over at Josh and he smiled, obviously in his element. Within seconds of our entrance people began greeting us with hugs and hellos. It was a shock. The feeling of acceptance rushed over me like a tidal wave that I had not seen coming. Before I sat down, seventeen people had introduced themselves. I was staring at them, tongue tied and grinning like a real moron. On stage, a man announced as "Pimp Daddy Supreme" belted out a classic Steely Dan song, while another man wearing a black leather hat adorned with a skull and crossbones toggled the lights on and off, and played air guitar as needed.

"That's Bad Boy Breeze," Josh said, pointing to the man in the black hat. "I work with him at Wal-Mart."

"I thought he looked familiar," I said, having visited Josh at work countless times.

"Tim, in this place, everyone is familiar." He patted me on the back reassuringly, sensing my discomfort. "It's magic, isn't it?"

I didn't know how to respond.

At the end of the night, I left, confused. Not just confused but overwhelmed. The people I met had sunk into me somehow, becoming a part of me. I felt protective of them.

"No one ever told you growing up that queers and atheists are actually loving people?" Josh asked, smiling, as we walked out the door. The derogatory labels jumped out in a way they hadn't before.

"No," I answered, shaking my head. I thought about the young activist who told me he loved me, and it occurred to me again that he had really been honest. My head didn't stop shaking the entire way home.

Summer 2008: Doubt perfected

Two years passed quickly after the first time I found myself in that little bar, and I spent those two years attending *Lesbaoke* more faithfully, even, than church. I had found a new home, where everyone was the epitome of loving, and where the voice inside of me was forced into silence. The regulars at that bar became a family of sorts, tied together by something stronger than blood: a combination of cheap beer and the rocking hits of the

'70s, '80s, and '90s. And while those were two of the best years of my life, they were also two of the hardest. In our dive, I became a witness to countless victims of my kind of religion. None of them spoke negatively of God; it was always the Christians who'd maligned them. I was not as outspoken a Christian as I had been in the past, at least not at karaoke, but these instances of hurt I witnessed made me feel guilty, and I did not know why.

"Tim, can we talk for a minute?" The tug on my sleeve was delicate and dainty. Elizabeth, a fairly recent newcomer, looked upset, and I nodded yes and followed her onto the covered patio in the back.

"What's up?"

Her face looked fluid, like she was a shape-shifter, barely able to hold her form.

"How can you be a Christian?" Her voice was shaky, and I could see she was falling apart. "How *can* you, and still be so happy to be here? I don't know any Christians that would be. They'd shun this place like it was contaminated. *Fuck!*" She stomped her foot and lowered her eyes.

"Their loss," I said. "Lizzy, what's wrong?"

Looking up at me through watery eyes, she said, "I came out to my family yesterday…" Tears began rolling down the softness of her cheeks. I knew she was on the verge of a breakdown.

"What? What happened?"

She reached up to wipe her eyes, allowing the sleeves of her sweater to slide down her wrists, and I could see that the silky white skin of her hands had already been stained by what I could only guess was smeared eyeliner. She had been crying a lot, apparently.

"My dad told me to get my stuff out of his house, and that he wouldn't pay another dime for the education of a 'faggot daughter'! And my mom told me to come back when I was 'fixed'…" Her face found my shoulder, and my arms wrapped around her comparatively tiny body. She felt delicate, like papier-mâché that had not fully dried and was still soft to the touch.

I betrayed her, then. Without even thinking, I betrayed the soft creature crying endlessly on my shoulder.

It was a subtle betrayal, but a cruel one: I was silent.

She did her best to compose herself. "Now I have to leave. I'm moving to a friend's. She's my only friend that my dad doesn't have any control over. I'm going to Texas tomorrow…" Her voice trailed off.

Tell her what Leviticus says about homosexuality. Read her Romans 1! Go on, Tim, it is your responsibility as a follower of Christ to help her see the error of this choice. The voice inside me had a distinct tone. It didn't sound like me. It didn't even sound like it knew me, yet it was powerful and opportunistic. It was a voice of rejection, telling me to reject Elizabeth. I realized that I hated Lizzy. Not because she was a bad person, but because she liked other women. That one facet to her being was enough to spark remarkable animosity toward her, animosity I could not comprehend.

The Bible tells us to love one another as ourselves. How could this voice be Jesus? And if this voice wasn't Jesus, what voice was it? Whatever it was speaking to me, I knew it wasn't guiding me in love, and that could only mean one thing. The voice had to die.

Elizabeth left the bar with tears still in her eyes, but they were tears of goodbye, not anger at my lack of understanding. Had she been oblivious to my inner turmoil? I stood silently, staring blankly at the door she had just walked out of. The din from a Styx song caught my ear but not my attention. Nothing could steal my attention; gut-wrenching feelings of shame brought tears to the corners of my eyes. I found my way to a booth and sat down.

And that's when I saw him for the first time, sitting across the table from me, smirking like a schoolyard bully. He looked like me, dressed in khakis and a black button-up shirt, but he seemed to bleed arrogance. I wiped my eyes and shivered.

"Who are you?"

Why didn't you tell Liz the truth? Why did you waste an opportunity to help her see her choice for the sin that it is?

I felt heat. It began in my toes and moved slowly upwards.

Cat got your tongue?

"You can't be serious. I hurt her enough with my silence! I should have held her, cried with her, loved her, but I didn't. That wasn't Jesus."

How do you know it wasn't Jesus? Sure, Jesus died for her sins just like anyone else, but she's not His child. You were right to think what you were thinking. Go get your Bible—there's still time to run after her.

I felt his words in my bones, in the very marrow of my bones. He was manipulative. He felt wrong. I felt like I had that day at Liberty, standing off against Soulforce.

Someone had to say what Patrick couldn't.

That day broke my heart. *I* was supposed to be the one who loved, not the one that rejected a group of people because they were gay. I was wrong to offer such empty condemnation. I should have disagreed differently.

No, you weren't wrong. You just weren't committed enough.

I shook my head and wiped the sweat from my forehead. No, I wasn't right. I had not been right then, and my condemning silence with Liz wasn't right, either. The memories of my theological instruction flashed through my mind like images on a television. But I didn't see myself in these images; I saw the condemnatory creature, the Pharisee, who sat across from me.

And then it dawned on me, and a weight lifted from my shoulders: *I might have been wrong all along.*

The figure across from me shook his head, judging my thoughts as quickly as I thought them. But the Pharisee's finger was fixed, pointing cruelly at me. I stood up, but he remained seated, smirking. I was repulsed. I had to get rid of him.

You can't.

I had to! Something drastic needed to happen, something that would test my beliefs on a foundational level…And then it came to me: Walk in Liz's shoes—the shoes of the very people I had been taught to hate. Live with the label of *gay*.

The implications of the idea were overwhelming. To do so would ruin my life. But what kind of life did I have, if such a barrier existed between me and the people I knew I should love? I felt the idea growing, rooting itself in me, like the decision had already been made, and I could almost see the path that was in front of me. I was meant for this. It was a calling I neither wanted nor understood, but I could not ignore the overwhelming sense of divine affirmation in it.

I needed to come out of the closet as a gay man.

1 coming out, into the closet

January 1st, 2009

My brother's face betrays concern, and it seems impossible to force the words from my mouth. He's not just concerned, he's worried. Each second passes as if time has been slowed, almost to a stop. My thoughts race incoherently, and my mission appears only in glimpses before diving back beneath the chaotic surface of my consciousness.

Andrew and I share similar features, but we are opposites in stature and personality. Whereas I am the typical husky American, my brother appears carved from marble. The lines of his face angle downward and his eyes are an expressive blue. He is confused. Years of learning have taught me to understand, at least, his mannerisms.

Over the past three months, I've stood in front of my bedroom mirror and practiced the speech, for this exact moment, no less than five thousand times, and I thought I had it memorized. But fear has wiped my memory of anything I hoped to say. My palms are sweaty, and even though it is the middle of winter, a bead of sweat forms on the crease of my forehead. I feel nauseated, my stomach a pot left unwatched and about to boil over. No amount of preparation could have prepared me for the moment that I look my only brother in the eyes and tell him I am gay.

My sister-in-law, a recent addition to the family, stands next to her husband in the kitchen of their house, rubbing his back empathetically. She eyes him protectively, bracing herself for the moment I finally speak.

The second hand on the clock above the entryway reaches each marker with the force of a hammer strike. The dog drinks loudly from his bowl, lapping up water with a curled tongue and an animated jerk of his head. Friends are on the covered porch nearby, smoking cigarettes and laughing about something, I wish I knew what. The dishwasher clicks, switching cycles on the first load of dirty dishes from our pancake breakfast. Loads two, three, and four are stacked neatly in the sink; leftover syrup drips over the edge of the top plate. I feel my subconscious preparing for another attempt at my speech.

Still nothing audible escapes my lips. I cannot speak. Finally, out of nowhere, it happens.

"I'm gay!"

Those two simple words are sharply punctuated by the silence that follows them. My lips sting as I realize that my hand has smacked them closed. I am in shock. Two words, and no immediate response from my brother. My life has changed forever. Waiting to say the words was one kind of hell, but waiting for my brother to respond to them is a second hell that makes me long for the first. My eyes are on the verge of releasing salty, wet tears, and the fear inside me is growing. I feel cowardly as I lean against the counter, petrified, one hand still covering my mouth.

"Are you joking with us, Tim?" My brother's voice sounds different. It is not his normal voice. It wavers and almost cracks as he speaks, and I can tell by the look on his face that he is trying to decide whether or not I'm serious, hoping that the next words out of my mouth will be *Got ya!* or *Just kidding!*

"No, Andrew. I'm not." The words are slightly mumbled through my hand, but they are understandable. My resolve is weakening, but the words I've spoken are out of my control now. They are alive as I am alive, and they cannot be undone. Even if I were to take it all back and tell my brother about my experiment, the wound of this moment would always remain. My body begins shaking as I wait for the backlash.

I never anticipated that coming out as gay would feel this raw, this emotional, this terrifying. It isn't a fear that life won't go on; rather, that life won't resolve in some way. The questions and the stereotypes, and fear for all of the relationships I might lose, consume me. I don't want to lose my friends, and I don't want my family to hold me at arm's length. I do not want to be the black sheep of the family, or the *different* gay brother or son. I want to be me. But having been raised in a conservative religious home, I know these hopes aren't reasonable. Living in the culture of the "Bible Belt" makes the prospect of feeling simultaneously normal and gay likely impossible. I cannot imagine what coming out would be like if I were really gay. One year may seem like a long time, but a lifetime…That would be more than I could ever adjust to.

The look on my brother's face as he processes my revelation is proof. Nothing about this year is going to be easy.

Then my brother's wife, Maren, looks at me with the grace of a sister, and Andrew's face takes on a beautiful look of sympathy and protectiveness. I don't know why he's looking at me that way, but it is not threatening. I have never seen it before, and it surprises me, knowing what he must be thinking. Then I feel guilt; not just because I'm intentionally allowing him to go through this with me, but because I am selfish. I am selfish because I treasure that look on his face and what it shows me—I really am important to him. In some indescribable way, I feel that he actually needs me.

Is he afraid of losing me? Why that look?

Why now?

For the moment my nerves calm and my fear abates. My sister-in-law moves next to me and playfully grabs the scruff of my neck. "Were you actually afraid we were going to push you away for being gay?" she asks as her hand rubs my still very rigid back. I can feel my pulse. It hasn't stopped racing since I told Andrew and Maren that we needed to talk.

"Honestly, I didn't know how you were going to react," I reply, still shaking.

Andrew moves next to me and puts his arm around me. I'm in the middle of these two people, and I feel like I hardly know them. Have I been too hard on them, assuming that my brother would react to my coming out the way I might have if he had come out to me? I don't know what to think. Surprisingly, neither of them asks questions. I have been told most family members ask questions after finding out for the first time that a loved one is gay. But they do not ask me how long I have known or "felt this way," and they do not ask me if I have a boyfriend. Instead, they just let me be. It is a beautiful thing that in spite of everything I believed would, or at least could, have happened, in our case, blood really does run thicker than dogma.

I hear the sliding doors to the porch open. The sound is a salvation of sorts, as I am ready to go outside and smoke a cigarette. The group of friends walk into the kitchen and immediately engage my brother and his wife in conversation. I slip quietly out to the porch.

It is cold, too cold for anyone without a jacket. I am without mine but unwilling to go back inside without taking a few minutes to myself. I put the cigarette in my mouth and reach for my lighter, but something comes over me before I can light it. I feel physically sick, like I am neck-deep in a pit of quicksand, like I have just committed a murder and am waiting to be found out. My worry turns into nausea, and my nausea becomes a forward movement to the screen door, which I wrench open just in time to vomit into the bushes. My nerves manifest themselves into a bought of physical sickness.

And then I see him, the Pharisee, standing at the bottom of the steps with a disapproving look on his face.

Why are you lying to them? We both know you can't maintain this lie.

Leave me alone.

I just don't understand why you think lying to your family is going to accomplish anything. You know lying is a sin, just like homosexuality. Now you might as well be gay.

His continual use of the word *lie* is intentional, but I'm too overwhelmed to pay him any attention. I look down at the throw up on the winter-stripped bush and start to cry. Deceiving my brother is the hardest thing I have ever done. I feel like I've stabbed myself in the heart.

Six months of planning hasn't prepared me in the least.

June 2008: Six months earlier

I had not heard from Lizzy since that fateful night at karaoke. I didn't need to, though. I had made an unorthodox decision, a path inspired by her conviction. Something about my thinking was wrong, something about my immediate desire to preach at her instead of comfort her…It had to be wrong, or I would not have felt so guilty. But making the unorthodox decision to come out as gay and actually coming out are two entirely different monsters, and the second was much more intimidating to face. It was late June 2008, and my course had set.

The idea was simple enough, or so I thought: come out as gay to my family, friends, and church, and see how the label of *gay* would affect my life. It would be the ultimate chance to test everything that two decades of programming in the Independent Baptist Church had taught me.

I'd lived in Nashville since I was two and loved it. Like most Southern cities, we lived at a much slower pace. It was a place where iced tea was the drug of choice and being a member of this church or that was more prestigious than belonging to a country club. It was also a place filled with people who thrived on bringing faith and Republican politics into conversation whenever possible, and I was an expert at injecting my extreme brand of faith into even the most mundane small-talk.

Growing up I was the little boy single-handedly responsible for the success of the clip-on tie industry. I was the kid who logged more hours in church than most pastors. Television shows like the "Power Rangers" were off limits because of the worldly music (not the violence—go figure), as were the movies like *Free Willy* because of their "environmentalist, liberal agenda." I was never allowed to believe in Santa Clause or the Easter bunny, and not once on Halloween did my parents allow me to dress up to go trick-or-treating. They said it was an "evil" holiday, and I was too young to protest. None of this really mattered, though. I'd just wanted to be normal, even though I was not quite sure what normal really was.

One of the earliest Sunday school lessons I remember was "Sodom and Gomorrah." I could not have been older than seven or eight. I stared in awe at the display board showing the destruction of the city, rendered in felt. The Sunday school teacher placed the "fire reigning from the heavens" pieces on the board with care, like she treasured them. Each piece, including the people, looked like something you'd see in a science fiction movie. It was a disturbing image...until the felt buildings fell off the board. They only stuck half of the time, and my laughing always got me in trouble.

Memories from my childhood had plagued me since that night at the bar with Liz, but none of them held the same novelty as before. Now I saw them for what they might actually be: the spiritual boot camp that taught me how to use the Bible to hurt instead of love. I had been raised a Bible thumper, a homophobe; my decision was not an easy one.

Acting on an idea is not as simple as one might think, especially one that is as deep as adopting the label of gay. I hadn't expected it to be an effortless process, or anything; I just thought that the mental hurtles I'd have to jump would be a little bit shorter. I thought I would meet the most resistance externally, but nothing could have been further from the truth. I suffered through anxiety, insomnia, and a heightened sense of nostalgia for the things I might lose. I was unraveling before the journey even began.

My first week of sleepless nights followed my decision to move forward with the experiment. I became an insomniac zombie, obsessing over every nuance of the experiment. Not only did I suffer insomnia, I became a hermit. My lack of contact with the outside world worried my best friend Josh, who hadn't heard from me since karaoke, and it didn't take much waffling before I drove to his house to tell him everything. It was his fault I'd started going to karaoke, after all—and I was going to make him participate, whether he liked it or not!

After some brief small talk, I hesitantly told him. "By the way, I've decided to 'come out' to my family and friends."

"What? But you aren't gay!" He looked shocked, and the confusion on his face almost lightened my mood. "*Are* you…?"

"Of course not! You know me better than that," I answered. "You know my story, about how I was raised and everything."

A look of recognition blossomed, and his demeanor changed. "That's perfect!" he said without my having to elaborate. "If you walk in their shoes, you might not be such an asshole to them."

"Hey, now! I am not…Well, yes, basically. But I don't want to be an asshole anymore," I said as Josh smiled at me. "It's just that, well, I'm not sure that I should…" I voiced my hesitation, wondering if he would tell me to drop it or encourage me to go through with the idea.

Josh saw my hesitancy. "If you don't do this, I'm going to find someone who will. This is the best idea you've ever had, and it needs to be done. Tim, this is your chance to question everything you've ever been taught! It's your chance to grow a heart. This is going to change your life!" He knew me too well.

I knew I didn't have a choice.

Josh leaned against the wall of his balcony, twisting the hair of his black goatee between his thumb and index finger. His expression was pensive, and I knew he was working out what exactly he wanted to say next. I looked off the balcony at the lights of downtown Nashville and lit a clove cigarette. The sweltering June heat, and the humidity even so late at night, had me consistently wiping my forehead with my t-shirt while I waited for him to speak. The cigarette was nothing more than a tar-soaked filter and my shirt was damp before he finally spoke.

"Tim, you know if you do this, you're going to have to establish some pretty strict rules for yourself." Josh's exultant expression had turned serious.

"Like what?" I said.

"Well, for one, you won't be able to date women. You won't even be able to flirt with them! That's what will make or break this project," he said, taking another hit of the clove nestled between the fingers of his left hand.

"Why not?"

"For several reasons. First, the duality of this experiment is hinged on the fact that while you're out as gay, you'll be in the closet as straight. You'll be completely imprisoned to this new life—repressed like gays and lesbians are, before they come out. It will bring you closer. Also, it minimizes the risk of being found out by everyone. People talk, and if you're dating someone, they won't be able to keep things a secret. Plus, you'd be cheating yourself out of the most important part of the story if you did. Relationships just complicate things. You wouldn't be able to handle it."

Josh was right, as always, and with his words the burden on my shoulders became much heavier than before.

"I understand," I said, looking down at my feet.

"Do you?"

"Yes, I really do. It's going to kill me, but you're right." I felt powerless.

"No relationship drama for a year. It'll be a blessing in disguise. I promise."

"I guess," I said.

"So when are you going to 'come out'?" he asked, putting his hand on my shoulder.

"I really haven't given it much thought." The idea alone had been almost more than I could process.

"You'd best get those details hammered out, bro." Josh tossed his clove over the stairwell and I watched it fall, the cherry dimming as soon as it made contact with the damp leaves below us. "Come inside and we'll figure it all out."

January 1st, 2009

Maren's sudden presence on the porch startles me. She hands me a can of Sprite and tells me to come inside where it's warm, her hand patting my back reassuringly. I don't know if I can. I don't even want to move, even though I've lost the feeling in my nose and ears. I feel tears and snot frozen on my facial hair.

"Tim, you can come inside. Don't be afraid. What you told us isn't going to ruin the rest of the party." Her hand still rubs my back reassuringly, and I feel connected to her for the first time. She is my brother's wife, my sister-in-law, but until now I hadn't see her as my friend. I follow her inside, tossing the cigarette into the ashtray, unlit.

I spend the rest of the morning sitting quietly with everyone, sipping coffee and trying not to fall asleep. I'm exhausted and feel like sleeping for days, but before I can sleep, I still have to come out to my mom and stepdad. The thought presses me even further into despair, and I fight the urge to throw up. Again.

And then before I know it, I'm saying goodbye to Andrew and Maren. Both hug me and tell me they love me, and I reciprocate. As I hug my brother, I pull his head down and kiss the top of it. It is something I've done for as long as I can remember, but as I pull away and say goodbye, I hope he doesn't think I do that because I'm gay. The paranoia is already beginning. I get into the car and drive away from the house. I lean my head against the window and feel warm tears contrasting with the icy cold window against my cheek. It is 11:34 a.m. on January 1st, and I have 364 ½ days to go. The calendar on my phone looks more like Mount Everest to me than a simple list of days.

I don't know if I'll make it.

Before going to my mom's house, twenty minutes north in Hermitage, Tennessee, I stop at my friend Hope's apartment. I slept very little the night before, and I need to rest for a few hours before I see my mom. I walk inside and wash up before going to the kitchen. Hope pours me a shot of vodka while I am in the bathroom. She hands it to me, and one gulp later and my chest warms as the clear liquid moves through my body.

"What's next?" she asks.

"I'm going to ask my mom if she'll go to coffee with me, and then I'll tell her."

"Sounds good. You going to rest awhile?"

"I don't think I can."

"You need to try," she says.

"I'm going to call her in a few minutes and try to get her to meet up with me," I say.

After another shot and some small talk, I dial my mom's number and press the phone to my ear. It feels like an eternity before my mom answers her cell, and I feel my eyes glaze over, resigned to the possibility that I could break her heart.

"Hey, mom, can we get some coffee or something, later? I need to talk to you about something." A part of me wonders how she'll respond. I cannot help but wonder if she'll even believe me.

"Tim…I know what you're going to tell me." Her voice, usually whimsical and high-pitched, sounds somber. It sounds like she's been crying, her voice hoarse and broken.

"What are you talking about?"

"I know you think you're gay. Andrew called earlier." She seems to be waiting for confirmation, so I give it to her.

"*Think* I'm gay? Mom, I *am* gay." I can't help but respond defensively. Why would she say *think*? *Thinking*, as she put it, would leave room for error and doubt, and if I know anything, it is that no one would have the gumption to declare their orientation to the world if they just "thought" they were gay. It is too life-changing and painful to do haphazardly. Not only that, but it also negates the declaration in itself, a declaration that takes time for anyone who makes it.

"Just come home, Tim. We'll talk about it here." The edge in her voice is gone, and I reluctantly give the nod to Hope that it is time for me to leave.

I arrive at my mom's house. As I pull into the driveway, I see her standing on the front steps waiting for me. She has never greeted me like this. Part of me feels relief at the thought that she already knows; but another, larger part feels angry that I have lost the opportunity to tell her myself. I get out of the car, grab my bag, and walk towards her. As I reach the top step, she holds her arms out to hug me.

I fall into them like a child who has just scraped his knee, and she holds me.

"Tim, I love you. You know that don't you?" she asks while my head rests on her shoulder. I can't help but be proud of my mom. This is how I should have treated Liz.

"Yes, but I know this isn't something you want to hear from me."

"We'll figure it all out. I'll love you no matter what. Just give me some time."

"Okay." I can't say much in response. I am too tired, but happy that she is making an attempt to show me she cares. We walk inside and sit on the couch, saying very little as we both adjust to something new. Eventually she speaks.

"Have you told your dad yet?"

"Not yet. I'll email him. I don't have the energy to have another conversation today."

"You don't have to do this all in one day," she says.

"I know," I say.

I try to imagine how much harder things would be if she and my brother hadn't cared enough to show me they love me still.

My heart breaks for those who have actually lost family after coming out of the closet. I cannot imagine feeling this vulnerable only to be abandoned by the people who are supposed to be there no matter what. I think again about Lizzy that night at karaoke, six months earlier, and I wish I had known. I wish I had known how this feels, I wish I had wrapped my arms around her and grieved with her, and accepted her in her pain. Overcome by guilt, shame, and sadness, I walk upstairs to go to bed. It's 4:26 p.m., but I'm ready to sleep.

Anything that incites the kind of fear that I've felt this day requires courage to overcome. I had never believed coming out was an act of courage. Until today, coming out as gay has always represented cowardice and a sense of giving up. I believed it was an easy out for people who didn't want to overcome the perversion and sin in their lives. But if today has shown me anything, it is that the act of coming out itself and risking the life you have always known is a courageous thing, an act worthy of respect.

2 not in kansas

A little more than a week has passed since I came out to my friends and family, and, well, they seem to be adjusting to the idea. Yesterday my brother finally felt comfortable enough to ask me questions about my sexuality, and although I would have been more than happy to oblige his curiosity…The truth was, I did not know how to answer him. Not actually being gay means that I am ignorant of what *being* gay is actually like. And I will always be oblivious, no matter how much I experience this year. The limitations and restrictions of my project are constantly in my thoughts. I can only hope that the one aspect of the alternate orientation with which I am now associated provides enough insight for me to answer some of the tougher questions I have struggled with.

What does it really mean to be gay? Is it really so simple as an attraction to the same gender, or is it something more? And if there is some deeper meaning behind it, do I have to ask what it means to be a heterosexual? Growing up, I had always recognized a palpable fear when people brought homosexuality into the discussion, and that fear often became fuel for anger and hatred towards the supposed "gay agenda." A little over a week has passed since I came out, and so far all I've seen is that same tangible fear.

In the eight days I have been out, that fear has permeated every social sphere I have been part of. I have been rebuked in the name of Jesus, lost four friends who refuse to be close to an "unrepentant homosexual," and I have even been told that Jesus does not love me. Perhaps the most disheartening response I received was from my former pastor.

I wrote to him via email that I hadn't been attending church because I was gay and knew he wouldn't approve. I told him that I was celibate—a fear-induced copout. I told him that even though I questioned everything in my life lately, I had not questioned my faith. I told him he could share my email with whomever he felt needed to know, that I was out of the closet now and wouldn't hide it from anyone. I ended the email by telling him that I loved him and wanted to get together to talk. It was an extremely difficult email to write. Jim has been a mentor and a friend, and I served at his church as the college and singles coordinator for over six months. I left a few months ago, before I came out, so no one would be relying on me when I left, as I would almost inevitably have to leave the church. I felt completely vulnerable as I clicked *send*...and even more vulnerable when he responded an hour later:

For some reason, your news does not surprise me. My discernment meter starting going off when you told me of your frequent visits to the gay bar near Centennial Park. I just didn't want to believe it. To be frank with you, you have been hanging around the wrong crowd. The enemy has used that to influence you to make really bad decisions. Yes, this is a decision, not a 'gene.' You have read the Bible enough to know homosexuality is a sin. I will be praying that the enemy's spirit will be rebuked from you in Jesus name!! As you read this, the enemy will fight back...but you must stand up and break free! All this said, you are welcome as any other sinner to our church. We are a gathering of imperfect people who worship a perfect God. There is no sin greater than the other...lying, adultery, gossip, homosexuality, and more. However, I can understand the 'anonymity' issue with something like this, which may make it easier for you to attend another church. Whatever...you've got to get back into church!

I tried to read the email as objectively as possible, but every thought jumped off the screen in a negative way. They were the very thoughts I had wanted to voice to Liz that swelteringly hot summer night, the very thoughts that I didn't say because I knew they would have done more harm than good. I felt betrayed. I reread the message, scanning the email in its entirety four times before my eyes recognize the most upsetting detail. Five words underneath his name spoke louder than even the message itself. Displayed prominently below Jim's name were the words *Sent via BlackBerry by AT&T.*

Not only did he rebuke me in the name of Jesus, tell me I was hanging out with the wrong crowd, and declare that my lifestyle was "a decision, not a 'gene'"...He did so from his cell phone? He didn't ask if we could meet up to talk more about it. But all of that was somehow okay because he was inviting me to worship with all of the other sinners in his church. I mulled the words of his message inside me like a bad breakup, and I wished he'd just tried to talk to me in person.

But more painful than any of these reactions, I have been ignored by the majority of my conservative Christian friends I reached out to. Martin Luther King Jr. once said, "In the end, we will remember not the words of our enemies but the silence of our friends."

And so far, that silence has been more hurtful even than judgment.

It is difficult to describe the range of emotions I have felt thus far, but loneliness is the most acute. My phone no longer rings with calls and texts like it did only a short week ago. I have been waiting, preparing myself for numerous conversations about my revelation, but so far most friends seem to desire only distance. It is that distance, I think, that has pushed so many people over the edge, the excommunication from believers, friends, and loved ones that disagree and disengage. My news spread like a plague, but I was the only real casualty.

I remember seeing gays out in public as a kid and looking at them like animals on a safari. They were a rare sight to see—at least the ones whose appearance gave them away—and I remember not being the only one who stared at them as if they were a sideshow act. But more than seeing or hearing about homosexuals, I remember being taught about the insidious *homosexual agenda*. They "wanted children," they "owned" the media, and even MTV had to have one of them on every show so as to desensitize the younger generation to the dangers of their abominable agenda. Oddly enough, even that poor purple Teletubby, Tinky Winky, was nailed to a wall!

Now I wonder why I spent so much time focused on the intentions of others, on the "agenda." I am still me. Even though the label of my orientation has changed, I know that if anyone has an agenda, it might just be to live their lives. I am interested to see how this aspect of the journey unfolds. Will I discover the actual existence of a "gay agenda," or will I discover that life for gay men is really as benign as life for heterosexual men?

~~~

Twenty seconds at the gay club and already I feel uncomfortable. After eight days of this experiment, I am ready to move forward and see what the LGBTQ scene in Nashville is all about. Club Play is the only LGBTQ club I have heard of in the religious circles I traveled, so it is the place I have chosen to go first. And almost instantly it becomes clear why I have heard about *this* place and not the others.

Walking into a gay club for the first time is a surreal, almost alien experience, and it only slightly resembles the straight clubs I've been to. The lighting is bluish, switching every so often between green and orange and yellow, like the stained glass windows of a church, a combination of disco reflections, neon, and the colorful wardrobe of men peacocking about. I look toward the bartenders and see all men. They are well built and almost always shirtless, like the opposite of a strip club or Hooters. This place was made for gay men, or at least caters to them. Above the loud thumping techno beat, I hear my heart rapidly churning like I have just run up a long flight of stairs.

The Friday night crowd is more diverse than I've seen anywhere. It's a melting pot of different kinds of people. I see a man wearing business slacks and a button-up dress shirt dancing with a man in leather with both nipples pierced. I see another guy in a tight t-shirt and skinny jeans dancing with a transvestite. *Toto, I've a feeling we're not in Kansas anymore...*

I walk towards the bar and get a kiss on the cheek and "Hello, stranger," from a man I've never met. He quickly moves on to the next newcomer. *Now I know we're not in Kansas!*

I am uncomfortable, but I have a purpose and know I need to be here. I think the strangest thing about this bar is the flamboyance of the décor. It all fits the stereotypes I have heard about gays, and I wonder if the reason the stereotypes even exist is because of the appearance of the environment, rather than the people *in* the environment. I hope I can get past the look of the place, because initially the look is very hard to get past. I walk into the club wearing more than just a Tommy Hilfiger button-up and Perry Ellis jeans. I walk in wearing a chip on my shoulder; I see that much. Why do I feel superior to these people? I feel incapable of impartiality or objectivity, and I wonder if I am going to have to learn a tough lesson the hard way.

Lady Gaga's "Poker Face" finishes and a Brittney Spears song begins. I order a beer and sit at the bar as inconspicuously as possible. It is an odd feeling to hope that people will not detect that I am straight; I try to act as gay as I know how with my demeanor and mannerisms. I think back to every stereotypical example of gay on television and movies, and I try to adjust my behavior accordingly. But I am still paranoid. What if I'm not doing it right? This first time out is meant to be more a fact-finding mission than an actual experience, but I am so worried about how I am acting that I do not know if I can learn or experience anything.

On stage a drag queen lip-syncs the song "Womanizer," and the crowd is going wild at the irony. I try to focus on details instead of the big picture…details like the fact that I've never seen a woman with as toned a midsection as that of the drag queen, details like the queerness of the décor, details that won't make me confront my growing irrational fear.

Why am I so uncomfortable? I try to breathe and calm myself, but it feels impossible. I wonder if this crowd would feel the same way if they were at church. Well maybe not *church* in general, so much as the kind of church *I* feel comfortable at.

I look next to me and I see the Pharisee with a wild look in his eyes. With every second that passes, the look becomes more pained. He is uncomfortable to say the least, much more uncomfortable than me, if that were possible. I feel good knowing that he is in this position, that he is so out of his element he cannot even focus on me. Instead he is focused on everyone else, looking at them like they are less than human. I feel sorry for him. But I have to feel sorry for myself, too, because what I see on his face, I feel inside myself.

I track the Pharisee's gaze to the man next to me. The guy is wearing daisy dukes, a choker, and his lip is pierced. As he talks, I see his tongue is, too. I follow the tattoo of a merman from his shoulder down his arm to the light blue drink he is sipping. It is a loaded drink. I can smell the alcohol from three feet away. "You go, girlfriend!" he yells towards the drag queen on stage. He spins around to the bar and orders another drink, his movements graceful and feminine. On a nervous whim, I try to spin around the same way and clumsily spill part of my beer. I feel ridiculous and embarrassed, and he smiles at me. It is a warm, disarming smile, and it makes me feel a little bit better.

"Another beer for the new guy!" he says to the bartender, pointing at me. The shirtless man behind the counter winks, uncaps a longneck, and puts it on a napkin in front of me.

"Thank you." I finish the rest of my spilled beer and take a sip of the next.

"No problem. Just don't spill that one!" The man smiles and lightly slaps my ass as he walks away. And then for a few seconds I lose it. I want to punch the guy for touching me, for presuming that physical contact would be okay…even if he believes I am gay. I take a few deep breaths and compose myself, hoping that nothing else happens to push me even more outside of my comfort zone than I already am. I hope, but then *it* happens.

Across the room, another man's eyes lock on mine. His eyes are intense, and it is only when he is halfway to me that I see he is shirtless and covered in baby oil and glitter. Oh, shit…

The Pharisee looks at me with a sense of immediacy, of panic.

Leave! Let's go!

Before I can move or respond, I feel a man's hand gripping my wrist firmly, and I begin to panic. Adrenalin courses through my body and my legs feel unsteady, like they are about to give out beneath me. I am unable to free myself, and the shirtless man aggressively pulls me onto the dance floor in the adjacent room. I never stood a chance.

It happens too fast for me to react.

One second I am standing at the bar, sipping my beer in a room full of people I irrationally hate, and the next I am on the dance floor with a shirtless man covered in baby oil and glitter while a Beyoncé song roars through the speakers on either side of the room. I feel my body forcibly turned around and positioned away from the man dancing with me. Panic and terror wash over me as I stare at the mirrors on the walls, reflecting an image of utter violation that causes my stomach to turn.

The shirtless man now behind me rides me like a cowboy. I struggle to understand why he thought I would make a good horse—or dance partner. I feel more like a jackass as I watch myself lose my precious innocence. Instead of running, I decide to dance, or at least attempt to dance, but having been raised

Baptist, I have very little experience with rhythm. I feel like a fool. I probably look like one, too. My attempts amount to little more than the awkward swaying of my hips and a few offbeat finger snaps. It is difficult to focus as the man dry-humps me; I feel his every touch on my body like I'm being groped by a pervert.

Of course this experience isn't unusual for him, or for anyone else here. I look around the bar and see gay men and a few women, all dancing just like we are. The man's hand grabs my chest and he squeezes forcefully. I jump in reaction to the pain. "Oh, yeah, my bucking bronco!" he leans in and whispers in my ear. I want to escape. I want to vomit. I need a cigarette. I feel like beating the hell out of him.

One song bleeds into two without my realizing it, and something weird begins to happen. It's as if I've mentally snapped, unable to fight the situation or even just the overly aggressive man behind me. The music draws me in hypnotically and I got lost in it, like everyone else.

The song ends, and I feel violated, slimy, used. I cannot blame anyone but myself that I let it happen or lost control. I walk away from my suitor without saying a word. "Bitch!" he says, just loud enough for me to hear. Maybe I am being a bitch, but I do not care. I feel like washing my hands, washing the baby oil and glitter off of me…which is probably more easily said than done.

As I leave the dance floor, I look back and my eyes meet his again. He looks rejected and upset, like he was having fun and I ruined it. It is not the look of a predator or a pervert. It is a vulnerable expression, and I feel as though I have deeply misunderstood him, allowed my discomfort to exaggerate my perceptions of his intent. I feel a pang of disappointment in myself. The Bible says that man looks at the outward appearance but God looks at the heart. Have I judged this man's heart because of how he danced with me? Have I fallen so quickly back into my ways that I frivolously presumed him to be a predator?

Once more I am startled by his eyes. He looks *into* me, instead of at me, like he is searching out the truth of who I am and why I am here. Finally he looks down, and I take the brief moment to run from the club. I am overcome with regret, and as I walk to my car I resolve to change. If I am going to do this, to *really* do this, I cannot merely mask the judgment inside of me—I will have to leave it at the door. I will save the judgment for myself, and try from now on to meet these people on their turf, with an open mind and heart.

~~~

Minutes later I'm standing in front of Josh's house, still rushing from the adrenaline and still depressed by my own behavior. I knock and the door opens.

"So? What happened?" he asks before I can even walk inside.

"You had to ask…!" I sit on his couch and light a clove. "I spilled my beer trying to spin like a guy next to me, got dance-raped by a shirtless guy covered in baby oil and glitter, and to top it all off, I made a fool of myself by acting homophobic in a gay bar!" The frustration on my face is apparently too much for Josh to handle and he laughs hysterically.

"I would have paid to see that," Josh says, trying to breathe. He isn't laughing with me, he's laughing *at* me.

"No! It was awful. It was like I was a piece of meat."

"You *are* like a piece of meat—an especially big piece of meat with 'bottom' tattooed on your forehead!" He's still laughing.

"I would not be the bottom!"

"I think you would be." Sandra, Josh's wife, wanders in, apparently just as amused.

"That's right, honey, you tell 'im!" he says to her, grinning.

"I think I need a boyfriend," I say. "I need someone who can take the target off my back and teach me how to act in those types of situations." I hope Josh will agree.

"Actually, that's a really good idea. But who? And would they be in on things?" He stops laughing, momentarily thoughtful.

"Well, Shawn from karaoke is a great guy, and he's gay. I think he'd be perfect."

"Like a gay Yoda?" he asks.

"Like a gay Yoda."

"Protect your ass, you must!" Again, Josh bursts into laughter and I get up to leave. As I close the door behind me I hear Josh and Sandra laughing raucously.

"*Bitches!*" I say under my breath.

3 shawn

I have always loved women, always been fascinated by their mystique and beauty. My mom will tell you that when I was a little kid, I used to run up to women and wrap my arms around their legs, saying, "I like your chubby legs!" Most of the time their legs weren't chubby, but because my mom used to pinch my legs and say the same thing, I thought chubby legs were what everyone had.

As I got older, my mom hoped I'd learn how to conceal my pleasure with the opposite gender more readily, but to her dismay, it only got worse. At six years old I had my first girlfriend, but unlike most childhood romances, mine had passion. My mom always tells people about the night the family was driving to Uncle Bud's—a seafood joint in the South that I remember fondly—and about the 167 kisses that took place in the back seat of the minivan while we drove. Timmy and Kimmy, we were a match made in heaven.

Several months later we were on a summer vacation with my "girlfriend's" family, and Kimmy's parents told us we had to break up because we were getting too old to date and kiss…But I wasn't going to let her parents salt my game. Five minutes later I went over to Kimmy's older sister, Bethany—who happened to be my brother's "girlfriend" at the time—and I asked her out. She said yes, and my brother was devastated, but Bethany was a foxy nine-year-old, and I wasn't going back to the single life, no matter what.

Because of this project and because I'm in the closet as a straight man, I can't be who I've been since I was a kid. But being cut off from women this year isn't yet as much a problem as I had thought it might be. I'm too distracted and off balance to even notice, really—but tonight that will change. Tonight I'm asking Shawn to go out with me, and I'm going to ask him to be my boyfriend. I've also got to tell him about my project and see if he is willing to help me on this journey.

It has been two days since my first club experience, and I am nervous about venturing into another gay bar. I don't like being nervous. I don't like being afraid of where I'm going and who I might meet along the way, but I don't have the option of turning back. Shawn has graciously agreed to meet me at Tribe to talk, and I try not to fixate on the purpose of our meeting. This is my first time asking a man to be my boyfriend, and if he agrees, it will also be the last. Oddly enough, my nerves have less to do with Shawn and more to do with the environment I'm meeting him in. After my first experience the other night, I feel as though my homophobia has gotten worse, and I am not sure why. I was the one at fault there, but I can't stop thinking about how violated I felt being touched the way I had been on the dance floor. But Shawn is different, and his style of interaction has always been respectable. I have always seen him as just as another friend. Springwater karaoke will do that to you, or at least it did that to me. It is a place where labels don't survive very long.

The more I think about Shawn since that night, the more I know he will be the perfect boyfriend for me. I've known Shawn for a little over a year and always enjoy our talks. But even more than our talks, I enjoy listening to Shawn sing. He has a beautiful voice, the type that grabs you and places you in the very lyrics of whichever song he's chosen to sing. His voice sounds like velvet feels. It is smooth, soulful, and deeply moving. Growing up in Nashville, I am not a stranger to listening to undiscovered talent, but Shawn isn't just talented. He sings with every fiber of his being, with every cell in his body. It is magic. I have never been more impressed by an artist than I was the first time I heard him, and that was how our friendship began.

Shawn is adored by everyone who frequents karaoke. He has a personality that puts anyone at ease—and he's the first openly gay man that I've ever felt such a connection with. I remember the first time we talked. He was walking off the stage, barely a step above the ground, and I grabbed his hand and told him how impressed I was by his voice. He hugged me. He hugged me like a lifelong friend would hug, deep and meaningfully, and he thanked me for the encouragement. His vulnerable nature and appreciation for a simple compliment was very moving, and I was suddenly faced with a gay man I was incapable of disliking or writing off. And now I can only hope that he won't be offended by my project or write me off for asking him to help.

Club Play and Tribe, the gay bar where I'm meeting Shawn, are attached. Also attached to Tribe is a restaurant called Red. I don't know how a restaurant can be gay, exactly, but it is. Everything from the food and the drinks to the employees are gay or gay-themed; the result is a line of three gay establishments, encompassing a small city block.

I walk into Tribe and marvel at the bar most straight people wouldn't dare enter. The bar doesn't fit my preconceived stereotypes. It's classy, well-lit, and clean—an upscale place to grab a drink after work. I've been told all gay bars were dens of iniquity, places where men gathered by the hundreds to pair up and have the fleeting one night stands indicative of those that are sexually promiscuous. At first glance, a few of the men seem to have those stereotypical motives or are at least dressed that way, but most aren't. This isn't Play. Most of the crowd gathered tonight look like normal people, business men meeting friends for a beer after work, wearing suits or business casual. Even the drinks look more traditional. If I were to attempt to paint a visual, I'd say that Tribe looks like a cross between an Applebee's and a P.F. Chang's, with better lighting. I am much more comfortable here and feel less pressure from the environment itself. I could get used to this place.

I make my way to the bar and order a pint, and the bartender is very friendly. Unlike Play, he's not shirtless. He's wearing a nice collared button-up shirt and dark pants. His hair is spiked and he has several piercings in each ear, but for all intents and purposes he looks like a normal bartender.

Inside Tribe one finds two separate rooms, both with bars, and a third in the adjoining restaurant. After taking a sip of beer I walk into the second room and see Shawn waiting for me at a table. He's wearing a black, vertically striped button-up and nice jeans. When he sees me, he smiles. Shawn is a handsome African-American man, bigger but well built. I know it is going to be an interesting dynamic. Black, gay, and we live in the South. Might as well kill two birds with one stone, I think. Shawn is also several inches taller than me, and as he stands up and hugs me, I feel like I'd imagine a girl would feel hugging me. There's a sense of safety in his embrace, a sense of comfort that says everything is and will be okay…and I hope that proves to be true. Shawn's demeanor is calm as I explain my experiment to him. He appears to be waiting to react. I wait for his response the way I waited for my brother's when I came out. This is the first time I'm telling a gay man about what I'm doing, and I nervously hope he won't be offended. Shawn takes a few deep breaths, and I take a few deep gulps of my beer.

"Wow…I don't really know what to say." His words are slow and deliberate: "First, I want to say that I think it's an incredible idea and I'm happy you are doing it." I exhale a sigh of relief and wait for him to finish. "And I'm really happy you told me."

"Why?"

"Because you're in it deep right now and I'm glad I know, so I can be here for you." Shawn puts his hand on mine and his expression is reassuring.

"Well, it's funny you should say that," I laugh nervously.

"Why?"

"Because I need to ask you a huge favor."

"Uh huh…" he says.

"I was in the club a few days ago, and I don't exactly know what happened, but I was pretty aggressively forced into an uncomfortable situation by a guy. I didn't know how to react, and

I think I was as offensive as I felt offended. I don't know how to act in gay bars and clubs, and I need to learn," I say in a rush. Shawn looks at me thoughtfully but doesn't say anything. "I guess what I'm trying to say is that I really need someone to teach me. Shawn, I want you to be my boyfriend." I down the rest of my beer.

Shawn waves to the bartender and he comes over. "I'd like to by my friend another beer," he says.

"Sure, babe. What kind?" the bartender asks.

"Blue Moon, please," I answer.

"I think that is a really good idea, Tim," Shawn says to me. "It'll at least give you an excuse to turn down the guys who will ask you out, which minimizes the damage you could potentially do to their feelings. You need to make sure you don't take advantage of them. Just observe and interact, and pay attention to what you see."

"I would never want to hurt anyone or take advantage of their feelings. Besides, no guy is going to ask me out!" I laugh.

"Sure they will! I would, if you were really gay," he says.

"So you'll be my boyfriend?" I ask again.

"Let me get this straight. You aren't gay *so* you want me to be your boyfriend?"

"That's pretty much the gist of it."

"Okay. I'll do it." Shawn half giggles to himself and takes a sip of his drink.

"Really? Are you sure?" I ask.

"Of course I'm sure," he says. "This is going to be an interesting year!"

"It already is."

"I can't begin to imagine."

The bartender brings my Blue Moon and I drop the orange slice into the beer.

Shawn and I make small talk, letting the gravity of our new relationship sink in. His tone is reassuring. I tell him about what it was like coming out, and that I've emailed and texted a few people but haven't heard anything back. I feel rejected, like I have a disease or something, and they won't come near me. I am in the South, so I guess I do have a disease, albeit a social one. I would probably be ignoring me, too, and that fact shames me. But Shawn understands, and it is nice to talk with someone who understands. I tell him more about my first time at the club and how uncomfortable I was. Like Josh and Sandra, he laughs at me and agrees that I acted like a big piece of meat, and for the first time during my year, I actually forget where I am and what I'm doing. For the first time, I'm just another guy in a bar, sitting with a friend and enjoying a beer.

"Okay, boyfriend, teach me," I say.

"First things first," he says. "See that guy over there at the bar? He's been eyeing you since I got here."

"What? Gross!" My reaction is subconscious and instantly I see that I've offended my friend.

"Gross? Tim, it's not gross. It's not even remotely a bad thing." Shawn thinks for a minute. "It's as natural as you being attracted to any woman you see."

"He's probably not even looking at me. He's probably looking at you!" I feel like an idiot.

"Seriously, he is! You're going to need to learn that men and women look for different things. And you're hot."

I don't know if I should take Shawn's words as a compliment or an insult.

"You're going to get a lot of attention, and the attention you're going to get is a lot different from the kind you're used to. You can't act put off by it, or even uncomfortable. You have to learn how to embrace it. Just think about it this way: If a guy gives you attention, even if it's unwanted, it's a compliment. He's saying he thinks you're attractive and worth his putting himself out there, just for the chance of getting your number. If you think of it that way, you won't feel nearly as uncomfortable."

"So how do I turn them down without giving myself away?"

"Use your common sense. If a guy has just put himself out there, realize and appreciate that fact. Be gentle and gracious and tell him you have a boyfriend, but thank him and flirt a little bit."

"*Flirt?*"

"Yes, Tim, flirt. If you think you'll be able to last an entire year, night after night at places like this, without pinching a butt or two, you're not going to make it!"

"Me pinch a guy's butt?" I feel sick at the thought. It's hard enough for me to be touched by a gay man, much less flirt with one.

"The rules of flirting are virtually the same here as they are at a straight bar. Be suggestive without being too aggressive, and be playful. Flirting between gay men is almost more about validating that other person than it is about hooking up with them. Think of flirting as the ultimate encouragement."

"But what happens if they are *too* encouraged by it...?" I ask.

"Tim, you aren't going to get raped! Is this really what you think about gay men?"

"No, but you've gotta try to understand how hard this is for me."

"Stop thinking about everything in terms of *you*, and think about it in terms of others. You aren't in church. You're on different turf, and it's not your place to be put off by an advance, no matter how unwanted it is. When a guy comes up to you, realize that he's doing so because he sees something in you that he likes, and that's never a bad thing. Take it as a damn compliment!"

"Okay, I'll try. And I do understand." An awkward pause follows and I can't help but stare at two men a few tables away making out. The sight turns my stomach.

Shawn sighs, seeing my discomfort. "And if you're worried about it going too far, don't be. Just remember that no means no. It's a genderless word. If you're courteous about it, you'll most likely get a free drink, even if you say no."

"So what do I do about that guy at the bar? Is he still staring?"

"Not for long." Shawn smirks. "If I'm your boyfriend, then let me do my thing."

Shawn looks intently at the man staring at me. It's not a mean look, but it's possessive, and it's not long before the stranger turns away, apparently having gotten the hint.

"Now he knows we're together." Shawn seems happy with himself, confident and playful.

"You really are a gay Yoda!" I'm amazed at how subtle Shawn's body language was. "Have I mentioned how much I love you?" Shawn laughs and I know I've made the right decision. Not only do I get at least a small measure of protection and an awesome excuse to avoid potential suitors; I also get to spend time with someone who defies my Pharisee, someone I actually trust.

"So how's this relationship going to work?" Shawn's voice brings me back to the moment, and I'm at a loss.

"I don't really know..." I say. "I won't be dating anyone else." The no-women rule of my year weighs heavily on me as I speak.

"You know, the only thing you really need to understand is that the people you're going to meet and have relationships with this year aren't any different from you."

"But we believe so differently." I can't help but argue internally over the semantics.

"You'll figure it out, sooner or later." Shawn speaks from experience. His coming out was a radical one, though not of his own volition.

Shawn was raised in a single-parent household, and his mother was all he had. Much like me, he had been very active in church growing up, but when a close friend who attended the same church "repented" of a physical relationship they'd had on a few occasions, Shawn couldn't hide his orientation any longer. He was outed in the worst possible way: by a former lover, confessing to a group of leaders in the church—a group that included Shawn's own mother. At the time of his friend's confession, Shawn was walking past the quad to practice for a theater production, and his cell phone rang. It was his mother, calling to confront him about what she had just been told. And Shawn told her the truth and bore the overwhelming stress with grace. He even forgave the friend who outed him and remained in the church, taking a stand that I would not have had the courage to take. Shawn inspires me.

Not only does he inspire me, Shawn makes me question myself. Why do I believe I'm any different, any better, than anyone else? Why do my beliefs give me a sense of entitlement? Everyone is human, fallible, and flawed, and it is not my job to determine who's better or worse. It is my job to be myself and to learn as much as I can from anyone I meet. This year is about that, and Shawn is showing me that I need to experience the discomfort, especially since I've put myself into this position.

"Just remember, be kind but be unavailable." Shawn's tone is serious, and I know he is trying to spare me future awkwardness. "And if you ever need me, just call my cell. If I can make it, I'll be here to help out!"

I feel like I may have bitten off more than I can chew. Adopting the label of gay isn't enough to understand gay. I have to know how to interact and what not to do. The other day, I probably sent all the wrong signals, probably made an ass of myself by being the me I'm hoping to change. I feel remorse for letting down everyone, even if they don't know it.

Have you ever wondered what it'd be like to wear another person's shoes? It's not easy. The setting of my life's story is changing at a pace I can barely keep up with, and I know this is just the beginning. Going from homophobe to boyfriend is a huge leap, but it feels right. I feel like I am finally understanding *life*, and my time with Shawn is a huge step forward.

Tribe's crowd dwindles as we talk. It's a weeknight, and people have to work, including Shawn. We settle the bill and make our way to the patio while we finish our drinks. It has been a different kind of night than I anticipated: I was faced with the fact that *I'm* the weird one, and that my beliefs make *me* the alien. Going from the majority to the minority isn't what most people would consider doing, but I know I have to learn that life really isn't about me. Even the thought of this is refreshing, and I am excited to see how this plays out.

My boyfriend (*boyfriend!*) hugs me as we separate, and I cannot thank him enough. He has spared me the possibility of falling on my face while I'm getting used to the LGBTQ nightlife, and he has increased my chances of changing my life for the better.

4 will

There is a fine line between tolerance and rejection. Waking up to that fact has cost me dearly. In the past three weeks, I've received emails and text messages from people whom I always believed loved and valued me. But now I know the truth. Instead of speaking with me in a personal way to understand my decision, many of these people took the easy path of judgment, and they did so using the impersonal and soulless tools of social networks and email to do the dirty work.

Upon hearing the news of my coming out, multiple friends voiced their concern over my "evil" decision; but instead of speaking to me in person or even on the phone, they resorted to black letters on a white page—and not the kind I can touch and feel, and fold up to put in my pocket. They manifest their worldviews so impersonally that I am left wondering if they ever really loved me to begin with. On the other hand, I also feel relieved. I don't know how much more I could handle right now.

Patrick, my old nemesis from Liberty, messaged me the other day and asked me how I could claim to love Jesus and be gay. I told him that I did love Jesus, and he told me that I may love Him, but Jesus doesn't love me. Just like that, because the label of my orientation changed, he says that the gospel doesn't apply to me anymore.

Four of my other friends got together and let me know with one clear voice that they could not condone my decision. They said that upon my "repentance," not only would my relationship to Christ be restored but also my relationship to them. But until that day, they could no longer, in good conscience, continue to be my friend.

These were just a few of the responses that I received after sharing the news, but these few hurt the most. Pastors, friends, enemies...

Karma really is a bitch.

~~~

I take Shawn's advice, and in the weeks following our conversation I spend as much time as possible in the small gay district of Nashville. I read books in the LGBTQ bookstore and drink coffee in the LGBTQ café attached to the bookstore. I eat dinner and drink beer and spend more time with Shawn at Tribe, and I try to make friends whenever possible with the only community that doesn't judge me for who everyone believes me to be. I feel benign resignation, and with each trip I make to Church Street, I become more comfortable. The people whom I always considered moral pariahs are becoming my grief counselors, the "abominable" my only support structure in a time when I need love and acceptance the most.

On Wednesday nights at Tribe, from 6:00 to 8:00, well drinks are only a dollar, and the result is a crowd. A huge crowd. A huge gay crowd. I still find it slightly unnerving to go from a life in the pew to a life on the barstool, but I am content with the change. I approach the bar in the third room, attached to the restaurant, and see someone I know. Tending bar is my childhood best friend! When he sees me he grins.

"Tim?"

"*Will?* Oh, my God, is that you?"

Will runs from behind the bar and hugs me. "I was so happy to get your message. I was hoping I'd see you one of these nights," he says excitedly. After coming out, I'd e-mailed him to share the news, and I have hoped for weeks I would get the chance to reconnect with him.

"How've you been?" I ask. The reunion brings back a flood of memories from my childhood…and, more recently, the day I found out *he* was gay.

"I'm great. Still in school. I don't know if I'll ever graduate!" Will is dressed in a tight t-shirt and jeans, and his hair is spiked. He looks good, and he looks happy (contrary to everything his mom has told me). "Let me buy you a beer. I want to hear how life has been since you dropped the bomb on your family."

~~~

I met William when I was six years old and we were in Cub Scouts together. Our mothers became instant friends, bonding because they were both homeschooling their young children and because of their conservative faith. So for years, Will was a big part of my life. We played t-ball together, did our school work together, and he came to my high school graduation. But Will was always different from my other friends.

Two years before my experiment, I bumped into Will at an American Eagle in the same mall I worked at, and he introduced me to his fiancé. But after talking with him for a few minutes and then hearing the news about his engagement, I felt perplexed. Will wasn't like the guys I surrounded myself with, and I even wagered with a co-workers who knew him that he was secretly in the closet. I hope he's not just another queer, I remember saying; but in the back of my mind I always had the suspicion. Several months later, Will got married, the mall I worked at closed down, and we lost touch once more. I decided I was probably wrong about his being gay.

A year passed, and I bumped into Will's mom at the grocery store. She seemed very upset when I asked how Will and his wife were doing, quickly changing the subject without answering. I gave her my phone number, but just like that, my childhood friend was once again out of my life, and my curiosity about Will was again left unanswered.

In February, four months before the fated night with Liz, Will's mom called me, and it didn't take more than a few seconds to hear her crying on the other end of the line.

"Oh, Tim…" She took a deep breath. "I've got a problem and I need your help."

"What's wrong?"

"Will's marriage is over. His wife caught him making out with another guy, and they decided to get a divorce. And now Will *thinks* he's gay, and you're the only one who could get through to him. I know he's devastated…We are all devastated about it. I just know that the devil is influencing him." She paused for a second, taking a few deep breaths.

"Me? What could I possibly do?"

"Would you please talk to him and try to help counsel him out of this? You're in ministry—if anyone can do it, it's you. Please just try." She sounded desperate, and her confidence in me inflated my ego.

"I'll try. What's his number?" I took down the number and told her I would pray for her and for Will. "I'll do what I can, and I'll try to show him that what he's choosing is going to hurt him, but that's all I can do."

For the next two months, I called Will nearly every day, multiple times. I left voicemails and sent emails. I showed up at his work (he wasn't there at the time) and I talked with his Christian friends about him. I even met up with one of his closest friends and had a strategy meeting about how we could "show him the light." And all this time I was talking with his mom about him, trying to get the latest intel on what he was doing, so I could finally catch and convert him.

But nothing happened. Will never answered his phone, never responded to my emails, and even stopped talking to the friend I had met with. Looking back, I can only say I am happy he did. My approach wouldn't have done any good because it was not the approach anyone ought to use. There was no love in my methodology. I became an Inspector Javert, trying to hunt down a moral criminal. Though I believed I was fulfilling my moral obligation, I became an antagonist in the story of Will's life.

~~~

"So how'd your mom take it?" Will asks with concern.

"She seems to be taking it okay, but it's obviously not what she would have chosen for one of her sons." The understatement of the century.

"At least she's trying."

I know what Will is inferring. "About that…" The pang of guilt washes over me. "Will, I really need to apologize."

"Why? Tim, you don't need to apologize to me."

"Yes, I do. I harassed you! I was trying to change you. My intentions were flawed from the beginning. Your mom called me when you came out and wanted me to help counsel you out of it. I feel like an idiot."

Will's eyes show sympathy. "I appreciate that, but don't worry. You weren't the only one. She still refuses to believe that I'm not that perfect little child she always thought she had, but she'll figure it out eventually." Will smiles. "I'll be okay. And Tim, you're forgiven."

"I saw you, and the first thing I felt was guilt because of how I treated you."

"I've been treated much worse, believe me." Another understatement.

"So I saw you've got a boyfriend! He seems like a nice guy. Has your mom met him yet?" I ask.

"Yeah, but she won't have anything to do with us together. He's not even allowed at my house, and they won't see us together," he says. I can see that he's struggling with his mom's less-than-warm welcome. "God only knows why he's putting up with it. Makes me love him more, though! I see him dealing with my parents who don't like him, and I can't help but be thankful for him."

"So he treats you well?"

"He's a prince." Will's face lights up when he talks about his boyfriend, and I can see he's in love.

"You deserve a prince."

"I'm just going to give my mom time. She still thinks her ex-gay therapy groups will straighten me out; but until she realizes I'm being me, we won't be able to move forward."

I can't imagine. If my mom tried to shove ex-gay literature at me, I'd probably throw it right back at her. *Reparative therapy*, they call it. They should call it "repression therapy."

"Well, it looks like you've got a line of thirsty men," I say.

"And a few that want a drink, too!" he says with a laugh.

"It's awesome seeing you. We need to hang out soon."

He nods. A few steps back towards the bar, he stops. "Oh, and one more thing: Do me a favor and realize that in every community there's good and bad. Don't get caught up in the bad, now, no matter how much you may want to."

"What do you mean?"

"You're free of the closet, but don't lose yourself by acting out. Take your time acclimating and don't rush into anything. I see too many guys come out, and in the happiness of it all, make some very unwise decisions. Break the stereotypes, Tim. This is an opportunity to break the stereotypes." He turns and walks back to the bar where a line of people wait to order drinks.

"I will," I say, even though he is too far to hear me. I'll have to ask him to elaborate, but for now I am so caught off guard by Will's concern for me that I don't know what to say.

I wonder what's worse: rejecting someone for being gay or accepting him with ulterior motives. Will's mom, who has always been very sweet and caring, is not only permitting a wall between herself and her son—she's helping to reinforce it. I just don't get it. How can someone separate themselves from another person, especially a child, using theology as bricks and dogma as mortar? It makes no sense.

I think that's a problem with conservative theology: it allows one's beliefs to keep one from a relationship. And unfortunately, she has fallen into the trap. Will is her son, and by keeping his boyfriend at arm's length, she's keeping her son at a distance. I feel distraught for Will, and I wish his mom would love him without trying to change him. Even more, I wish the same for myself. Loving without motive seems like the more Christ-like way to go, but maybe it is more easily said than done. Maybe this year I'll get to a place where that is not only my mindset, but my habit, too.

5 church street

One of the great theological fundamentals, instilled in me for as long as I can remember, is that we are all born into this life with an albatross of sin hanging around our necks. This weight and pressure is designed to force a sense of spiritual immediacy and urgency as we live and share the Gospel of Jesus. It is a belief that says all of us are broken and unable to enjoy a relationship with our creator until we repent and turn away from our sinful selves.

Coupled with this idea that we are unable to know God until we repent is the idea that those "living in sin" are incapable to knowing salvation. For gays and lesbians, it doesn't matter if you've been raised in church, love Jesus, and are fluent in the religious language; God's truth will simply evade you until you turn away from your same-sex attraction and give your struggle to the Lord. That is, you cannot know God and be an unrepentant homosexual.

So I am surprised as I eavesdrop on a conversation at the bar. It is more of a religious debate, really, between a well-dressed man drinking a cranberry vodka and a bartender with both nipples pierced and wearing a spiked dog collar.

"I'm just telling you," the businessman, a regular, says, "that I believe that what the Bible says is true. I don't believe that we could evolve in trillions of years, much less billions. Randomness doesn't allow for that kind of order."

"Ben, get serious. I'm not saying the Bible isn't a great book, I'm just saying that I don't think Genesis 1 and 2 should be taken literally," the bartender says. "Or much else, for that matter."

"If you think it's a great book, why can't you have faith in it?"

"I'm not saying I don't agree with a lot of it! Just saying that I think this planet has been around a helluva lot longer than six thousand years!"

Is this even possible? Are they actually debating young-earth creationism? The implications of this are overwhelming to me. I'm in a *gay bar*, for Christ's sake! I wish my high school Bible teacher were here...though I doubt he would be listening. He used to refer to bars and lounges as "upholstered sewers."

"I respect your opinion, don't get me wrong," Ben says. "I've just found that the evidence people cite for evolution doesn't seem to hold much water."

With each second that passes, I lose patience. It is the first time I have been at the bar and heard people speaking my language. I have to interrupt. "Excuse me, but are you guys actually talking about young-earth creationism?"

Both men turn towards me, and the bartender nods. "What do you think?" Ben asks me.

"That's an irrelevant question, I think. I wasn't there, so I don't really know how everything came to be. I definitely believe in God, and I'd like to think the creation accounts are literal, but I don't really know what I think, nor do I really care." I was inundated with young-earth creationism in science and college at Liberty University. To believe in evolution was tantamount to being pagan. If the first two chapters of the Bible aren't true, then how can anything else be? At least that's what my teachers always said, coming from the perspective of biblical literalism.

"So you're a Christian?" Lance looks at me, engaged and genuinely interested in what I might say. The bartender, sensing an opportunity to escape, moves towards another regular at the other end of the room.

"I am a follower of Jesus...But honestly, I don't know what that means anymore." This is the truth. Several weeks have already given me a sense of disillusionment, and I am overcome with doubt. If the people of God, who claim to know him better than anyone else, would treat me the way they have, it is hard for me allow myself to believe blindly what I have been taught by them.

"I completely understand. It sounds like you're searching." Ben smiles and moves to the stool next to me.

"You have no idea."

"If you're searching, you will find the answers. I'll pray for you."

It is the first time in weeks that *prayer* has come up without a deeper motive attached.

"Thank you, but…Would you mind if I ask you a personal question?"

"Not at all," Ben says, sipping his drink.

"How can you be gay and still be so conservative in your faith? I was listening to your conversation and you sound, well, you sound like a Southern Baptist."

Ben looks down thoughtfully before answering. "I'm fairly conservative in that I take most of the Bible literally, but I don't believe the Bible addresses 'gay' as we know it. I guess I just try to follow the two great commandments above anything else. And yes, for the record, I do go to a Southern Baptist church."

"So what would you say in defense of your being gay and being a Christian?"

"I believe God knows me more than I can even know myself, and I believe He loves me more than I can ever love myself. And if that's true, what else is there to know?"

Ben's humility is a breath of fresh air, and it takes me a second to remember I'm not talking to a typical believer. But is his faith really legitimate?

"Fair enough," I say, fearful of the direction the conversation might take me. If it is possible that Ben actually has a relationship with God, then what the church has told me all along could be wrong—and the consequences of *that* are something I do not want to contemplate right now. I am not ready for it. I am still struggling to understand the effect of what I consider to be un-repentant sin on a relationship to God.

"I saw you talking to Will the other night. You guys old friends?"

"Yeah. We grew up together but have just reconnected," I say.

"He's a great guy. A total lover. He loves everyone who comes to this bar, and everyone loves him back."

"That's not hard to imagine."

"So what's your story? Are you new to Nashville?" Ben asks. His enthusiasm is contagious.

"No. I've lived here since I was two."

"Why haven't we met here before?" Ben probes innocently.

"Well, I just came out in January," I reply nervously.

"*Really?*" Ben's inquisitive expression turns into an all-out grin. "I'm so happy for you!" And before I can respond, he hugs me. Of the thousands of hugs I have had in my life, this one feels different. I feel a totality of acceptance, a sense of overwhelming support, and I feel valued. Ben isn't just hugging me; he is shar-ing his heart with me, and I am ill equipped to respond. "Devon, get Tim here another beer. We are celebrating his coming out!"

"Seriously? This one is on the house." The bartender pours me another Blue Moon and puts an orange slice on the edge of the glass. "Welcome to freedom," he says, putting the beer in front of me.

"Cheers to your new life, your search for faith, and to gor-geous men!" Ben toasts and our glasses clunk together, spilling a few drops of beer on my thumb. I cannot help but laugh.

"Hell, yeah, to gorgeous men!" I say.

"Here here!" the bartender says.

~~~

After another hour of conversation, I'm convinced of two things. The first is that Lance is perhaps one of the most interesting men

I have ever met. The second is that Ben defies most of the stereo-types I have ever held about the faith of an openly gay man. Un-til now, I had not met someone who claimed to believe the Bible literally and still openly referred to himself as gay. I was taught that gay Christians are Universalists (meaning that if there is indeed a Heaven, then everyone goes there, regardless of their deeds, beliefs, or sexual orientation); that they hold a non-literal view of the Bible (to hold a literal worldview would mean their sexuality is a sin); and they only attend churches whose parish-ioners are predominantly gay or lesbian. But Ben seems to be every bit as conservative as I am, and he goes to a run-of-the-mill Baptist church. Not only is he a young-earth creationist, he believes in the divinity of Jesus, the necessity of repentance in salvation, and, most surprising, he believes in a literal Hell.

But how can he reconcile his life and his orientation while living the life of a social and theological conservative? One thing is sure: I have lived my life in a bubble. The fact that there are men and women who share Ben's beliefs demonstrates how broad the social spectrum is within the gay, lesbian, bisexual, and transgender community. It is so broad that I hesitate to use the word *community*—a word that Ben explains negates the profound intricacies of the queer-associated populace.

Ben makes a point to introduce me to the regulars that he says I should be friends with, and one of them really makes an impression. Phil is in his forties, balding, and wears glasses. Phil is the epitome of soft spoken. Even his handshake is gentle and friendly, and I feel as though I will break his hand if my own handshake is too firm.

"Tim just came out of the closet," Lance tells Phil.

"Oh, wow. Congratulations, Tim. How's it been for you so far?" he asks, tilting his head down towards me. He speaks in a soft, almost inaudible voice, and his demeanor doesn't leave any room for discomfort.

"I guess it has been pretty smooth. I've only lost a few of my friends…and the church I used to go to."

"Bless your heart, hun." He puts his hand on my shoulder and takes a deep breath.

It strikes me as interesting that I used to shun the touch of anyone I perceived to be gay, like they had some sort of disease I could catch. Additionally, if a man called me *babe* or *hun*, I would have been irrationally livid. But now it feels okay. Not only does it feel okay, it feels encouraging. It feels human.

"So, what's your story?" I say. I've found myself asking about people's stories a lot more lately.

"Well, I came out at thirty, and my parents weren't too happy about it. But I don't blame them. They were taught by people who were taught by people who didn't understand that being gay isn't a psychological malady. It really is easier for you younger folks nowadays."

"Have they warmed up to it since then?" I ask.

"Well, my dad died four years ago, and my mother was absolutely devastated. She moved into my house with me and has been there ever since. She's figured it out, but it has taken time. I don't know if she ever would have, if my dad hadn't passed."

"I'm glad she's figured things out." *I wish I could.* "Do you have a boyfriend?"

"No, but I'm happy. I don't want to settle for someone that I'm not supposed to be with. I may never find someone, but that's okay." Phil speaks in such a way that I can see he's reliving his life as he chooses the words to answer my questions, and I can tell he has made peace with the ghosts of his past. But saying that it would be okay not to have love in his life stirs something deep within me, and without thinking I speak.

"I hope you *do* find someone. It'd be such a waste if a beautiful man like you didn't find love." And what surprises me even more is that I actually mean what I am saying.

"Tim, I can tell you have a good heart, a gentle heart. Don't let life make you cynical and take that away. Stay you no matter what, because I can see grace in you." Phil doesn't attempt to hide his emotion and hugs me.

Once again, I feel the same connection and sense of kinship that I did when Ben hugged me, a bond that I would not have anticipated with a stranger, much less a gay stranger. And I don't know what surprises me more: the connection I feel with these two men, or how much I hope Phil *does* find someone. To wish that, after all, would mean I hope he remains homosexual—which in terms of my religion would be completely morally wrong and unnatural.

But is it? Both Ben and Phil are gay. There's no sidestepping that, no sweeping it under the rug. It is confusing to feel fondness for two guys who are so different from what I was taught to expect. Nothing about their orientation feels unnatural. They aren't at the bar on the prowl for a one-night stand—in fact, both are against casual sex—and neither has had more than two or three drinks. They are only at the bar to meet other empathetic souls, people who won't judge them for who they are, and both seem to have looked inside me and validated who I am beneath the hardened dogma. Phil even tells me that he believes I'm gentle and hopes I never end up cynical. Maybe beneath all of the bullshit, I am. Maybe they can see what I cannot even see in myself. I hope so…otherwise how will I ever accomplish anything?

I say my goodbyes to Ben and Phil and drive home in silence, stunned by the gaping holes in my assumptions. I do not just feel ignorant; I feel cheated, like I have been held back from people that could have spoken hope to me all my life, but I was not allowed listen just because of their orientation. Tonight, I found friendship. I found camaraderie and kinship. Tonight, I found fellowship. Tonight, I found pain and loneliness, but also hope. Tonight, I found a part of myself in a gay bar on Church Street.

6 the mirror

I wake up and see the signs of spring all around me: life, the smells of green and yellow and red, drifts into my window, just daring me to get out of bed. But I can't. Last night I cried myself to sleep. I cried myself to sleep, and even now the wetness from those tears has left my pillow damp to the touch. The novelty of my experiment, if there was any to begin with, has worn off—but I am still here, left to question and live out a life that does not belong to me. I cried because I was alone, and I stay in bed because I don't know if I'll be able to make it another day.

The other night I was with family, watching sports. The game was at a pinnacle moment where the next team that scored would most likely win, and fortunately my team made the goal.

"*Jesus Christ,* that was a good play!" I yell.

My mom sighs and I can hear her frustration. She's next to me on the couch, sitting Indian style with a pillow behind her neck, and her head leaned back.

"What?" I ask.

"Do you really have to say *Jesus Christ* like that, or is that just another sign that you've turned your back on God?"

It isn't so much the words she speaks as much as the tone behind them, and the implication of what she is inferring crushes me. Until that moment, my mother has not only done her best to make me feel accepted, she treated me like the daughter she never had. But in the moment, in *that* moment, I realized it must have been a lie all along.

"Excuse me?" I was blindsided by her words.

"Where did my little boy go, the one who always wanted to be a pastor and have a family? Now you're gay and sitting on my couch taking the Lord's name in vain." She had been bot-tling this up for weeks now, I could tell, and it was finally coming out. At least she was being honest. I was beginning to wonder if I had just imagined everything about my religious upbringing—the upbringing I had to be punished by in order to understand its true nature.

"If God is anything like the people who follow him, and I'm talking about you right now, mom, then yes, I'm proud to say that I've turned away from Him, and for good." I didn't wait around to see her reaction, or for my family to step in and mediate an argument. I stood and walked out of the room.

I meant what I said. I really did. If the God I claimed to serve was anything like the people I have encountered who had an adverse reaction to my being gay—like the me that probably would have said something very similar to what my mom just said—then I did not want to know Him. And if *He* was like *them*, then all of that love talk in the Bible was most assuredly bullshit, and one can only stomach so much bullshit in one's life.

The front door slammed behind me and I walked down the stairs and up the short path to the driveway, trying to hold back tears. I was not so much upset by what she said; I was upset that she seemed to have hidden so much from me.

But maybe for a woman who believed her son had hidden so much from her, it was only fair.

~~~

After deciding I that I have moped sufficiently enough for one day, I know it is time to get out of bed, pick myself up, and ignore the funk. I recently moved back into my dad's house in west Nashville, and the transition has been difficult. I still have boxes to unpack, but those can wait. I don't feel like unpacking. It is and odd thing to once again live in the house where I grew up. Unfortunately, the massive recession has given me no other option.

The move back to my dad's house has been awkward but also somehow cathartic. He is gone most of the time, always with my step-mother-to-be, and so I am alone with only my memories to keep me company. I walk into the kitchen, make a pot of coffee, and watch shadows of my former self running through the house with Nerf guns chasing my brother, or kissing ex-girlfriends on the couch, or sitting at the dinner table with a mom and dad that are still together. The phantoms command my attention more than the mug of coffee I sip. The hot black liquid spills on my hand. *Damn it!* I turn on the faucet and run cold water over the wound, but the physical pain is only a fraction of the pain I feel inside, thinking about the past. And now I am here to dismantle even more of that past, living in the home where the youthful sponge I was became so weighed down with dogma that I was practically broken in half.

I would not be who I am if my family had not fallen apart. I know this. I would probably still be attending the church I was raised in. I try to see the good in the past, but it does not make anything easier. Nothing about life is easy, I've found, but that is okay. Twisted, but okay. I wonder what other phantoms my mind would chase in this house, if I had experienced more home, more normal, more opportunities to live in that blissful ignorance when I thought my parents infallible. It is hard not to dwell on these things now. I am living in the closet, cut off from a once-flourishing social life…and detoxing from the most potent drug I have ever known: estrogen.

My dad's cat reminds me that he needs food. I set my coffee down to fill his dish. He's a wonderful cat. He sits with me on the couch when I am watching a movie or surfing the internet, and he sleeps next to my computer while I write. He makes me smile. I walk over to the couch and log in to my email, not expecting to hear anything from anyone. My inbox is not remotely what it used to be when I was in church. I feel stranded, cut off, because most of the friends I called family have not reached out or even attempted to contact me since I came out as gay. I'm desperately lonely, and it has only been six weeks.

I see an unread message, and my interest is peaked. Jennifer has been a friend since I attended Liberty, and I have not heard from her since I came out. I brace myself for whatever the message will say and take a deep breath. It reads:

Tim…You're gay? How on earth is that even possible? You are the last guy on the planet I would have suspected…But I wanted to tell you that I'm happy you are. We've been raised in similar churches all of our lives, and we are more similar now than ever. I'm gay, too. Should I say lesbian instead of gay? Either way, the whole thing is confusing to me and I haven't told anyone. I've struggled with this secret for so long that I've felt lost. I'm sorry that I didn't tell you sooner. I was just worried what "pastor Tim" would think and say. You were really hardcore before, and I didn't want to let you down. When I heard the news last month it was like a light at the end of a tunnel. I've been so depressed for so long, and it has been killing me. I am constantly overwhelmed and feel like I'm mentally and emotionally shutting down. Just wanted you to know, so that you know you aren't alone. I'm proud of you. Pray for me. I'll see you when I visit home.

Your friend,
Jennifer

I stand up and start pacing. This is too much. One set of friends emails me saying they will not support my "decision to be gay" or even be friends until I "seek repentance," and the rest have chosen to ignore me…But I never expected to hear from anyone actually living in the closet! Is *everyone* hiding who they are? Nothing I thought I knew about anyone is turning out to be true! Have I really been so blind and so oblivious? And worse,

I feel that my lie about being gay might now hurt Jennifer, because she only confided in me because she believes I am gay. She probably wouldn't have told me otherwise. I hope when she learns the truth about me, she won't feel angry. I never understood how my decision would affect others. *Lord, help me...*

I cannot get the line "I didn't want to let you down" out of my head. Was I really that scary before, that religious zealot who abused my friends for anything I did not agree with? Am I completely different than I have always perceived myself to be? Sure, I know how to find Ecclesiastes at the sound of a whistle, and I know how to recite the books of the Bible in less than twenty-five seconds—but for what? My own friends do not believe I love them and even fear being honest with me! I feel like a monster.

~~~

A few hours later I drive to Tribe to meet up with Shawn. As usual I am early, but that is okay because more than anything I am out searching for pity, for an ear to listen and tell me how right I am for feeling so angry at my mom. It is comforting to be around people who don't judge me, who understand what I am going through and accept me regardless of our differences. It is the way I always wished church could be.

After parking in my typical spot, I walk inside and see Will at the main bar. He's shaking a martini for someone, and as soon as he finishes he comes over and gives me a hug.

"How're you doing, bud?"

"I've been better."

"Oh, yeah? What's wrong?" he asks.

"The other night, my mom said some things that really hurt me." He looks at me sympathetically, and I don't wait for him to ask before saying, "I don't know how to get past it. I just don't understand her sometimes. I just don't understand how my being gay would change how she sees me so radically." Will hands me a beer and I take a sip.

"What is so hard to understand?" He pauses. "Tim, have you ever tried to think about it from her perspective?"

His words catch me off guard. "What do you mean?"

"You know what I've gone through, but what I haven't told you is how I can accept and love my mom, even though she doesn't accept me." Will pulls out a dish towel and starts wiping down the bar. "Initially when I came out, I felt like you do now, like she didn't love me because she doesn't accept me. But it's not that way. She loves me, *so* she's trying to follow her beliefs about me. Even though I don't agree with her, I can't hold it against her. Some may call her a bigot for how she treats me, but I call it being my mom...And fortunately, I was raised in the church, so I know that her motivations aren't evil. She isn't trying to spite me or make me feel like a freak; she really is genuinely concerned. It sounds like your mom is, too."

"How do you do it, though? I just can't imagine being able to do that."

"I just try to put myself in her shoes. If I believed what my mother believes, and I had a son come out as gay, I would be mortified because that would mean my blood, my offspring that I love unconditionally, was going to Hell. Now think about Hell from a conservative Christian's perspective. Wouldn't you do whatever you could to steer your child away from that path? It is simple enough for me. Her belief separates us, but her motivation helps me understand and accept her, even though it hurts me." Will steps away for a second and makes a drink for another customer. He finishes and walks back over. "The other thing I do is try to think about what my orientation takes away from my mom. I think about what she's lost."

"What do you mean, you think about what she's lost?"

"Tim, I'm my mom's only son. Your mom only has two sons. Think about how much it must hurt them to know they won't be able to go to our weddings or hold and babysit our biological children. It can't be easy. And let's be realistic: Our country probably won't come around for a while. Our moms will never have the 'normal' life they dreamed of. We don't have to agree with their beliefs, but we can sympathize with what they have to give up so that we can be ourselves."

"So what you're saying is that they care more about what they are losing than they do about us being gay?"

"Yes and no. Their spiritual beliefs about our lives and their personal sense of loss that is a result of our lives make them act this way. Try not to take it personally. I truly believe that it will get better for both of us, if we just give our mothers time."

"I understand and agree with you, for the most part, but I still can't help but feel gross that a religious belief would give someone 'cause' to treat me this way—especially my own mother."

"We live in difficult times. Be angry at the belief all you want, but the second you stop seeing people as people and see them only for their beliefs, you become guilty, too. I've been through hell over the past few years, but that much I've learned. I'm not just 'gay Will,' and my mom isn't just 'uber-conservative Christian mom.'"

"So does that mean I have to interact with people who believe I'm abominable?" I ask.

"Hell, no! I'm just trying to say that if you come into contact with anyone who holds those negative spiritual beliefs about you, don't forget to smile and show them the respect you wish you were shown. Karma, non-violence, the golden rule, and especially grace—these are all universal principles that will give you peace. Our families are captive to a more conservative way of thinking about things. That's the unfortunate part of this whole thing. We really are slaves to an idea that hurts us."

I came to Tribe to vent, and instead of blindly supporting me, my childhood friend is trying to help me think from a different perspective. He has shown me that we can empathize without budging on our worldview; and that if we do not empathize, we are as careless as the people whom we are at odds with.

Being a second-class citizen feels like being a tenth-class citizen. If I really were gay, I feel like my life would become such an issue for people that I would be constantly exhausted. Gays and lesbians are looked at as different, perverse, and the label alone seems to illicit an association with the lowest dregs of society, morally speaking. No one wants to be thought of that way! Is it really so unrealistic to let people's actions speak for them rather than the stigmatized label?

Experiencing the other side of prejudice is more painful than I anticipated. Worse, I feel as though I am constantly being faced with my own face in the mirror: the image of a Pharisee who has not thought to look past labels and orientations to see people for who they really are. Had I not gone through with this experiment, I probably would have always believed the lie that I really am better than the other, and my life would have been characterized by a shallower understanding of humanity. At least now I can see what I really look like, and, Lord willing, I may yet change the image staring back at me.

7 revive café

I never could have anticipated the social complexities within the gay community of Nashville. It is rich in people from all different walks of life. There is no one set of beliefs or opinions, no one particular political party to which every one ascribes, and no particular religion, for that matter. There is no hierarchy, and there does not need to be. Everyone seems to be at peace with one another. I am unaccustomed to such place of coexistence.

My life is changing as the season changes, and as winter slowly becomes spring and the weather outside begins drawing people from their homes, so does Nashville's humble gay district change. During the winter months, the community seemed only to come out at night; but now, only making my way to Church Street as the sun finally sets, I feel like an outsider. The quaint strip of businesses come alive, and I see families with two dads or moms, enjoying each others' company for story time at the bookstore or concerts at the café. For this reason I began applying for jobs in the neighborhood over the past few weeks.

It is just another Thursday when my phone rings. The number is not one I recognize. To my surprise, it is the manager of Revive Café. Revive is perhaps the coolest java spot in the city, and the idyllic bohemian décor meshes nicely with the flare that gays seem to bring to everything they touch. If I get the job, I will finally be able to work and spend full-time hours in the community. It would be my own rainbow-colored avatar experience—and a much more casual opportunity to finally ask the questions I have not been able to ask at the bars. *Revive Café: Virgin Drinks, Hot Treats, and Happy Endings*. The sign on the front window says it all.

Applying at Revive was not as easy as I had anticipated. While filling out the application, the realization struck me that something as simple as applying for a job had somehow become more difficult than ever before. Sure, my name, address, and phone number were all the same. My social security number had not changed, and my work experience looked pretty damned good on paper. But it was not until I reached the education history that I started wondering if I would be found out. Could I really put down *Pioneer Christian Academy* for my high school, and even more nerve-wracking, admit I attended Liberty University? Can you imagine the irony, applying at a gay café in the heart of the gay district, knowing that my college was founded by the man responsible for the Moral Majority?

It took me a full minute to write *Liberty University* on the application, and without thinking I drew an arrow from the name of the college to the margin of the paper and wrote: *PLEASE DON'T HOLD THIS AGAINST ME.* I walked out of the bookstore thinking I would never possibly get the job.

I answer the phone, still crossing my fingers.

"Is this Tim?"

"Yes."

And then there is a moment of silence, followed by the sound of paper shuffling.

"I just wanted to say that I won't hold it against you!" the man says, laughing. "This is Brent from Revive Café. I have your application and wanted to see if you'd come in for an interview this afternoon."

"I would love to!" I say, utterly shocked.

"Four o'clock work for you?"

"Of course!"

"Great. See you at four."

I press end and smile. Finally, my past is doing something to help my project.

I arrive fifteen minutes early and sit on the couch next to the front entrance. There are only a handful of people drinking coffee and reading, and I feel nervous. A minute or two passes and Brent makes his way over to me. "Tim?" he asks. "Give me a few minutes and I'll grab your paperwork and we can go to the patio."

A few months ago, the mere thought of working in a café frequented by a predominantly gay and lesbian clientele would have left me nauseated. Now I feel excited, hopeful, and the anticipation of working here has reinvigorated me. Besides, the Christian friends and community I spent years building seem to have forgotten about me. So many people have disappeared from my life that it is almost as though they never existed. Fair-weather friends? No, just people firmly stuck in their bubbles, I think.

On the other hand, the people I am meeting now seem to accept me more than anyone ever has. Perhaps that is because the gay men I spend so much time with don't judge me by my piety but let my actions speak for themselves. If I make them laugh, they like me for my sense of humor. If I am kind, they like that I am sensitive. Those are earned actions. It is nice not to be judged for my gauged ears, or for the fact that I didn't read as much of the Bible as a fellow parishioner. It is nice not to be judged by how well I can present a righteous façade. Shawn said it would happen. He said I would lose friends but not to lose heart because I would meet a host of new ones—and he said I would feel a certain level of authenticity that I hadn't before. Once again his counsel has proven correct. I hope I get the job, so we can go out and celebrate. After all, that is what boyfriends do.

"Ready? Would you like a latte while we interview?"

"Of course!"

Brent grabs a large mug and thirty seconds later, after pouring the shots and steaming the milk, he hands me my first free latte.

"I could get used to this."

"It is definitely a perk."

We walk outside to the patio and sit at the table closest to the door. The sun is shining, but it is still relatively cool outside. It is perfect weather for an interview. "First, I wanted to say that I loved your application. After reading sixty or so of them, I saw yours and it woke me up."

"Thank you. I was worried you would read my education history and I'd be blacklisted." I take a sip of the latte, and the creamy liquid tastes smooth.

"So, Tim, what is your story?" Brent asks.

"Well, I don't want to keep you here all day..." I try to think about how I can possibly answer. "I was raised in a very conservative church and went to very conservative churches. I just came out in January, and I thought it would be healthy for me to be around the community I was always taught to hate—to be around my people."

"That sounds like a really good idea. How is your family handling everything?" he asks solemnly.

"Okay, I guess. They haven't shunned me or cut me off, but my mom and dad keep asking if I will consider therapy. My brother and his wife have been really cool, so far."

"That's good to hear. You would be amazed at how bad some families react," he says, looking down at the application.

"So I've heard."

"What makes you want to work at Revive? Why did you apply to be a barista?"

"I just want to be around people. I have always loved coffee, so I thought making coffee might be just as enjoyable."

The interview seems to flow smoothly for another half hour or so, and in the process I feel a strong kinship with Brent. We spend more time cracking jokes and laughing about the people walking by than simply asking and answering questions. As we wrap up the interview, I know I will feel terrible if I do not get the job. I feel called to this place.

"Tim, you have a great personality and sense of humor. I think you would be perfect for the job, but I still have a few other people to interview. Give me a day or two, and I will call you and let you know if you have the job." He touches my shoulder reassuringly and we walk back inside.

I walk over to the counter and set the empty mug down in the dirty dish tub. A group of four men are sitting nearby around a small table, playing cards. "Brent!"

"Yes, Kenny?"

"You'd better hire this one. He's hunky!"

I blush.

"You might get your way if you stop yelling across the room at me!" Brent says with a laugh. "Those are the Bears. They meet here pretty regularly."

"What is a Bear?" I ask.

"Wow…Tim, you have a lot to learn, and you had better learn fast, because you are going to be target number one for them." Brent laughs, but I still don't get it. I will have to look it up online when I get home.

"Talk to you soon. Thank you for giving me an interview. It means a lot," I say. Brent winks at me and I walk out the door. If I get this job, not only will I be able to talk with people over coffee, I will actually be the one making the coffee! I can barely contain myself.

~~~

The next night I am standing on Josh's porch, smoking cloves and telling him all about the interview. It is hard to speak in complete sentences, and Josh seems happy for me. He laughs when I tell him what the guys were saying as I left.

"Like I've always said, you've got *bottom* tattooed on your forehead!" He laughs.

I ignore his teasing and take another drag on my clove cigarette. My phone rings. The name *Revive Café* pops up on the caller ID, and I take a deep breath and answer.

"Hello?"

"Hey, Tim. It's Brent. Just wanted to let you know that you got the job and you can start tomorrow."

"Seriously?"

"I think you'll be a perfect fit here, and I am looking forward to working with you."

"Me, too!" I can barely contain my excitement.

"Come by at noon to fill out paperwork, and you'll be working from 3:00 p.m. to close."

"Perfect!" I say. Josh is smiling and pats my back.

"See you then." He hangs up the phone, and I scream.

"Damn, are you sure you aren't really gay?" Josh says, laughing at my reaction. Once again I ignore his friendly teasing.

I drive home and get ready for bed, grateful for the good news I have received. But the excitement is short lived. I look across the room and see the Pharisee sitting at my desk, tapping a pencil on the cover of an old theology textbook from Liberty.

Congratulations. You get to work at a café that's attached to a sex shop.

It's attached to a bookstore.

And a sex shop.

So what?

Make coffee for perverted people all you want. It won't change anything. There is no goodness in people that don't know and follow Christ. You know this!

I don't believe that anymore.

Yes, you do. You're just caught up in the emotions of this whole thing. Eventually the Spirit and your conscience will win out. At least I pray they will.

I'm getting sick of you telling me what is and isn't true. I'm finally seeing things as they are—and no, I don't have all the answers, but I'm on the right track.

Homosexuality is unnatural. You might think you love your new friends, but you are forgetting that these "good people" will be going to hell. You should be warning them of the consequences of their sin, not serving them coffee.

Maybe just serving them coffee is all the Lord requires of me. Maybe loving them and listening to them and asking them about their lives, maybe that's what Jesus would do.

Next to a sex shop?

Have you read the gospels? I roll over in my bed and try to close my eyes. Whenever good things happen, I always end up arguing the merits of it all. It is exhausting. I close my eyes and think back to the last time I worked with an openly gay man, and I am overcome with grief.

~~~

The last time I worked with an openly gay co-worker, I was sixteen and working at a neighborhood fast-food restaurant. The gay man was my manager. His name was Todd, and from day one, I did not like him. Not only did I not like him, I felt a subconscious pull to make his life miserable. His voice was nasally and much higher than I believed a grown man's voice should be, and he a handlebar mustache straight out of an '80s porn flick. Todd was a prime target for my teenage aggression.

One of my best friends had gotten me the job, and though he disliked Todd for different reasons—he was agnostic and an anarchist who waged a war of passive aggression against any authority in his life—we both found a common enemy in our manager. So we concocted a plan. We decided to wait for the moment Todd did anything that could be construed as sexual harassment, and then we would blackmail him in exchange for "job security." My opportunity came one night while doing dishes. The sink was located in a very narrow hallway, and Todd, attempting to squeeze passed me, inadvertently brushed my backside with his crotch. I immediately accused him of thrusting, which he had not done, and because I was a minor he knew he had no defense. He could lose his job.

What started with these gross lies against an innocent man's character became bullying on par with any you might read about in a newspaper. Together my friend and I made our poor manager's life a living hell. We urinated on the door handles of Todd's car and vandalized it with eggs and cellophane, we purposely messed up his orders to make him look bad in front of customers, we incited others against him every shift we worked...We did everything we could to add stress to his job.

One afternoon as I was ringing people up on the register, I saw Todd out of the corner of my eye. He was cleaning a counter with disinfectant and restocking condiments for the dinner rush. I saw him and I felt my blood begin to boil. Why did he *choose* to be gay? Why would anyone *want* to be a sissy? I didn't just dislike him because my Bible said he was abominable; I didn't like him because he was different. I was the wannabe jock, and he was the queer, middle-aged fast-food manager. I grabbed the microphone that we used to call for backup when we were busy, and I pressed the button. The speakers shrilled the abrasive whistle of old technology, and I took a breath.

"Paging the faggot!" I said into the microphone. "*PAGING THE FAGGOT!*"

Other teenagers in the crowded dining area burst into laughter, and I saw Todd's face shift with emotion. He ran for the microphone and sent me outside on break with a wild look in his eyes. His lip quivered and his eyes filled with tears.

Eventually my antics lost their appeal and I became bored. I left the restaurant and began a new job working for a hat store in the mall. Six months later, my friend and fellow bully came to visit me at work. I greeted him with a smile, but the look on his face was somber.

"What's wrong?" I asked.

"Todd's dead." He took a deep breath. "Heart attack. Todd was a smoker, but they say it also had to do with an extremely high level of stress."

It could really only be stress and smoking. Todd rarely ate the food from the restaurant. He worked out, or at least talked like he did. He wasn't overweight. I stood there thinking through the news, processing it as I was able.

"What do you think?" my friend asked.

"I think it's sad that he is burning in Hell."

He snickered at my response. What I really wanted to say was that, although I was only partially to blame for Todd's death, I felt wholly responsible. And then I went back to work, my friend left, and I buried my memories of Todd and my profound guilt for torturing another human being.

I do not think I am able to describe the pain I feel now, looking back on these memories. Only now do I understand that he was a child of God, and that I will be the one to answer for my immaturity and cruelty. I am to blame, and I will never forgive myself for my actions against a man whose only offence was his orientation.

Why I am including this particular memory? I'm not sure, except to say that I will always live with guilt. It is my cross to bear, the consequence of thoughtless actions and a despicable mentality. And maybe, just maybe, one day I will be able to make amends. I have only one life to live, and I will always remember the warmth and kindness of the man who did me no wrong. Rest in peace, Todd. I never fully will.

~~~

Finally I fall asleep, knowing that tomorrow is a new day. Tomorrow is the beginning of a new season in my experiment and in my life. It is a season of revival. Not the kind of revival televangelists speak about before asking for money, but a revival inside of me. I hope I continue to see where I have gone wrong, and perhaps I will have the opportunity to atone for my sins.

Spring has arrived, and it has brought with it a gift. For the first time this year, I do not feel so afraid. Life has reached a sort of plateau, and I feel a sense of "normal" again. I even feel normal being known by the label of gay. Each day brings a certain amount of simple acceptance. I have stepped out of my life and into another. So far, the stereotypes I expected have not been applicable. Gays and lesbians, bisexuals and transgendered people...of the hundreds I have met, no two are alike. And tomorrow I will have the opportunity to meet and learn from even more of them.

Meanwhile, the label of gay has forced me to think more deeply about things I probably never would have otherwise. My homophobia has been replaced with questions. Now my focus is on discovering how many things I have always claimed to *know* are actually false. And most important, will I be able to relinquish what I "know" if experience shows me otherwise? Maybe not. But at least I am finally open to the idea that I may have been wrong all along.

Part II: The Old Testament

"If you want to improve, be content to be thought
foolish and stupid."

—Epictetus

8 a difficult truth

It is a beautiful spring day, and the sun reflects off of everything, casting a greenish blue tint to every window, car, even the street. I am driving downtown for my first shift at Revive Café, and my hopes are high. The atmosphere of Nashville's gayborhood is calm and quaint. After dark Church street comes alive, but during the day everything is sleepy, hung-over, and subdued. I drive behind the series of buildings that house the bookstore and café, park on a gravel strip big enough for only four or five cars, and walk around to the front sidewalk.

The café is attached to Nashville's only LGBTQ bookstore, and it is unlike any bookstore I have seen before. The store is divided into three main sections. In the front, one will find books on almost every topic related to the LGBTQ population. The back section is split by an invisible line and holds movies for rent and purchase, as well as t-shirts and other trinkets, almost all bearing a rainbow, human-rights campaign logo, or snarky message. The third section is closed off. It is a shop unto itself: sex toys, leather outfits, and porn. I curiously peek into the space but cannot convince myself to venture inside. Something tells me I am not ready for that yet. Maybe tomorrow.

The café is attached via two doors on the right wall of the bookstore. Inside, it feels like a different venue altogether. The walls are painted dark red and the wood around the bar is well polished oak. This café is classier than most. It definitely beats the café chains one finds on every street corner of Nashville. It is large, intimate, and unmistakably gay in theme and fashion. On one of the couches, a golden merman manikin, dressed in a Mardi-Gras appropriate outfit and mask, reclines. He is definitely not the Little-Mermaid type, unless Ariel had a gay merman cousin the movie didn't mention. He faces the door, checking out every customer walking into the café. I swear he winks at me as I set my messenger bag on the countertop. He gives me the creeps.

"Isn't he hot?" a voice from behind me asks. I turn and find a young man, mid twenties, wearing a red sleeveless t-shirt with silver letters spelling *QUEER* from waist to collar. He's also wearing a small gold chain with a cross.

"Who?" I am startled.

"Our merman! We got him from a local fashion boutique that went out of business. I mean, look at his abs. Spectacular, aren't they?"

"To die for. Too bad he's not real."

"Shh! Don't tell him that! Marco, don't listen to him! We all know you're real." The man smiles at me, obviously amused.

"Sorry, Marco." I try not to laugh.

"That's better. Now what's your name again?"

"I'm Tim." I reach out to shake his hand, but he pulls me into an unexpected hug and kisses me on the cheek.

"We don't shake, hun, we hug. We're a family here," he says. "My name's Mark. You are replacing me because I'm moving."

"Where to?" I ask.

"New Orleans. *Mardi Gras*, baby!"

"Congrats on that! I hear it's an amazing place."

"Yeah, but I'll miss Nashville. There are a lot of amazing guys here," he says thoughtfully. "Ever work at a café before?" Mark tosses me an apron. "I'm supposed to teach you to wear this, but no one does, and you'll never get in trouble if you don't. Just wear it today, and *I* won't get in trouble."

"You're direct. And no, I've never worked as a barista." I put the apron over my neck and can tell I'm going to like this job.

"Oh, honey, I'm always direct! Life is too short to waste on the bullshit. And speaking of bullshit, if my ex comes in—his name is Ryan—spit in his coffee! He's a real prick." Mark is sassy.

"You're going to have to teach me how to make the coffee first," I say.

"Good point. Let's get this sausage train open!" Mark walks around the counter and helps me log in with the time clock, and all I can think is how oddly comfortable I am around this guy. He's crude, entertaining, and someone I think I could be good friends with. Too bad he's moving to New Orleans.

Two hours pass, and a few customers come into the café that Mark tells me are regulars. Mark introduces them as Scott and Jason, a couple that can most aptly be characterized as an "April-September" romance. Both order sweet tea and immediately start interrogating me.

"Who are you, handsome?" Jason asks with a furrowed eyebrow.

He is trying to be seductive, but any discomfort I feel is diminished by the humor in his tone. He is gentle, albeit aggressive, and I imagine that he is the more free-spirited one in the relationship.

"Don't mind him. He's always trying to bring guys home!" Scott says.

"Am not!" Jason says, hitting Scott on the arm.

"Bitch!"

"It's okay, but I'm already attached," I interject, thanking God for Shawn. "I'm the new guy. I'm Tim, but you…" I look at Jason coyly. "You can call me whatever you want." I wink at him, and he is taken aback by my flirtation. I am even a bit surprised at myself.

"Mark, this one's a keeper," he says, fanning himself with his hand. "Is it me, or is it hot in here?"

"It's you." Mark laughs.

"So what's your story, hotness?" Jason puts his hand on mine, still laying it on thick.

"I'll give you the abridged version. I came out in January, and I thought it'd be fun to work here, so I could be around my people."

"Oh, my god! Are you serious? I never woulda thought..." Jason winks at me and makes a kissy face.

"Leave Tim alone, he's new. Show him some respect," Scott says, only partially rebuking his lover. "You'll have to pardon him, Tim. He lacks what most would call *tact*." Scott smiles. "And your boyfriend is a lucky man, I must say."

"Well, thank you." I set the glasses of tea in front of them, wipe the counter with a dishtowel, and return it to my shoulder.

"So how are you enjoying being out of the closet? Being yourself is freeing, isn't it?" Mark asks.

Being yourself, my ass!

I look over and see the Pharisee sitting on the couch against the wall, next to the Merman. The contrast is enough to make me smile and I ignore him.

"It's great," I say nervously, wondering what they would think if they knew how in the closet I am.

"How'd you do it?" Scott asks.

"I guess the normal way. I told my brother and his wife, and they told my mom before I could."

"Not cool," Mark interjects. "That is your privilege."

"I was just happy to have it over with," I say.

"Is your family okay with it? How'd they take the news?" Scott asks after taking a sip of his sweet tea.

"They're handling it okay, I guess. Not allies yet, but they're working it out day by day. Why does *everyone* keep asking me that?" I ask.

"Ask you what?" Jason says.

"About my family's reaction."

The mood in the café shifts in an instant. What was a light-hearted and flirtatious conversation becomes somber. It is a palpable change, and I feel it in my body as goose bumps race across my skin. Jason's face becomes serious, almost sad. He is not flirting anymore. His flamboyance seems to dim and his demeanor becomes more quiet.

"Tim, a really high percentage of suicides in this country are committed by people who are in the closet and feel they can't do it anymore. The closet kills people. And families can do a lot of damage early on, to those who've just broken free." He pauses. "Everyone asks because everyone is worried about you." His speaks very slowly, walking on egg shells with each word, gauging my response with his eyes.

"We're just happy you're okay," Scott says with the same solemn tone. "Just make sure and let us know if anything less than comfortable happens for you. We take care of each other, all of us."

"Thank you." I do not really know what to say, but gratitude seems appropriate.

I look over and measure my Pharisee's response.

He smirks. *This is why it's so hard for gays to see the light. They stick together so they don't have to face the spiritual ramifications of their unwillingness to repent. They don't judge because they don't want to be judged. It's not authentic support.*

No! It's deeper than that. The gays and lesbians I have met may have different standards of morality than me, but wanting to support each other is pure. No matter how much I could try to psychoanalyze it, I cannot discredit the idea. You're wrong.

He leans back against the couch and sighs. *I know I'm the villain for saying it, but guilt is what causes people to commit suicide. Not the "closet."*

Think whatever you want. And yes, thinking that does make you a villain. Where is your heart?

I try to refocus. Jason pinches Mark's butt and laughs when Mark jumps. They are like kids playing...a different kind of humor than I am accustomed to.

I never would have imagined that strangers would take such an interest in me, much less my family's reaction to me. The relational investment they demonstrate makes me feel like I have accidentally stumbled upon a sacred detail of the community. This cohesive empathy may be difficult for me to understand but it seems old hat for them, and I wonder how many people they have known who have gone through a much different experience than I have thus far. I wonder if I will ever understand.

Has my "absolute" view of gay been too narrow? It seems to be flawed, never considering the many intricacies and details that have shaped the lives of the people I meet so regularly now. It does not seem to consider the difficulty of coming out, the social stigma one faces as an openly gay man or lesbian woman—or a transgendered or intersex individual, who must struggle in ways I will never understand. Never for a minute did my ideology consider the life of belittlement and degradation that one faces for the remainder of one's life after coming out. It only claims one thing: Same-sex affection is unnatural and should therefore be rejected in all respects. For many conservatives, equal rights for same-sex marriage and adoption should not be given because equality in marriage and adoption would be looked at as approval or acceptance of the lifestyle, and that approval violates the moral imperative of the Bible. At least that is how it was explained to me.

I think about those trapped in the closet who see only two options: stay miserable in life or seek peace in the hereafter. And I wonder what Jesus would do. Would he go door to door campaigning for Proposition 8, or would he rebuke the Pharisees who dole out condemnation like a commodity, for missing the point? I think he would do the latter. But do I think that only because I have lost my focus on what my former pastor used to call the "panoramic landscape of the gospel"? My Pharisee said as much. But it just doesn't make sense. Life is too short to live out two-thousand-year-old prejudices from Leviticus, Greece, or Rome. Either way, I am starting to believe that people have the right to believe as they wish. *My* finger pointing has to stop, and thanks to Revive, I am starting to see why.

I finish my first shift at Revive and feel as though life is finally looking up. The people are fantastic—the epitome of entertaining—and I love the coffee-making process. Lattes are my favorite. Milk steamed to velvet perfection, poured delicately into a mug with two perfectly timed shots of espresso, add a sprinkle of cinnamon on top, and you have a little slice of heaven. I am learning quickly.

I leave the café and cannot stop thinking about the look on Jason's face, the look that said, *Congratulations on coming out of the closet! Stay in too long, and you could have died!* He did not seem to be exaggerating. I always thought that the people who found out about my coming out were buying me drinks because they were happy to have another queer-associated Southerner in the community, but now I think they are just happy to have one less closeted gay in the graveyard.

9 it's hard to be gay in spring

It's hard to be gay in spring. Well, probably not for someone who is *actually* gay, but for me, springtime poses more than a few problems. The rising temperatures result in rising skirt lines, and trying to keep my true orientation a secret is beyond frustrating.

I decide to go to church for the first time in months, hoping for the spiritual equivalent to a cold shower. The church I choose is a mega-church in town with thousands of members spread across several satellite campuses. For those unfamiliar with the idea, a *satellite campus* is a church that broadcasts the message of a pastor to multiple locations. The names of the churches are the same, they have the same non-profit status, and each has its own campus pastor; but essentially the structure allows a head pastor to be in multiple churches at once.

The location I am attending is the main campus, and the pastor is a young, good-looking guy with spiked hair and trendy clothes. He is a really nice and genuine guy, and, having spoken with him several times in the past, I know his heart is in the right place. The whole model of satellite churches seems kind of impersonal to me, but right now, the multitude of parishioners is the reason I have chosen this particular church.

After being greeted at the door, I walk into the lobby and am comforted by the fact that I am just another face in the crowd. Hardly anyone knows me, and that is a good thing. I am not here to be known, just to feel a little bit of normalcy before getting back to my new life. But seldom do well-intentioned plans pan out.

Upon reaching the café inside the church lobby, I am confronted with an overwhelming number of young women wearing incredibly revealing clothing. There are skin-tight jeans, short shorts, short skirts, and short shirts, and midriffs are exposed everywhere. Either I have never seen so much skin in a church before, or I never noticed because women have never been off limits. I rush to the bathroom and splash cold water on my face. I should probably splash water elsewhere, but that might be awkward for the other men in the bathroom.

I look in the mirror and see him behind me. His expression is sympathetic but coercive.

I've got to leave.

Don't leave. There is nothing unnatural about your looking at women. Besides, it's been a long time since you've let yourself see what you're keeping yourself from. It is the way God designed you to be.

No. And that feels like the wrong way to view women.

I cannot handle the visuals, the temptation, or the hormones raging through me. Staying in church would be tantamount to self-flagellation, self-torture, so I decide to leave the church and get coffee elsewhere. I was looking for a spiritual cold shower, and I got the spiritual equivalent of a *Girls Gone Wild* video.

I walk out of the lobby doors and shiver. It may be sunny and unseasonably warm, but I feel cold.

No, Tim, don't leave!

My Pharisee looks at me from the door, but I keep walking. Not today, buddy. Not today.

I drive to Starbucks and settle in with a venti coffee and a copy of the *Times*. It is my new Sunday morning ritual. Add to the combination Puccini's greatest hits, and what I get is better than attending church, nine times out of ten. After coming out as gay, I wholeheartedly expected to merely switch churches. I had thought that even though I would receive some nasty responses, my desire for church would remain. But it hasn't. After receiving the email from my pastor, after facing the plethora of responses, either rebuking me or ignoring me, the desire in me for fellowship has shifted. I want to spend time with people, but I feel sick to my stomach when I think about attending church. This feeling makes me understand why so many of my gay friends have left the church altogether. I can only imagine how much more severe my aversion would be had I received a worse reaction. So my replacement for my former Sunday morning tradition is to live a life of routines. I am amazingly content with just my coffee and paper and "Nessum Dorma" playing on repeat. For an hour or so every Sunday morning, I forget that life is not what it used to be, and the distraction is welcome. I sit and read a few compelling news stories and listen to a compelling piece of music, never forgetting that at any moment, the *Times* might remind me, vigorously, why I am living this life.

Today's *New York Times* has a story about LGBTQ teens committing suicide because of being bullied, and another about the never-ending saga of California's anti-gay marriage bill, Proposition 8. These two stories snap me back to reality. I read the story about teen suicide twice before pausing my music and praying for the families and the victims of bullying, and for the hearts of the bullies to change—and also my own heart. It is the only form of church I can muster today.

It is hard to comprehend that if I were actually a gay man, entire populations of socially conservative people have control over my fate. Religious organizations could raise enough money in a month to hinder my freedom in real and tangible ways, for the duration of my life. This is a reality for LGBTQ folks every-where. In California, religious organizations, primarily the Lat-ter Day Saints, covertly raised millions dollars to fund Propo-sition 8. Millions of dollars were spent raising an army of vol-unteers to canvas tens of thousands of homes with anti-gay literature and to engage voters in door-to-door confrontation. And for what? Passing Proposition 8 did not stop LGBTQ cou-ples from going to sleep that night with their partners. What it did accomplish, however, was remind the gay community once again that they are not looked at as equals, that the God of so many does not love them. I saw this as I watched the live coverage of the protests.

I have always allowed my beliefs to blind me to the reality lived daily by other human beings. I have let my opinions and interpretations of scripture to take away my compassion and God-given common sense. I am guilty of thinking in the stark black and white terms of my theology and politics, but never from the standpoint of real, living and breathing people. The picture at the top of the article breaks my heart. It is a photograph of two normal men, holding each other with tears in their eyes as they console one another.

I leave the café as hoards of church-goers show up, some of whom are the same girls that drove me out of the church in the first place. They prance around, ignorant of the effect they have on me. The chemical reaction inside me is enough to make me question what in the hell I'm doing, and I fight to look away. I shake my head in the despair of it all. It really is hard to be gay in spring.

I always wondered what it would be like to suppress my attraction to such an extreme degree. As I attempt it, I realize I have to suppress more than just physical attraction. I have to suppress *myself* to live within the mentality of the closet. And the closet is so much more severe than its name would have you to believe. It is not even closet-like. It is a self-imposed exile from the reality of who you are. It is a roadblock to anyone trying to have any semblance of a normal life. Were this experiment to last longer than a year, I would have to talk to girls discreetly and hide those relationships from everyone. It would be impossible for me to live without enjoying the company of another person. The only way I am able to handle this forced abstinence from women is by reminding myself daily that this project will only last a year. But others do not have that luxury.

Harder even than not gawking at girls is the act of forcing myself to live in an almost constant state of paranoia. Paranoia seems to be, for me, the key to staying in the closet. When people look at me now, my first thought is to question their thoughts. When I am with my family or friends, I have to make sure I control what I look at and where my eyes wander. And even when I am in the clubs, I have act totally comfortable, even when I'm not. This means forcing myself to maintain composure even when I'm receiving the most shocking types of attention from unwanted suitors. Being in the closet means I have to try to monitor every action and reaction before it becomes external, deciding whether it will give me away.

Being at church today reminds me of a story told by my friend James from Tribe, who grew up in the closet and had to shower day after day with his football team after practice. He had to will himself not to get an erection every time, because if he didn't, he would have been bullied, possibly to death. It was not safe for him to be himself. I am starting to understand why. "My life felt like a pornography I was forced into," he said. "And I learned to keep my eyes closed and shower like it was a sprint."

I have also begun tracking what I can only describe as a phenomenon. Several women frequent the gay dance clubs, trying to sleep with gay men. I am not sure whether they are doing so out of insecurity or for sport, but seducing a gay man seems to be a trophy of sorts: The only reason you're gay is because you haven't slept with me. They use this line or a variation almost every time. Every time it has been used on me, I have to laugh, walk away, and force myself to stay in the bathroom for several minutes so I don't end up taking the bait. It seems that no matter where I go, I am faced with my hormones and with the primal attraction of my orientation. I am not safe anywhere.

Another facet of the closet—the most difficult, for me—is the restrictive power it holds over my life. Being single was never something I worried about, but the moment the option of a relationship became off limits, I felt like I was in solitary confinement. I could never have imagined that being forcibly single would rob me of so much joy.

The closet is beginning to get to me, really get to me. I do not know how much longer I will be able to handle this.

10 recruited

It is just another Friday night, and I am at Tribe. Fortunately my shift at Revive ended in time for me to grab a beer and see some friends whom I have not been able to spend time with for a few weeks. Ben and Phil are both on the patio when I arrive, and run over to hug me. I am comforted by their presence and blessed by their happiness at seeing me. The ambiance, the very mood, at the bar is unusually relaxed. It is the end of a work week and everyone is looks tired and ready for the weekend. Maybe they should be drinking shots of espresso instead of vodka.

I find my way to Will's bar and order a drink. Next to me, two of the regulars are already four drinks in. They are loud and joking raucously about their sexual conquests, trying to bring others into their game. When they see me, the "virgin gay," they call me, they begin inching their way towards me. But I am not the fool I was that first night at the club. Shawn has taught me how to handle myself with these kinds of guys, even in unsettling situations.

"Hey, sexy!" The first man moves next to me and lays it on thick. "So we've been wondering something."

"What's that?" I ask, staring straight ahead at Will. We seem to be having a conversation without words, and Will is telling me to ignore them.

"Your earrings are four gage, right?" he asks.

"Twos, actually," I answer, still looking ahead.

"Well, we were wondering if your ears are all that's pierced."

"What's your name again?" I ask.

"Whatever you want it to be, babe."

"Cut the shit. What's your name?"

"I've told you three times since you've been coming in here. I'm Trey, and he's John." He seems upset I did not remember.

"Pleasure to meet you, again." I finally look at Trey and he smiles. "And to answer your question, maybe I have other piercings, maybe I don't. You'll never know."

"Ooh, he's feisty!" John approaches me from behind and starts massaging my neck. It is not a gentle massage. It hurts. I feel simple panic wash over me. It comes from somewhere inside, the place inside where I thought I had banished my homophobia.

Before I can react to the massage, I feel Trey close to my ear. He breathes heavily, trying to turn me on, like he is going to suck on my earlobes. I flatten my palm and slide it up in between my ear and his mouth, but he reaches up and lowers my hand. I feel angry and disgusted, but I cannot give into my revulsion.

I am on the verge of overreacting, and overreacting might give me away. This is too much. My hand tightens into a fist, and I want to hit John in the mouth. I want to punch Trey, too. The unwanted advances creep me out, and I feel more uncomfortable than I have felt in months. But unlike that first night at Play, I think rationally. I take three deep breaths, and an odd sense of calm covers me. I see their game for what it is. They are two lonely guys who have had too much to drink and want something they know they cannot have.

"You know, I feel really bad for you guys."

John stops massaging me and looks perplexed.

"What? Why?" Trey asks.

"There's only one reason you act this way." I pause and sip my beer. "Neither of you feel loved, so you look for any substitute possible to fill that void. But I want you to know that both of you *are* loved. I love you, and God loves you, and I hope you figure it out soon."

Will looks up at me from behind the bar and smiles. He nods his head in approval.

"How you figure that?" John asks.

"It's just the impression you guys give me. Like I said, I really hope you realize that there's more to life than crossing the line with a guy you barely know." Without thinking, I put my hand on Trey's shoulder and smile at him. "I hope you aren't offended."

"No…" He looks down thoughtfully. "We aren't." Trey seems surprised by my reaction.

I do love them. I really do. I feel their sadness inside their false confidence. I have always used religion to mask my insecurities, but never sex. Sex does not change anything. Both sex and religion are equally wrong when you use them as a substitute for being honest with yourself.

"Will. I'm going to the bathroom. Will you watch my drink?" I say.

"Sure thing." He smiles.

Before the bathroom door is closed, I have dialed Shawn's number. I need a buffer, and he is the only one I can think of who can help me out. He answers and I do not bother with pleasantries.

"Shawn, remember the two guys at Tribe that hit on anything that moves?"

"Yeah, baby."

"I'm here, and they're really coming on strong. My neck hurts from John trying to massage me—"

"I'm on my way," he says.

I take a deep breath and lean back against the wall.

Quite the situation you've gotten yourself into, the Pharisee says, resting against the sink.

Yes, it is. But I can handle it.

How could you justify their behavior? It's disgusting, and—How shall I say it?—abominable. "…the men likewise gave up natural relations with women and were consumed with passion for one another, men committing shameless acts with men." Romans 1:27 suddenly seems to make sense to you, does-n't it?

I don't agree with what they're doing any more than you do, but I refuse to call them *abominable.* You use your beliefs as an excuse to write people off too quickly, and you use your Bible to write them off too.

You're the one who has to deal with them, so think whatever you want. But I know they're unnatural. The goose-bumps on your skin tell me you do, too.

People are people, and if I were at a straight bar or club right now, I'm pretty sure I would be seeing guys act the same way as Trey and John.

I wait in the bathroom for ten minutes before going back to my seat. I am not scared of Trey or John flirting with me anymore; I just know I want to enjoy my night, and dealing with them in tandem is not my idea of a good time. They work so perfectly together, their comments and physical advances like those of one person split into two. They remind me of the lions from *The Ghost and the Darkness,* except that instead of predators, they are just a couple of obnoxious guys trying to have a good time. For the first time, I imagine what it must be like to be an attractive woman, and I am convicted. Have my methods of flirtation ever been that insensitive? Have I ever made a woman feel like the object I feel like right now? It is something to think about.

By the time I reach my seat, Shawn is already at the bar and I wrap my arms around him. His presence brings peace to the situation, and I am thankful he is a part of my life.

"Hey, baby! I'm glad you called," he says in his typical velvet tone.

"You have no idea how glad I am to see you!"

"I bet. I was down the street for work, so coming here was perfect," he says.

I lean into Shawn, putting my head on his shoulder.

"This your boyfriend?" Trey and John eye Shawn up and down.

"As a matter of fact, I am," he says, putting an arm around me. I still have not figured out why Shawn's touching me does not illicit feelings of discomfort. Maybe it is because I trust him. He knows I am not really gay and is helping me out…but, still. To the old, Tim his motives would not have mattered. He is gay, and that is the only thing I would have considered.

"You want us to leave him alone, don't you?" John asks timidly.

"Well, being that I haven't seen him all day, I would appreciate it." Shawn plays the part perfectly, speaking with the perfect combination of grace and protectiveness. The guys seem to get the point and back off a few feet.

"You're my hero!" I whisper to Shawn.

"No, I'm your boyfriend. You aren't ready to deal with guys like that," he says soothingly.

"I think he is." Will's voice comes out of nowhere and across from us. "I told Tim he needed to be careful when he's out. New guys are defenseless."

"True," Shawn says in agreement.

"But he handled them well enough. You would've been proud!" Will smiles.

"Believe me, I already am." Shawn hugs me again.

There is something humbling about going from total confidence to the total lack of self-assurance. In church I know the language, the order, and the procedure; but here, I am lost. Will and Shawn have become my teachers, and they are teaching me that with any group of people group or social sub-sect, there is inevitably good and bad. Such is life.

~~~

Shawn leaves after an hour and once again I am left at Tribe alone. Not a bad place to be, but it is always more fun to know who you are drinking with. I move to the second room and sit on a couch, waiting for something to happen, timidly hoping I will not have to initiate conversation. Making friends has never been an issue for me, but while straight Tim does not know a stranger, gay Tim leans towards introversion. I cannot help it. I am comfortable around the people who I know I can hide from, who I can fool by wearing a mask of phony pseudo-righteousness. For better or worse, religion is still my comfort zone.

The authenticity and humility I find in my gay friends is convicting. Will, Shawn, Ben, and Phil seem protective toward me. They care. To be cared for by people I have never allowed myself to care for...well, it makes me feel so incredibly ignorant.

After a few minutes, a young man with a clipboard makes eye contact and approaches me. He is dressed in dark jeans, black leather shoes, and what looks to be a baseball jersey. He smiles and sits next to me. Behind him, I notice John and Trey working their next victim. Apparently I am not longer a target—or an option. Thank you, Shawn!

"My name is Mike. What's yours?" Mike extends a hand, almost formally.

"I'm Tim."

"Ever consider playing sports?" he asks.

"I played all through high school."

"I mean now. I'm with the Metro Nashville Softball Association, and we're looking for people to play this season. Interested?"

I think about it. "Actually, that would be great!"

"Just put down your name and contact info, and we'll be in touch this week!" he says. I write down my name and phone number and hand the clipboard back. "Glad to meet you, Tim. We'll let you know which team you're on and when your first practice is."

I look down at the flier Mike gives me, excited by the prospect of playing sports again. Signing up feels like the right thing to do, another opportunity to immerse myself in the community. And if there is one thing I am confident in, it is the fact that I am not completely un-athletic!

At least you can finally say you were recruited by a homosexual! The Pharisee laughs, amused by himself.

Really, a joke?

I used to think that all gay bars were 99 percent stereotype and 1 percent people. I thought that I would find loud techno music providing the beat for hundreds of sweaty, shirtless men that all wanted to hook up with each other. I had imagined that a gay bar was almost like a bathhouse, it was the foreplay to some main event. Surely there would be alcohol, and obviously there would be crowds of people, but their intent would be what I was always taught in church. *Lascivious.* But these stereotypes are only true of a select few at Tribe on any given night, and with the exception of John and Trey, no one else acts any different than the crowd I would find at any other bar. So I am faced with the simple reality that stereotypes are only true of a select few, if any—a select few that we seem to remember and focus on more than the rest.

To be fair, I have noticed that negative stereotypes of gays and lesbians are promoted almost as much by pop culture as by the conservative church. Television and Hollywood have taught us that every gay man is an avid fan of show-tunes, speaks with the effeminate voice of Jack from *Will & Grace*, and dresses in clothes that are always just a bit too tight. We are taught that lesbians are a bunch of butch, radically feminist man-haters. And of course these stereotypes always lead back to sex.

If there is one stereotype that I have found holds truth, it is that both conservative religion and pop culture are hyper-obsessed with gay sex; and I, too, have bought into the lies. The vast majority of gay men and lesbian women desire nothing more than love, commitment, and a normal life. I also recognize inside myself a man guilty of projecting his imaginary world onto others instead of looking at individuals as unique teachers of their own life experience and truth.

John and Trey saunter over, and I look up from the softball flier. Their faces are meek and conciliatory. "We just wanted to say that we're sorry for before. Can we buy you a beer?" Trey's voice betrays a much changed and more respectful tone.

"I would love that, guys. Thank you," I say. The Pharisee looks as though he has just lost a bet, and I feel hopeful for another chance to get to know new people. We walk back into the third bar area where Will is preparing drinks. He looks at me and smiles, and I know I am on the right track. Apparently even the stereotypes are not so stereotypical.

11 what david felt

I step off of the train at Penn Station in awe of my surroundings. Of all the places I thought this experiment might take me, New York City was never on the list. It hadn't occurred to me that I would leave Nashville. Even more intimidating than the hustle and bustle around me is my purpose. I am here to protest with Soulforce—the very organization that I adamantly opposed four years ago at Liberty University.

Even more surprising than finding myself in the ultimate concrete jungle is how I came to be here. The round-trip plane tickets were purchased for me by a church located a mile away from my house. The River at Music City is an open, affirming, artistic body of Christ-followers led by Donny McGuire and Reba Rambo McGuire, who have enjoyed long and successful careers in gospel music. When a friend of mine who attends the River told the pastor about my opportunity, the church graciously provided the one thing hindering me from attending. Amazing.

I emerge from the mouth of Penn Station with only the clothes on my back and a backpack hanging over my shoulder. I packed light, knowing that I will be walking most of the week in New York. The weather is miserable. Sleet and rain pours on the thousands of city folk rushing all around me, most of whom look as though they are late for a meeting. I examine a guidebook that I purchased before leaving and begin the 119-block trek to a Starbucks on the upper west side. An ex-girlfriend of mine moved to the city four months ago and arranged for me to stay at her boyfriend's apartment my first and last nights of the trip. I look both ways before crossing the street and begin my walk into an experience that will change my life.

~~~

Three months before my experiment began, back in October, I read every book possible on coming out of the closet. The small collection of books I amassed was topped, however, by one book. *Stranger at the Gate: To Be Gay and Christian in America*, by Mel White, was the most poignant of them all. The irony of Mel's story and the beginning of my journey left me unsettled. The memories of that spring day at Liberty played through my head after every chapter, and something inside of me said that I needed to apologize for my behavior. Not only that, I felt compelled to ask for Mel's blessing.

Without much effort I was able to reach him by phone.

Mel was very calm and personable. There was an ease in our conversation, and as I laid out my plans he graciously listened to every word.

"I want to ask your forgiveness for what I said about you, and I want to know if you think going through with this whole thing is offensive, or justified, somehow…" I said, nervously pacing in the front yard of a friend's house.

"Tim, I'm glad to forgive you. Thank you for wanting to apologize," he said.

"And the other thing?" I asked, shaking.

"I really think you need to follow your heart and your gut. If this is what you need to do to question your upbringing, I think you should do it." Mel's warmth and sincerity was encouraging.

"I really think it's the right thing to do."

"I'm eager to see how this plays out. It's a ballsy idea." He half-chuckled, and I felt like I was talking to an old friend. Not someone that I once called *enemy*.

"I'm just hesitant about lying to the people I'll meet."

"Well, in this case, I think it might be safe to say that the ends could justify the means."

Mel's blessing was a match to a fuse, and in that moment the reality of my experiment became all the more real.

Five months after that first conversation, and two months into my project, I received an unexpected call. Mel's voice was a pleasant surprise. Mel had kept touch with me by e-mail and offered me words of encouragement and advice as I dealt with the initial backlash of my coming out as a gay man, but his phone call was a surprise.

"Tim, I wanted you to know about an action Soulforce is doing in New York City. I'd really like you to come."

"I'm not sure how I'd get there, but I'll do my best," I said excitedly.

"I'll be praying it works out for you. In the meantime I'll email you the information."

"I really will try to be there."

"I know you will, and I promise to keep your secret. I think you need to see what Soulforce is really about. It might help you answer some of those nagging questions you've been wrestling with."

Mel's invitation was an unexpected gift. More than that, it was a revelation. I began to think about how perfect the opportunity could be. I felt a renewed sense of purpose and reveled in the idea of having the opportunity to experience Soulforce for a second time. Not only that, but I would finally be able to speak out against an injustice, and I would get to do so in my first ever, non-violent protest.

"I appreciate it, Mel. Thanks for calling and letting me know!"

"No problem. See you in New York." Mel hung up the phone, but it took me a few seconds to follow suit. I just stood there with the phone to my ear and a grin on my face.

~~~

The first twenty blocks of my walk are painful. My feet and hands are numb from the cold, and I chide myself for not checking the weather before leaving for the airport. I might have packed warmer clothes, or at least worn long underwear. I'm wearing only a hoody and baseball cap. A few blocks past Times Square, I catch my reflection in the glass of a first floor office window. My nose and ears are red, and I wonder what I will look like after walking another hundred blocks. My only consolation is that I am meeting my friend at a café. *Coffee...* Just the thought makes me move more quickly.

After an hour of trudging through the metropolis, I reach the upper west side cafe. I am a soaked, frozen, soggy mess, and I hope my friend is able to recognize me. I open the door for a woman and she sneers. Maybe the stereotypes about New Yorkers are true. Or maybe she was sneering at the weather. I hope it is the latter.

Not long after I arrive and find a table, Amy makes her way inside. She looks around the café for me, so I raise my hand and wave. Her smile is contagious, and she looks better than I remember. It has been a year or more since I have seen her, and she looks classy and grown up. She looks like a New Yorker. It is amazing to me how an environment can change someone, like it has a godlike power over style and interests. Amy looks changed, and I wonder if the Southern girl I have known for so long is still there somewhere, under the designer clothes, makeup, and auburn hair.

I stand and Amy wraps her arms around me.

"It's so good to see you, Tim. What brings you to New York?"

"Didn't I tell you? I'm here for a protest."

"Sounds like a lot's changed for you since you came out. From church guy to gay activist; I must say I'm impressed."

Her comments catch me off guard. "You were more churchy that me!" I laugh. "No religion for you in this city?" I sip my coffee and welcome the warmth. I may be soaked, but at least I am warm.

"We have visited a few churches but haven't found one yet. What about you? Have you been to church since you came out?"

"Honestly? I've tried but it hasn't gone so well." I think back to my most recent attempt at church and shudder. Maybe winter would be a better season for it.

"Just remember that you are still you. And you love church."

Amy is different, but a good different. Somehow, after just four months in the city, she has grown up.

"Things are different. Maybe I'll go back one day, but I'm too busy trying to discover if it's worth it anymore. Nashville may not be rural Mississippi, but it *ain't* New York."

After thawing a few more minutes, we set out once more. We are still twenty-three blocks from her boyfriend's apartment, and I hope it goes quickly. I am exhausted, but my lack of energy is made bearable as Amy tells me how she met Nick while visiting friends for Thanksgiving. Three weeks after meeting him she decided to move, and the rest is history. She seems happy, but I question my decision. Staying with an ex-girlfriend's boyfriend is not something I would do if everyone thought me straight…but admittedly I am too afraid of hostiles. Too many creepy movies have ruined them as a viable option while traveling.

The apartment building is exactly what I pictured, and the architecture and design is probably early twentieth century. I also love the neighborhood. Amy tells me that the building three doors down is an old church converted into housing. She says she will prove it to me when I am in Nick's twelfth-floor one bedroom apartment, but all I want is to sit down.

"Your feet hurt?" Amy asks sardonically.

"Like hell," I answer.

"After a few weeks you get used to it. I walk everywhere. It's the cheapest way to get around."

"After a 142 blocks, I've decided to buy a subway pass!"

"Good idea," she says laughing. "Don't get pissed, but the elevator is broken. We've got some stairs to climb."

"Great! Trying to get me to lose weight?"

"Just trying to get you to a couch and a hot shower."

The words *couch* and *shower* are magical, and I catch a second wind. "Tell me there's beer in the apartment, and I might go straight and steal you from Nick!"

"Yeah, right! You're totally gay!" She laughs, and I smirk. If she only knew.

I count each stair as though I will be tested on the number of them later, and with each step my calves, ankles, and the soles of my feet scream in agony. The hallway floors we pass are black and white, checkered tile, and the décor is a retro mustard color with molding worn almost completely away. This is not the New York apartment building you see in the movies. This place is real and grungy, but still somehow appealing.

This is the New York City I have dreamed of since I was a kid, and it is perfect in all of its imperfections. It is a place alive with the spirits of the thousands who call it home, a place that digs deep within me and stirs the writer I have always wanted to be. This place, this old apartment building, inspires me.

As we reach the top step of the twelfth floor, I see Nick waiting by a door at the end of the hallway. He is tall and handsome, thinner than I had imagined. He looks the type of man who would wear long winter jackets with big black buttons, and shoes that don't have laces. His facial hair is patchy but not unkempt, and his blue eyes contrast vividly with the dark brown of his hair. I like this man. We have yet to shake hands, or even utter a word to one another, but I know he is good. And his goodness is confirmed by the look in his eyes as he sees Amy.

Before greeting me, Nick embraces Amy and they kiss. A pang of jealousy overtakes me. I am not jealous that he is kissing Amy; I am jealous that he is allowed to kiss and know and love the person he desires. The closet has robbed me of that option. But unlike many, I must endure it only for the rest of the year—a fact I try to remember every time I feel self-pity. So, so many have it worse than me.

After they separate, Nick introduces himself and pulls me into a hug. His friendliness draws me in, and it is easy to see why, after only three weeks apart, Amy would make the move from Nashville to New York. "Come in! Come in! Welcome!"

I make my way inside, following Amy, and Nick closes the door behind me and shows me to the bathroom so I can dry off and change clothes. The bathroom is cramped but quaint, and I welcome the hot water and soap.

After changing socks and pants, and putting on a fresh t-shirt, I make my way to the living room. Nick and Amy are playing video games and pause as I walk in. "Do you have a roommate?"

"Yes, I do. In fact, you might like him."

Amy slaps Nick on the shoulder, but I am not sure why.

"Why would I like him?" I ask naïvely.

"Well." Nick stalls for a second, second-guessing himself. "Dane is gay, too." He smiles, trying to take the edge off what he realizes to be an insensitive generalization. It is a generalization I have made many times, believing that just because someone is gay means they are sexually attracted to everyone of the same sex.

"I appreciate you looking out for me, bro, but things don't really work like that. I'm sure you don't want to sleep with *every* woman you meet."

"Well, most of them!" Nick says with a laugh right before Amy punches him on the arm.

"You guys are so cute, I could just shit."

Amy throws a pillow at me.

"I like this guy," Nick says, high-fiving me.

I take a seat next to Amy and she hands me her game controller. "What do you guys want for dinner?"

"Take-out Chinese!"

"Tim, are you sure you aren't from New York?" Nick asks.

"No. I've just spent years watching *Seinfeld* re-runs."

"You got it," Amy says, grabbing her coat.

"Need money?" I ask.

"No. Dinner is on me! You are our guest." She smiles and walks out the door, and I see it. I see the country girl in her, and the spirit that had always attracted me to her.

~~~

Dane bursts through the door like a force of nature, startling me as I take a bite of my General Tso's chicken. I try to keep from choking but cough it down, awkwardly covering my mouth with my hand. Nick hands me a beer and I take a gulp.

"You would not believe the day I've had! One meeting after the next, and those damn designers would not listen to me! I said we didn't have the right type of fabric for my new design, but *noooo*! They kept asking and asking as if I was hiding it just to be rude! Tha Queens!" Dane speaks without breathing in a voice an octave higher than I would have expected, and his energy reminds me how tired I am. The atmosphere, once conducive to conversation and rest, becomes tense and dramatic. I feel like I have been transported into an episode of *Sex and the City*. Amy looks at me sympathetically.

"Tim, grab the dumplings. Quick!" Nick whispers. I reach for the box.

"Ooh! Are those dumplings? I love dumplings! Do you have any of that sauce?" Dane moves towards the food.

"They are Tim's dumplings," Nick says.

"Oh, yeah. Okay! What else did you get?"

"You'll get used to it," Amy says to me.

"Get used to what?" Dane asks, but before Amy can answer, Dane is walking off to the bedroom with a box of kung pao and a pair of chopsticks. "Tonight, we're going to party with the new guy!" His voice trails off and the door closes.

~~~

Three hours pass and the four of us have emptied more than a case of beer. I know this because the room is spinning slightly to the left, and because I find myself strapping on black four-inch high heels. A few feet away Nick is doing the same.

"I'm going to kick your ass!" Nick says. "I walk faster in heels than any woman I've ever met!"

"Are you sure *you're* not actually gay?" Amy says to Nick, slurring slightly. She has had more to drink than Nick, and is handling it better too.

That there are heels that actually fit my feet amazes me only slightly less than the fact that I am able to stand up in them. My feet still throb from all of the walking, and I feel as though I am constantly falling forward. I do not stand a chance racing any-one, but the four of us walk into the hallway and Amy stands in front of us, *Greece* style, holding a scarf above her head. "Three! Two! One! *Run!*" She waves the impromptu flag, signaling the beginning of our sprint, and Nick proves his boastful claims to be accurate, surging ahead of me with little to no effort. In less than a minute I am the loser, and Nick is already challenging Amy.

"You look good in heels." Dane winks at me, and I know the look. It is time to start drinking water.

After lapping me and outdistancing Amy by several yards, Nick sits on the couch, pleased with himself, still wearing the high heels victoriously. In the next room, Amy and Dane are rolling out and inflating the blow-up mattress, and I realize that I will be rooming with Dane. I refill my cup with water three or four times before setting my pack in the room. Dane is stum-bling, alcohol impairing more than just his balance. He comes over and gives me a big hug and kisses me on the cheek. I look at Amy, but she does not seem to notice.

"Behave yourself, buddy," I say calmly in Dane's ear.

"*You* behave yourself, buddy!" he says laughing.

And in a matter of minutes, we are all settling in for bed. Amy gives me a hug and closes the door to the bedroom, leaving only me and Dane in the room. She is staying over, sharing Nick's bunk-bed in the living room. I put on my basketball shorts and my now-dry hoody, and crawl into bed. I stretch and position myself in the most comfortable way the airbed allows. My body finally seems to be happy with me.

A few minutes later I feel a hand brushing along the length of my arm, down to my hand. Startled and half awake, I roll over to find Dane kneeling over me, wearing only his underwear. I feel panic but take a deep breath. I have been through this before and know I can handle myself.

"Dane. What are you doing?" I calmly ask.

"Looking at you, I guess," he says. I can smell the beer on his breath and a hint of something else that smells like bourbon. "You look uncomfortable."

"I'm perfectly fine. Thank you."

"I think you should come sleep in the bed with me," he says, smiling.

"Dane, I have a boyfriend." I hope he will get the hint.

"Is he here?"

"No, but you are making me feel uncomfortable."

Dane walks over to the bed and sits down, and then I hear him crying. I know he is drunk and probably just overtired and horny, but for some reason I feel guilty. I get up and sit next to him on the bed, and he leans his head on my shoulder.

"I'm sorry. I'm just lonely. You have no idea how hard it is to find a relationship in this city. Finding sex is easy, but love…Finding love is impossible!" His tears turn into sobs, and I put my arm around him. Maybe I have been too hard on Dane… That thought disappears as I feel Dane trying to kiss my neck and put his hand in my crotch.

"Damn it, Dane! Stop it!" I push him over and get back down on the blow-up mattress, determined not to fall asleep until he does first.

A few minutes pass and I sit up, peeking in Dane's direction. I had thought the gentle cadence of his breathing meant he had finally dozed off, but instead I see the blanket moving up and down, up and down. Is he masturbating? Thoroughly uncomfortable I get up, grab my cigarettes, and walk into the living room…only to discover that I am trapped. I see Nick and Amy, and they are not *asleep,* either. My sudden presence does not disturb them, and they do not even pause to say hello. I hope Nick took off the heels.

Back in the bedroom I find my only avenue of retreat. The fire escape outside the window is somewhere, at least, where I can smoke. I crawl through the window and sit, leaning my back against the railing. I feel apathetic. I feel frustrated. It seems like too many of the stereotypes I was taught are either true or not easily enough disproven. Why am I even in New York?

The Pharisee is sitting a few feet away on a step, silently nodding his head.

I notice an interesting light. Over the tops of the buildings, a steeple tower protrudes from the middle of a roof, and it looks beautifully out of place. The lights of the city form a backdrop that illuminates the forgotten marker to a house of God, and the sight of it makes me miss church. *Lord, help me see what you would have me to see.* I repeat the prayer to myself a dozen times, fixating on the forgotten symbol in front of me. *I want to see them the way You see them…I need to see them as You see them.* I take a drag from my clove and the smoke trails out of my nose and into the cold, almost dancing with the air as it ascends. I feel peaceful and content.

Twenty minutes and two clove cigarettes later, I crawl back through the bedroom window and shut it quietly behind me. Dane is asleep, and I walk over to the bed. The blankets are falling off him, and as gently as possible I cover him up and look down at his face. He is less obnoxious when he is asleep, less abrasive. But much more than that, he looks vulnerable and real, without façade or pretense. Twenty minutes ago he wanted sex, but now he looks innocent.

I feel myself love him.

A story in the Old Testament has always fascinated me. King Saul, ruler of Israel and the first king in the small country's history, is told that the shepherd David will succeed his throne instead of Saul's own son, Jonathon. Infuriated, the angry Saul dispatches an army of three thousand of his best soldiers to hunt down and kill the young shepherd. One night, fed up with being chased, David sneaks into Saul's tent to kill him and finds Saul asleep. God had given David the freedom to do as he wished with the jealous king, but as he watched Saul sleep, he decided against slaying his enemy. Instead, David cut off a piece of Saul's robe, mercifully sparing the king's life.

I have always wondered why David spared the life of a man trying to kill him and why he showed mercy. And as I cover Dane with the blanket and watch him sleep I think I understand. I think David spared Saul's life because in that brief and simple moment, King Saul had been stripped of his title and all that was left was the man. No longer was there the label of *king*, or even *enemy*, there was only vulnerability, peace, and humanity. David saw himself in Saul, a brother in the image of God, so David obeyed the voices of his better angels. David finally found his love for Saul.

I see the same as I look at Dane. I do not see gay, or horny, or abomination. I see myself, a brother, the image of God. I settle back into my bed and the countless aches and pains of the day course through me. Tomorrow I will learn the principles of non-violent protests, but for now I am content bunking with Dane and looking through the window at a forgotten steeple surrounded by city lights, directing my heart to the heavens.

12 living in the tension

I wake up. My eyes open and see the bedroom bathed in the dull blue light of an overcast morning. It is 5:15 a.m. and I have only slept three, maybe four hours. The blowup mattress is sagging. I feel the wood laminate flooring beneath me. It is hard and cold. Seconds pass and my brain re-activates slowly. Too slowly. Today is going to be a long day, busy and instrumental. How am I going to make it? I already want to go back to sleep. *Coffee.* The thought is enough to keep my eyes open and give me the strength to sit up. I look over at Dane. He is sleeping but apparently still horny. Thank God I covered him up.

I creep into the bathroom and take a quick shower and I hear Amy and Nick. They are up making breakfast; I smell the bacon as surely as I hear it pop and sizzle in the pan. It feels good to be with friends. Too bad my schedule is so packed. I would have enjoyed spending more than the first and last night of this trip in their company.

This evening I will be taking a class on non-violent protesting. It is a requirement for anyone participating in the action with Soulforce. Matthew 5:9: Blessed *are the peacemakers, for they shall be called sons of God.* It seems like common sense, but I have never felt like a peacemaker before.

After a quick bite to eat, Amy walks me to the subway and shows me how to navigate the city. I have decided to sightsee as much as possible before making my way to the church where Soulforce will meet, and my first stop is the Metropolitan Museum of Art. I have designated blocks of time for each section of the museum, but the majority of my five hours here will not be spent meandering the many hallways filled with suits of armor and weaponry or ancient artifacts of antiquity. I am drawn to the art galleries, the same galleries where my father once brought me at the age of thirteen. I walk through the maze with full-fledged nostalgia. A decade may have passed since then, but the hours I spent here with my dad are still some of the favorites of my life.

A lot has changed during that decade. My father and I relate differently than we used to, especially since the divorce. He has renounced the fundamentalist Christianity of my youth, read-opting the religion of *his* youth, Catholicism. Every week or so, I find brochures on the kitchen table about same-sex attraction and the idea of "freedom through celibacy." I know there's a broad spectrum of belief within the Catholic Church and not everyone believes homosexuality to be a sin. I just wish my dad would choose a more progressive parish, seeing as how his own son says he is gay. A lot of my dad's closest friends and colleagues are gay or lesbian, so I expected a little more support. But the worst part of it, for me, is that the pope he looks up to so much, the person the Catholic Church identifies as the mouth-piece for God, says I am an abomination and a danger to the human race.

I leave the museum in search of another boyhood memory with my father and find a street vendor selling *perogies*. I sit on the steps outside the museum, quietly eating my lunch and watching a young woman playing an accordion. She is European and beautiful. She looks like a gipsy, and for a moment I fall under her spell. Her song ends and the trance is broken. I throw a dollar in her basket and walk south to my next destination, the Central Park Zoo.

Much of the zoo is typical. The monkeys have their own house and the birds do too. Come to think of it, every animal I visit has their own house, except for the seals, which enjoy a large round swimming pool at the center of the park. But the real attraction of this zoo is the penguin exhibit. I have seen it a dozen times in movies but never in the flesh. I walk into the manmade cavern and am confronted by a colony of little chubby butlers. They are perfection. I sit down against the wall, staring at them as they waddle around the enclosure, only to launch into the icy water like bullets shot from a gun. Whatever awkwardness they exhibit on land disappears as soon as they are in the water. My eyes can barely follow them as they dart back and forth.

I wonder if God looks at us the way I look at those penguins, seeing the same basic creature with only the uniqueness of our markings to give us away. I wonder if he laughs at our awkwardness but takes joy in our ability to fly through the icy waters of our individual calling as we navigate life and love. I hope that is the case. I hope He sees all of us as the same, no matter what labels we bear. We are the same species after all, even if we do not want to admit it.

~~~

Three hours later and I am ready to plant myself somewhere and rest. I find my way to the church, sit on the steps, and light up a clove. I am nervous. My parents and pastors have always told me that activists were lunatics. I am walking into this protest completely blind, having never attended one before, and it is unsettling. Oddly enough, every time I have read the gospels I have thought Jesus personified the role of activist. His methods were unorthodox and his message was rejected by the pious wherever he went. But his truths resonated with ordinary people, and I think that is what separates the religiously pious from the activists. I wonder if being an ordinary radical is what this whole protest thing is all about—speaking loudly for those ordinary people whom the mainstream would rather silence.

After few minutes of sitting on the stairs to the main entrance of the old church building where we are meeting, I see Mel walking down the street. His assistant Samantha is next to him, and as he sees me, a broad grin spreads across his face. As he reaches the steps he holds out his arms and we hug. The man

I once considered my enemy is now embracing me as a friend, and I am humbled by his graciousness. I feel wholly accepted by Mel, and I wonder what he sees when he looks at me.

"I'm so glad you could make it."

"I'm so happy you invited me!" I say.

After a few minutes of small talk, Mel and Samantha go inside the church to set up. For some reason, I am not as ready. I wait around for a few minutes and another familiar face approaches. It is not familiar because I have met the guy personally, but we have spoken on the phone several times. The young man's tattoos are immediately noticeable. He does not look like a punk, the way he has been marketed many times in his life, but he definitely would not fit in in the churches I have always attended.

"Jay Bakker!"

"You must be Tim." Like Mel, he hugs me and I feel an instant connection.

"It's great to finally meet you."

"You too! This is your first action, isn't it?" he asks, adjusting the small messenger bag at his side.

"Yes." My meek response is met by Jay's warmth.

"Well, you are in for a learning experience. Soulforce does great work."

Jay is the only son of Jim Bakker and the late Tammy Faye, and he went through as much hell as a child can face after a devastating scandal hit the *Praise the Lord* PTL ministry of his parents. Growing up surrounded by scandal, Jay developed a drug and alcohol addiction, overcame those addictions, and found God in a way he never had before. God's grace, he says, set him free from the vices he adopted after his life was flipped upside down. After leading a church in Atlanta, Jay came out in support of LGBTQ equality; the mainstream church rejected him as harshly as if he had come out as a gay man himself. He lost everything. Jay is now the pastor of a small church called Revolution NYC, in Brooklyn. Revolution meets in a bar called Pete's Candy Store.

Jay walks through the church doors and stops when he realizes I am not behind him. I look up at the door skittishly and he waves me inside. I take each step cautiously, knowing that by entering this training, I am coming full circle in my journey. While Soulforce was once my enemy, now I will stand among them. I am unsettled. Am I traveling this road too quickly? Have I too casually dismissed the teachings of my youth? Or is this the first real moment where I am taking steps towards living out a more Christ-like grace? This experience might solidify some of the more negative stereotypes, or completely disprove them—and I do not know if I am ready for either to be revealed. Change has always been a difficult for me, and this change is the most difficult because it is possibly the most important change I will ever experience. The moment feels pinnacle. I toss my clove into the gutter and follow Jay inside. What in the hell am I getting myself into?

~~~

I find myself in a large room with maroon carpets and a unique assortment of people unlike any I have ever met. They are not the straight-laced conservative types—though most of them were raised to be. They are free spirits, in New York with the intent to stop a grave injustice that I have just discovered. This injustice takes place in countries all over the world, and as I listen intently, the revelation shocks me out of my ignorance.

In countries all over the world, gays and lesbians are not just subjected to religious persecution and second-class citizenship. They are regularly beaten, imprisoned, and even executed for practicing the *abomination of homosexuality*. I hear this from one of the organizers—a handsome thirty-something who helped organize this action—and I cannot believe my ears.

Matthew shuffles the paper in his folder and addresses the group. "Thanks, everyone. It's awesome to have all of you here. I think the first thing we need to do is explain *why* we are here. The following is a written statement that will be posted on Soulforce.org. Bryan, could you please read the report for us?"

Bryan begins to read: "In December, 2008, France introduced a Declaration to Decriminalize Homosexuality at the United Nations Assembly in New York City. The statement condemned violence, harassment, discrimination, exclusion, stigmatization, and prejudice based on sexual orientation and gender identity. It also condemned killings, executions, torture, arbitrary arrest, and deprivation of economic, social, and cultural rights; noting that in seventy-seven member countries, homosexuality is illegal, and seven other countries declare it punishable by death.

"Almost immediately following the Declaration's introduction, the Holy See issued a statement opposing it, suggesting that it could lead to same-gender marriage acceptance.

"In response, Soulforce pulled together a team to confront the Holy See. We sent a letter to the ambassador's office, asking it to withdraw its opposition to the Declaration and to meet with us to begin a dialogue on the destructive nature of heterosexism. By late March, Soulforce had negotiated a meeting with two of our representatives with Father Bene, assistant to Ambassador Archbishop Migliori. Fr. Bene, while friendly, appeared surprised to hear that American gays and lesbians experienced any kind of discrimination. During the meeting, we pressed for a meeting directly with the ambassador and were told the office would get back to us. They have not."

I listen in shock. I feel like I am living in the book of Leviticus. I feel the veil being lifted, and scales falling from my eyes one by one by one. It is almost more than I can handle. I feel angry.

"That is why we are here," Matthew says with a deep breath.

I wonder what my devout Catholic father would say if he read the report.

"The Catholic church has gone too far, and we now feel a need to respond. We are here for a reason. People are dying, and it's within our power to hold the church accountable. If you will each please take out the pledge card from the front of your folder, we are going to talk about the tenets of non-violent protesting. Please read along as we go into them. After we are done, sign and date your card."

One: As I prepare for this direct action, I will meditate regularly on the life and teachings of Gandhi and King, and other truth-seekers.

I grab my pen and make a slight note in the tenet. Before Gandhi I write the name *Jesus*, and out of the corner of my eye, I see Jay doing the same thing. "This is an updated version of Dr. King's tenets of non-violence from 1963," Jay whispers. "In the original, it only says *Jesus*." I nod my head.

The history of non-violent protesting is long but became an organized alternative to physical bloodshed in 1906 with Mohandas Gandhi and the South African campaign for Indian rights. Perhaps the most notable example of non-violence was the year-long Salt Campaign, where over 100,000 Indians were jailed for intentionally breaking the Salt Laws created by the British Empire in India.

The non-violent protest tradition in America is very rich as well. In the 1840s, Henry David Thoreau refused to pay the Massachusetts poll tax levied for the war. After being bailed out of jail and someone else paying the tax on his behalf and ending his protest, Thoreau wrote his political beliefs in a book called *On the Duty of Civil Disobedience*. He is famous for saying "Must the citizen ever for a moment, or in the least degree, resign his conscience to the legislator? Why has every man a conscience, then? I think that we should be men first, and subjects afterward. It is not desirable to cultivate a respect for the law, so much as for the right. The only obligation which I have a right to assume is to do at any time what I think right."

Thoreau was not the only one. By the mid twentieth century, non-violent protests were the primary tool used by religious institutions, labor unions, student groups, and anti-war activists. The South, my home, was changed forever by these non-violent protests, where race relations were the most notable issue of the day. Next to Gandhi, Martin Luther King, Jr. is perhaps the most important figure in the non-violence movement, a hero to anyone who has ever carried a picket sign.

"You are part of something much bigger than yourself," Matthew says solemnly. "Please understand, and be grateful for, the privilege we have to question the powers that be."

Two: I will remember that the nonviolent movement seeks justice and reconciliation—not victory.

"As human beings, we have a tendency to seek victory over compromise," Matthew continues, "but that isn't our aim over the next two days. We are here to show the archbishop who we are, so that we can work towards reconciliation and justice. Victory creates enemies; reconciliation creates unity." Matthew's words speak to me, not just in light of my politics but also in light of my faith.

For years I have sought victory by evangelism, not reconciliation between God and His children. I write down Matthew's words. *Victory creates enemies, and reconciliation creates unity.* We are on this thing, this journey, together, and we have only two options: cooperation or condemnation. I hope we all prefer cooperation.

Three: I will walk and talk in the manner of love and nonviolence. "We are not here to argue or condemn Catholics. We are here to be here, to love others, and to show a better alternative. Please, if faced with someone who wants to argue, speak lovingly to them and show them the respect you hope they show you."

Four: I will contemplate daily what I can do so that all can be free. "We are not fighting for ourselves, we are fighting for everyone. Think in terms of others, and don't fall into a mindset of complacency. Contrary to what some of you might be thinking, we can and will make a difference tomorrow. It may not be instantaneous, but our voices will be heard."

Five: I will sacrifice my own personal wishes that all might be free.

How many times have I ever thought about sacrificing my comforts for another person's freedom? The Bible teaches us to take care of those in need, to give freely. Jesus even said in Matthew 25:40, "*Truly, I say to you, as you did it to one of the least of these my brothers, you did it to me.*" I was taught this, but never had it spoke to me of social justice. If I was taught to take the Bible and apply it to my life, why was I also not taught that spirituality and social justice are connected?

Six: I will observe with friend and foes the ordinary rules of courtesy. "This is simply the golden rule reworded. Do unto others as you would have them do unto you. Don't be a jerk. It's too easy to be a jerk. It takes courage to speak love to those who condemn you."

Seven: I will perform regular service for others and for the world.

Eight: I will refrain from violence of fist, tongue, and heart.

"We can use our words for good or for evil. We can use them to build up others or to tear them down. Physical violence is destructive, but hateful words and a hard heart can be just as detrimental, if not more so. Non-violence dictates that we use neither our bodies, words, nor hearts to hurt one another."

Nine: I will strive to be in good spiritual and bodily health.

Seven through nine are read twice each, slowly, and they pierce my heart. I have spent years working on my spiritual life, but never my physical.

Ten: I will follow the directions of the movement leaders and other squad captains on our nonviolent direct actions. "This one is important," Matthew says. "Police officers will be present over the next two days, waiting to see if this protest gets ugly. They're also there for our protection. Please follow our direction and everything will go smoothly. We want to make a difference, and that means we all need to be on the same page."

Matthew calls for a break and I make my way to the bathroom. I do not have to go, but I need to solitude. I reach the first stall and practically fall onto the seat. All of this time, I have been taught that activists were godless robots, that they were hateful to anyone who had an opposing world view. The tenets of non-violent protests, at least Soulforce's tenets, are all about two things: reconciliation and respect. How could I have not known this?

I will sacrifice my own personal wishes that all might be free...

I feel an indescribable guilt for mentally painting these people as monsters, and worse yet, for treating them as monsters that spring day at Liberty University, years ago. I pull the list from my pocket and read it silently a dozen times.

And my mind begins to pin scripture references to each principles. They are scriptures I have always known but never applied. The sickening realization dawns on me that I have never really followed these ideals, all the while claiming to be a Christian. The people I condemned most heartily have shamed me by walking more closely with the faith I have proclaimed so boldly. Talk really is cheap.

If I am honest with myself, I have to admit that these people whom I have always felt prejudice against are better people than me. Living love is so much more tangible and powerful than speaking love. I feel inspired to follow suit. When I die, I want people to remember me as the guy who loved everyone—because if I loved everyone, then I really will have followed the example of the Jesus I serve. *Love your neighbor as yourself,* the Bible says. How foolish I was to pick and choose only my fellow conservative Christians as neighbors.

Lord, please forgive me for believing as I have, and for blindly condemning people I never even understood, I pray. I pull a pen from my pocket and steady the non-violence pledge card on the monstrous plastic toilet-paper dispenser. *I will do my best, Lord, to follow these in my life.* I sign the pledge and date it, and feel a profound sense of peace.

After a few more hours of talking, everyone who has a place to stay in New York leaves for the night, and those staying at the church, including me, settle down for the night. We are all sharing the big room with dark red carpets, and I pull two comfortable chairs together to create a makeshift bed in the corner of the room.

Mel looks over at me and smiles. He has the spirit and vitality of a man half his age, and I know that his work has kept him young. He cracks jokes and we all laugh, and he tells us stories of his work with Jerry Falwell and Pat Robertson, and others. His life has been unorthodox but impactful, and I am amazed by his humility. Mel, the founder of Soulforce, is here, but he never spoke at the meeting, contentedly giving others the spotlight.

We turn off the lights and curl up, ready for sleep. All is quiet save for a few coughs and deep breaths, and my exhaustion overtakes me. I feel something at the foot of my makeshift bed, and I half awaken to see Mel covering my legs and feet with a blanket so I won't be cold. He moves over to Samantha and does the same, tucking her in like a doting grandfather. I feel tears well up in my half-closed eyes and I weep silently.

I was *so* wrong about this man.

13 activist like me

Day one of the protest ends much as it began. The Vatican's embassy remains closed and locked, and even the mailman was unable to deliver the mail for the day. Neighboring businesses tell us that they have never seen the embassy closed like this during the middle of the week, and it is obvious they are doing everything in their power not to engage our group as we vigil on the sidewalk outside.

Before today, I never understood how simple a non-violent protest is. We take turns passing out flyers, answer questions if anyone asks, and hold signs that say *Stop Spiritual Violence. We* are led in song by Matthew and spend time in reverent silence. There is nothing about it that could be construed as morally wrong. It is a time of sincere peace. Several members of the group pass the hours in prayer, others in conversation.

The only thing I have a difficult time with is the rain. It is unrelenting and miserable. My feet are soaked to the bone. After our day ends, I walk to a nearby Walgreens and spend $12 on three pairs of fresh socks. I shiver uncontrollably while I swipe my debit card, and it takes me three attempts to put in my PIN and successfully make my purchase. Samantha stands next to me, reassuringly rubbing my back. I feel weak and hungry but am in good spirits.

After paying for my socks, Samantha and I decide to grab a bite to eat back by the church where we are staying. Brandon, another activist, decides to go with us. He is tall and dark with a shaved head and glasses, and he has the gentlest demeanor of anyone in the group. He was at the same protest as me, that day at Liberty years ago, and hearing his memories of that protest makes me feel even more like an ass, if that were possible.

We emerge from the subway and walk six blocks to the church. Changing into dry clothes feels like a rebirth, and as I am finishing, I see Mel changing into a suit.

"Looking sharp, Mel!" I whistle and Mel blushes.

"I got two free tickets to the opera, and I couldn't pass up the opportunity to go!" Mel sounds like a kid on Christmas morning, his enthusiasm contagious.

"Have fun!" I say.

"You too!" he says as he walks out the door.

Samantha and I are meeting Brandon at the sports bar three blocks away, and the walk allows us our first opportunity for privacy. "So you've read Kevin's book?" Samantha asks. Recently a mutual acquaintance of ours wrote a book about a semester he spent undercover at Liberty University. He wanted to see if the stereotypes about the evangelical right were true, and in the process he made friends with Samantha.

"Yes I have. It was really good. Ever think you'd be fooled again by someone 'undercover' writing a book?" I ask.

"Absolutely not! I'll smell an experiment like Kevin's a mile away." She sounds so confident.

"Yeah, you probably would." I hope she doesn't hate me when this is all over.

After a block or two, I broach the topic of sexuality. Samantha's devout Christian faith makes me curious about her opinion of the gay scene.

"I want my life to be an example. Conservative Christians perpetuate the stereotype that being gay means being promiscuous and godless, and then when their children come out, those stereotypes create barriers. I just want people to know morality has nothing to do with orientation. The everyday relationship we have with God is all that matters. The promiscuity you're asking about is a symptom, not the problem." As she speaks and I listen to the passion in her words, I know I can learn a lot from her.

"But what if the fundamentalists are right, and being gay is a sin?"

She stops walking and looks at me, grabbing my hand delicately. "Tim, if God knows my heart, then He knows how much I love Him and want to serve Him with my life. If being gay is a sin, then I'll just have to trust that when He said that *His love covers a multitude of sins,* He was telling the truth." She kisses my hand and smiles at me. "Have faith, brother. Just because the people in your life doubt you and are trying to change you doesn't mean for a second that they're right."

"You are an incredible woman," I say. She looks up at me, grinning. "Too bad we aren't straight," I add, squeezing her hand.

"Yeah, too bad!" She laughs. "But, for the record, you are kinda cute." She winks at me and we start walking again. And I feel as though I have found yet another friend for life.

The three of us sit at a table in the modest sports bar and I listen as much as possible. Listening is easy when you are eating the biggest burger you have ever seen, a twenty-ounce triple with bacon. Brandon and Samantha laugh at me as I eat the entire thing.

"Congratulations, Tim. You eat like a straight slob!" Brandon says, biting a cherry tomato in half off of the end of his fork. His salad is tiny compared to the plate of food in front of me.

"I'm from the South, and we Southerners know how to eat," I say, wiping burger grease from the corner of my mouth with a crumpled napkin.

"And you're proof of that!" Samantha laughs.

Several hours later and we curl up in our makeshift beds. Once again Mel makes sure the covers are keeping us warm, and I realize the oddest thing. I do not feel like I am at a protest with a group of gay activists. I feel like I am at a reunion, and these people are my family. There is much more to this than standing on a sidewalk with signs. This is as much for our group, in the moment, as it is for the people and cause we are advocates of. And I am having fun.

~~~

Day two of the action is much like the first, but without the rain. Once again the Vatican's embassy is closed and locked, so we stand outside and hold our protest signs. *Stop spiritual violence!* I hold the sign high, and a taxi-driver honks and gives me the finger. I see a rosary hanging from his rearview mirror. Go figure.

About three hours into the vigil, the mailman comes again to deliver the mail. He walks up to the gate and inserts a key that he did not have yesterday. Mel and I look at each other, trying to comprehend this sudden turn of events. We have composed a letter, out thoughts on the contradiction of the Church's Path of Peace with their United Nations veto, and we want to deliver our letter directly. This morning we decided that we had to get inside the building if possible, to deliver the letter, and this is our first and probably only opportunity. The mailman leaves the gate slightly ajar. "Tim, let's go!" Mel says urgently.

Mel, another activist, and I run through the gate and into the building. I hear nervous shouts from the police behind me, but we keep moving. We will probably be arrested, but it does not stop me. Let them arrest us if they want, for walking through an open door to deliver a letter to a man who thinks it is okay for people to die just because they are gay.

Inside the lobby, time seems to slow almost to a stop. I look up at the golden words on the wall of the lobby: *The Path to Peace.* It is the first time I see them unobstructed, and I think for a moment that I rushed inside the building because I needed to see these words up close. I need to see them without the bars blocking them, to see how beautifully the golden letters contrast with the black marble of the wall they hang from. I needed to taste the contradiction up close—the contradiction of the place, but more so, a similar contradiction within my own heart.

I have hated this building from the moment I saw it, because this building reminds me of myself. It is closed off, impersonal, political, and religious. The similarities are unnerving. There are too many to name. I stand inside the lobby and survey the inside of my own heart. Outside the gate, the Pharisee watches me. He is yelling something, but I cannot hear him. I choose not to hear him. I do not need anything distracting me from the palpable tension I am living, second by second, in this building. I feel outside my own body, as though I am watching myself stare up at that godforsaken lie on the wall, a lie I have lived all along.

When I tell my family the truth of my experiment, I will tell them about this moment. I will tell them that the lie I told them about being gay is nothing compared to the lie I have lived all my life in the church.

Can I truly claim Jesus and be at odds with his children? Are they even his children? I remember the scripture that says "by your fruit you shall know them." Yes. They are his children, as much as I am his child. Salvation is not a country club, and we do not have the right to deny anyone admittance. People and their relationships to God are their own concern, and no good can come from my shoving my theology down someone else's throat.

And then the answer comes to me: There is only either *a path to peace*—or a barred gate protecting an empty wall. Both cannot exist simultaneously within me.

I feel a hand on my shoulder. It is a police officer, and I know I am about to be arrested for trespassing. I hold my wrists behind my back, resign myself, and take a deep breath. If I get arrested, it will all have been worth it. I got to see myself under a microscope, and even though what I saw has shaken me, the moment seems fated.

"Why are you putting your hands behind you?" the officer asks as he leads me towards the door.

"Haven't I just broken some sort of law?" I look at his face and he smiles sympathetically.

"Son, I didn't see you do anything." He winks. "You look pale. Go drink some water."

I walk outside and a few of the Soulforce crew gather around me to ask what happened, but I can barely talk.

"What happened inside?" Samantha asks.

"I'm not sure."

I look over at the Pharisee and as he opens his mouth to talk. I glare at him. He closes his mouth and walks over to the stairs of the next building. Coward.

"I gave them the letter we wanted to give them. Mission accomplished," Mel says. He walks over to me and puts his hand on my shoulder. "Good job, Tim. I'm proud of you for charging in like that." His praise means more than I can describe.

"I don't understand. Tim, what happened?" Samantha presses me for an answer.

Mel smiles at me and I shrug my shoulders. Samantha drops the question and puts her arm around my waist.

And then, just as quickly as the drama began, the moment is over and we are back at our posts in the vigil line.

~~~

I am on the plane flying home. The experience of New York City and the action with Soulforce is something I will never forget. But as I lie back in my seat and close my eyes to rest, I still see those golden words. *The path to peace* felt more like the path to hell. For what the church leaders allow to continue to happen to gays and lesbians all over the world, it is hard not to wish ill upon them. I am thankful that the God I am finally getting to know transcends my prejudice, that He is able to show grace where I have a difficult time of it.

I flew to New York not knowing what to expect; looking back, I have to say everything culminated in that ever-so-brief moment in the lobby. I feel like I might just be grasping why I felt called to this journey in the first place. My life has been a lie, a lie even bigger than the one I have had to tell my friends and family in order for this journey to be possible. I can only hope my eyes will continue to open to the inconsistencies and lies I have believed all along.

Weeks later I receive an email telling me that there is news about the action on the Soulforce website. Five paragraphs down, I read the news I have been praying about since returning home:

...Several weeks later, as we persisted in trying to meet with the ambassador, we were able to persuade the ambassador to sit down with our representatives. The meeting was again cordial and the ambassador indicated that he would be discussing the Statement with the United Nations when they meet in Switzerland this summer for their summer sessions. This meeting was significant in that after eight years of trying to negotiate with the hierarchy of the Roman Catholic Church, this was the first time we have been able to sit down with a high-ranking representative of the Vatican.

Given the years of hostile rhetoric between the Vatican and the LGBT community, we are hopeful about the improvements we have made in helping the Vatican understand the sacredness of LGBT lives. Soulforce will continue to monitor the situation and will keep people up to date.

Some may read my account of New York and scoff at the attempts we made those days to help improve the quality of life for lesbians, gays, bisexuals, and transgendered individuals across the globe; to those people I offer only one thought: Jesus fought for the oppressed. If you claim to follow him, his mission is your mission. You do not have to agree with the organization that I protested with—or with me, for that matter—but if you can see a cause for what it is, a chance to live the gospel instead of just preach it from a pulpit, you will be able to share your faith in a much more tangible way.

I learned this because of Mel White. I learned this from Matthew, Samantha, Brandon, and others. I learned this after finally listening to that still, small voice within my heart, and I finally obeyed its call to stand up for something bigger than myself. I learned this from the "unnatural and abominable," and for them, I am thankful.

14 sticks and stones

Opening Day

Although my many stereotypes about gay culture have begun melting into the category of "fairytale," one has consistently rung true: gay men *love* drag queens! The instantaneous effect of a drag queen is both fascinating and contagious. It is a tradition of sorts, and a passion for many. Drag queens are a staple of the community, and I have never been as entertained as I have been by my friends who regularly participate in drag shows. In church I was taught that drag queens represented the worst kind of homosexual perversion, and I believed that. I believed it until I learned the role of drag in gay culture. Drag shows are vaudevillian talent exhibitions populated by uniquely beautiful people. I have even met heterosexual men who dress in drag, which goes to show that my programmed aversion had more to do with the shock of seeing a man dressed in women's clothes than understanding what drag represents.

I am standing behind the backstop of the main softball field, watching the first game of the season. It is a faux game of sorts among satirically dressed drag queens—many of whom, I am told, have never dressed in drag before. The weather is perfect, perhaps the nicest day of the year so far, and the park rented by the Metro Nashville Softball Association for the league games is packed. Vendors have set up tables and booths the entire length of the main field, and restaurants are selling food to the hundreds of families that have come out for opening day. Children are everywhere, and they look like they are having almost as much fun as I am, watching my friends play in this first game.

I also cannot help but notice how well-adjusted and pure these children are, with moms or dads following not far behind. The children's faces are painted and many hold cotton candy or animal balloons. Were any of these children from a prior marriage, I wonder idly, or were they adopted? Does it even matter? They are all so happy. As I people-watch I cannot help looking for signs of dysfunction. But everyone looks "normal." Even though I wasn't sure what to expect, watching them...but I didn't think I'd see "family" like I see right now. Maybe I was wrong. Maybe the "traditional family" exists in gay and lesbian households.

A friend of mine from my first softball practice walks to the plate, and I shout to him encouragingly. Roark looks over and waves. On the first pitch, he hits a ground ball to left field. The shortstop fumbles after the ball and my friend makes it to second base. I feel a deep love for him. The first time we met, Roark saved me from my own anger—and also from being arrested.

It was months earlier, on the first day of softball practice and my introduction into a world of sports I had no idea exists. After I stretched, I was paired with an attractive young guy wearing a pink dew rag and grey stretchy pants that looked like something one might find in the girls department at the Gap. His name was Roark, and he seemed cordial, extending a hand and asking my name before we warmed up and played catch. His voice was surprisingly deep, and I could tell by his build that he was extremely athletic. All around us, men and women warmed up. It was a sea of stretchy pants and sweatpants, as far as the eye could see. I didn't fit in. I was wearing basketball shorts and a t-shirt, and the cold weather made me wish I had dressed more appropriately.

"Is this your first year playing softball?" Roark asked as we tossed the ball back and forth.

"Yes, sir. I was recruited by a guy at Tribe." I tossed the ball back as nonchalantly as possible.

"Oh, that's Rick. He must have liked you. He always seems to approach the guys he thinks are cute." Roark threw the ball back to me, and it stung my hand through the glove. He smiled.

"Ouch! It's called *warming up* for a reason!"

"You'll live," he yelled back.

I looked down the hill adjacent and saw a man walking two small pugs. He was older, wore slacks and a grey vinyl jacket, and looked as though he hadn't shaved in a month. He glanced at the field, surveyed its inhabitants, and his gaze stopped on me.

Our eyes met, and he sneered.

"Humph, *faggots*," he said, just loud enough for me to hear.

My world froze. Something deep inside me that I had not known existed boiled to the surface. "Excuse me?" I said, shocked.

The word hit my ears and I lost myself. I had never been called *faggot* by someone attempting to hurt me, and I did not know how to respond. One second I was tossing a softball with Roark, and the next I was contemplating violence. I felt a new kind of anger, an anger wrought by immediate feelings of violation. The man's prejudice weaseled its way into my head and heart like a parasite, and heat flushed throughout my body. The heat numbed my judgment, and my instincts told me to fight. He had challenged me, that little man walking his equally little dogs. That *little* brain with its gigantic prejudice!

I wanted to beat him unconscious with the softball glove that was on my left hand. I looked down: the softball glove was on the ground and I was already moving down the embankment. I felt myself take those first steps towards the careless stranger who used a derogatory term to identify me. To identify all of us. My steps were deliberate and fueled by a white-hot hatred that gave me tunnel vision. And all because of a single word!

Before I could take another step, I felt a surprisingly powerful arm holding me back. It was Roark. I turned my head, met his eyes, and saw a look of severe empathy. He looked heartbroken. He rubbed my back and forced me to breathe. I felt conflicted.

On the one hand, I was intrigued by Roark's empathy, and the other I felt a deep sense of loss…a loss of innocence and self-esteem. One word. It only took one word to disrupt my equilibrium. The shock of hearing that word directed at me was worse than jumping into a frozen lake. It knocked the breath right out of me. Worse, it knocked the patience and grace out of me, too. I had been wounded and wanted to react out of that woundedness. But Roark wouldn't let me. He restrained me with his strength, and also with his empathy.

"You just came out of the closet, didn't you?" Roark's question was rhetorical, but I nodded my head yes.

"January," I said meekly.

"Hun, you have to get used to that kind of thing," he said, "'cause it sure as hell won't be the last time someone calls you a fag." I saw a tear in the corner of his eye. It moved slowly down the arc of his jaw line and he wiped it away quickly. He was speaking from experience.

He spoke with one hand on my back while his other arm restrained my movement. Roark had ushered me forward into a new reality that I had never known. It was a cruel reality, a reality where a single word could inflict untold damage, without so much so as a warning. I felt damaged.

"But *that's not cool!*"

My words probably sounded like a child's reaction to the injustices of life for the first time, and I was that child. It was amazing that one word could elicit such a wide range of emotions. I felt nauseated. I felt humiliated. Practice had not even officially begun and already I wanted to leave. I wanted to hide in my bedroom and scream into my pillow.

"Just breathe…" Roark said. He released me from his hold. "Besides, we're the ones playing sports up here, and he's walking two pugs! If anyone's a faggot, it's him!"

The dog walker kept moving but turned his head and frowned at Roark's words.

That was the first time since coming out that I heard that word and understood what it actually meant. It means that you are a lesser, a second-class citizen, and an anathema. It means that your life is relegated to a single word, and the details of that life don't matter. It means that your thoughts, experiences, loves, and struggles should be painted over because you aren't an equal, that yours isn't as valuable as other lives. It meant you are hated. Even though I am not actually gay, I felt that hate, and it still disrupted something sacred in me. *Faggot* denotes rejection and epitomizes unwelcome, and it was a vile epiphany that I came to. Without knowing anything about us, the man walking the pugs told all of us that we were not worthy to be in community with him.

Minutes passed before the adrenaline subsided. As I came back to my senses I realized that Roark had done me a huge favor. He brought me back into control of myself and saved me from making a terrible mistake. The man walking his dogs should send Roark a bottle of wine and thank God that someone cared enough to stop me.

I made it through practice and back to my car before I had an emotional break-down; while I rested my face against the steering wheel, I couldn't help but cry. I wondered who'd taught that man that behaving that way was okay. I wondered if he had hurt anyone else with his words. I wondered who had hurt him with theirs. Kierkegaard once said, "Once you label me, you negate me." And that, I believe, is why words can hurt us so powerfully. I think that was why I reacted so emotionally to the man calling me *faggot*. I hope I will never use words like that again, that I will never negate anyone with my words or attitude, no matter how much I disagree with them.

I am learning that words I always thought were harmless really do have power. I mean, they really can hurt people. I have use words flippantly, without much consideration of how they would be accepted. My aunt Michelle from Kansas City once tried to get me to go see the Broadway production of *Rent* with my cousins. I told her I did not want to go spend three hours watching a bunch of *fags* getting what they deserved. One of the first movies I watched after coming out of the closet was *Rent*, and I felt immensely ashamed. The line "Will I lose my dignity? Will someone care?" pushed me over the emotional ledge. How many times have I used my words to take away another person's dignity? How many times have I shown just how little I care…all the while claiming to serve the God of caring?

When I was a kid, I taught myself how to play the harmonica. It was a long process, and I still owe my parents an apology for the racket. But the funniest thing happened as I learned: I started hearing the harmonica everywhere. I heard it in TV commercials, in songs that I had heard a thousand times on the radio but never realized included the tiny instrument, and I heard it walking down the street as a homeless man in my neighborhood played the blues. Once I began playing the harmonica, my ears opened up and I became aware of the harmonica in a way I had not before. I think the same thing has happened this year. I never used to flinch when derogatory terms were used by friends, or when I spoke them. It all melted in to the background of every day speech and conversation. After coming out, especially after having the dog-walking man call me *faggot*, I tuned in and I cringe as words are thrown around like careless projectiles. Our words, once spoken, live. They live and float around our lives like the stars above us on a clear night, watching us. They are markers of who we are and have been, indicators of our character or lack thereof. My night sky is filled with these living curses.

I watch the opening softball game, spitting sunflower seeds from the bleachers. Roark's hit is good, and with two more batters, he reaches home plate with ease and walks over to me. He wraps his arms around me, tells me he loves me, and asks me how I have been. He actually gives a damn. I feel indebted to him.

But despite the festive atmosphere of opening day, I feel an emptiness, and nagging questions from my past: What if the people I went to church with actually gave a damn about me? What if I had given a damn about them? If we really cared about each other, would the church have a reputation for pious ruthlessness, if the religious could learn to love even the people who do not agree with them? If I had believed that the people I went to church with actually cared, I might not have chosen to walk the path I am on.

Roark wishes me good luck on my first two games and heads back to the dugout. Roark is proof that it really is that simple to love another person.

My performance on the opening day of softball is humiliating. I have never felt more feeble as an athlete or more inept at a sport. My team loses both games, but at least I have fun doing so, and that is what it is all about (I think). I get to lounge in the sun and talk to a couple that had just adopted their first child. I hold a little baby in my arms and see the looks of infinite love on her moms' faces. I get to enjoy community again on a Sunday, and it is a new and fresh experience. Joining the softball league is one of the better choices I have made this year; it presents an opportunity to see a more normal life for the gays and lesbians of the community, a life apart from the atmosphere of the gayborhood. I am excited to become even more a part of this community.

15 my first prom

Outside the café, on the window of the small community center next door, I see a banner. It advertises a prom—but how could an entire prom be held in such a small facility? I read the fine print of the announcement: an *all-inclusive prom*! I have never been to a prom, and I wonder how similar a gay prom and straight prom are. My ultra-conservative Christian high school was strict, and the administration had never allowed proms because they were *too worldly* and because dancing led to lust and lust led to teen sex. They opted instead to throw us a junior/senior banquet, where we had to dress formally just to eat dinner. I felt jealous of every kid in public school that night.

On the Friday of the all-inclusive prom, I see kids arriving next door as I smoke outside on the café's deck. They are not the type of kids I ever hung out with. Some of the guys are extremely delicate and feminine and look weary; I wonder if their weariness is the result of merciless abuse and bullying at school. The girls...well, they look like younger versions of the women I have met this year, many with short cropped hair and piercings. But one fact becomes immediately apparent. All of them look thankful to have their own prom, a night where they can be themselves and celebrate the end of the school year among friends.

I walk out of the coffee shop and over to the community center with a tub of clean dishes and utensils for the party, and I am greeted by a couch full of bright-eyes teens. Their life is refreshing, and their exuberant smiles and energy are infectious. I feel protective of them, like a big brother or chaperone...but I also feel a pang of helplessness and guilt. I would have bullied these very same teens if I had gone to high school with them.

"Having fun?"

"Hell, yeah!" several voices speak in unison.

They seem so innocent. Having been taught being gay is such an abominable choice, I would have expected innocence to be my last impression, even from kids. But they *are* innocent. They are young and unique, pure somehow, not at all jaded the way I would have assumed. They are the way I always wished my classmates could have been in my Christian high school, so themselves, so confident in who they are as people.

"Anybody want a latte?" I ask. "It's on the house."

Three of the kids jumped up as soon as they hear the word *latte*. It is the same reaction I imagine I would get if I took a six pack into an Alcoholics Anonymous meeting, and I smile at their energy.

All three follow me back to the café, and while I make the drinks, the kids tell me about themselves. They all have similar stories: all came out at thirteen or fourteen, and all faced tremendous fallout with family and friends, but all are happy to live what they feel is a much more "normal" existence. I am beginning to understand the *normal* thing. The closet is suffocating. Being in the closet is a constant source of negativity and mental oppression. It can be worse even than the rejection and abuse that come with being out of the closet—at least, I feel that way. I think about my friends. Most are still are not talking to me, just because they believe I am gay. I look into the eyes of these teenagers and know we share a bond. It is a bond formed by the pain of abandonment, and I know that what these young people have experienced is probably a thousand times as intense as anything I have, or will, during my short journey.

The last latte I make is for a young guy named Matt. He is thin and a bit lanky but seems solid. He has the build of a swimmer, and his tuxedo-print t-shirt tells me what kind of guy he is. He is the kind of kid who tries not to take life too seriously, and whether it is a defense mechanism or he is just being himself, there is something special about this kid. Matt stays after the others leave, and we talk. I am impressed by his eloquence. He is so intelligent that I have a hard time keeping up with him. More often than not I stand and nod my head, hoping he does not see how lost I am as we talk. Matt's passion is philosophy.

"I just want to make all of this bullshit make sense." He takes a sip of his drink and smiles. "This is really good!"

"Glad you like it," I say while I wipe down the counter and clean up the coffee grounds from the counter. "So, why philosophy?"

"I guess I study philosophy because I need it. Philosophy has taught me how to forgive, and I have a lot in my life I need to forgive," he says. "I don't want to be one of those people that can't enjoy life because I'm so bitter. You know?"

"I do, actually. I'm pretty bitter...but not as much as others, I guess. So what's your story?" I ask, steaming the milk for another latte I promised to take to another one of the teens.

"I'll give you the abridged version," he says confidently. "I came out to my family when I was in the eighth grade, and they didn't take it so well." He looks down, reliving the moment, I think.

"What happened?"

"Well, right now I'm living at my best friend's house. Her family took me in after I was kicked out."

"Are you *kidding* me?" The words *kicked out* sting my heart. This kid has been through a hell that I can never understand.

"No...Why would I joke about that?"

"I meant that rhetorically."

He looks at me and I see the child inside of him, the being that is not supposed to face this kind of pain so soon. He is the victim of the kind of life that no kid should ever know about. It is the position that insists he isn't good enough or worthy of love and support. The innocence of a child typically includes a much smaller reality, a sheltered reality. But Matt hasn't ever been sheltered. This is a tangible reality that a large percentage of LGBTQ youth in this country understand, but not me. I will never understand.

"I still get to see them at church on Sundays, but they don't know how to treat me. My mom hasn't looked me in the eyes for several years."

"That's a tough thing, hun. I honestly can't imagine." I am dumbfounded. I cannot imagine having to seek refuge with a family that is not my own. The milk for the last latte is ready. I can tell because the steam hisses through thickened white, silky 2 percent. I gently settle the milk by tapping the frothing pitcher on the counter, and I clean the steaming nozzle with a wet rag before pouring the espresso shots into the white paper cup. Matt looks on interestedly.

"Yeah, it sucks pretty bad, but I'll be okay," he says, looking curiously at the merman sitting on the couch.

"So you still go to church?" I ask.

"I love church! I sing in the choir, and no one there really treats me differently. They stopped bringing everything up after they saw that I wasn't going anywhere."

It makes me happy to know that he is not making the church an enemy because of his family, but it is sad because I know what is probably being said about him behind his back. They have not accepted Matt as a young gay man. No one in his church probably thinks they are or could hurt him. His family doesn't either. No one is the villain of his own narrative and no one understands the role he plays in the narrative of others. Matt's family probably thinks they are taking a stand *for him*. I doubt they understand that they are creating a barrier of hurt and pain between them that might never be overcome.

"So what do you miss most about your family?" I ask.

"I miss the hugs. I miss feeling my mom and dad hugging me." Matt looks down at the latte he is supposed to deliver to his friend. He sees the heart I drew with the steamed milk, and his face lights up.

A lot of my gay friends still go to church. They talk about wanting to have a relationship with Jesus, and they never fail to mention how important their faith is in their lives. It is always eye-opening when I hear their stories; but in this case, from a junior in high school, I am beyond surprised.

Matt picks up his latte and thanks me. "You should stop by the prom later. And if you can, you should bring the merman. He'd be perfect there!"

"Marco is pretty heavy, but *I'll* make an appearance."

"Thanks, Tim."

Before he walks out the door I give him a big hug and hold him tight. "Matt, I know you may doubt this, but your parents do love you. They are captive to a belief that says they can't be in relationship with you, and it's hard to overcome that teaching, sometimes…but never for a second doubt that they love you."

"Thank you. I'll try to remember."

As he walks out of the café, I walk over to the couch and collapse. Marco's body feels heavy next to me, his outfit scratching the exposed skin of my arms and neck, but I don't care.

How a parent could ever disown her child to such a degree scares me. It is a crime. I feel angry and sad at the same time. I think Matt goes to church because he wants to see his family, and I think he likes singing in the choir so he can see them without looking as though he is staring. That is what I would do, if I were him.

A few hours later I take my break and walk next door to the prom. Some of the kids from earlier pull me out on the dance floor and we laugh the whole time, trying to top one embarrassing maneuver with another. It may be odd for me as an ex-homophobe or a recovering Pharisee, but it is a highlight of my year.

Matt makes his way towards me through the crowd.

"Having fun?" he asks.

"I've never been to a prom before."

"Well, you're at one now!"

He is right! This is my first prom, and it is a gay prom with gay pirates as the theme. I feel a hole in my upbringing being filled, and it is a moment I will never forget. Even though this is so radically different than what I am used to, it is normal—and I feel normal.

I wonder what the world would be like if we taught our kids and each other that we should never be afraid of someone just because they are different. I wonder what would happen if we taught our kids more about the similarities in people than hyper-fixating on the differences. In that perfect world, Matt would not be living with his friend's family; his parents would know that he is still the baby whose diapers they changed, the same little kid they took trick-or-treating. At what point did Matt stop being their little boy?

All I know is that I would be proud to have Matt as a son.

16 outed

Late May

They say time flies when you are having fun. I wonder if they would say the same when you are living a lie. I think time passes more slowly when you live every moment in your head, when paranoia saturates every look, every word in a conversation, every encounter you have with the individuals whom you are deceiving. It's like I am waiting to fully live until I can be honest again, even though this experiment has a momentum of its own now. The learning curve has finally passed, but it has not gotten any easier. I feel the weight of this necessary evil every day, but I also feel peace. Even though my experience is different, I know that in some small way, I am finally beginning to understand the struggle unique to those living a closeted life. Every day, and with each new interaction with the gay men and lesbian women I spend so much time with, I am reassured that I can finally question my faith. But will I ever be able to reconcile my faith in God and the homosexual orientation?

I turn off the water from the shower and dry myself vigorously, feeling energized and excited. We just won our first softball game, defeating one of the better teams in the league. I played catcher and was encouraged to have done well for the first time this season. My team is filled with athletes, and having me on the team is probably sometimes frustrating for them. I wipe my head dry and look into the mirror. The image reflected is mine, but I do not feel like me. I feel the growing pains and awkwardness of transition. I feel like a man without a country, a man without a religion, a man who does not know himself yet. It amazes me that I have made it five months.

Even my boyfriend Shawn is surprised. After some of the earlier close calls in the gay bars, he is relieved not to have to babysit me anymore when I go out. Instead, our time has become more quality and less instruction. While we are out, we spend more time getting to know each other and less time focusing on the nuances of body language and flirtation. I learned the language of the community quickly, in spite of myself, and I feel better for it. I am not longer a stranger to the gay community of Nashville. I am one of them—or as much as I can ever be without actually being gay. I know names, stories, and, even more satisfying, I have allowed others to get to know me. Where I once felt guarded, I am finally able to trust the people I meet. There is an unwritten code in our humble gayborhood. Shawn helped teach me that code, and now I feel like we are able to invest in our friendship and our relationship more than ever.

I am brushing my teeth when the phone rings. I rinse and spit as quickly as possible. "Hello."

"Tim, it's Mom. Andrew and Marin know. They called and told me." Her voice is shaky.

"Know what, exactly?" I ask. My body begins to shake with panic and adrenaline.

"That you aren't really gay. That you are doing some kind of experiment."

She knows? *They* know? All at once, in the blink of an eye, I feel exposed, naked, and vulnerable in front of the people I have misled. My first thought is that I need to talk to Andrew and explain, but all I can do is collapse into a nearby chair as tears fill my eyes. If he has second-hand information, he won't understand why I have done this to him. It is a terrifying thought, the lid coming off of my experiment just shy of the halfway point. It is terrifying and devastating. My experiment isn't over! It feels like it has barely just begun. I am finally at the point where I am learning, where my feet are more than just wet. I am in the pool now, and my body has acclimated to the water.

I do not feel shocked, the way I imagined I would be if this ever happened. It is a different kind of guilt. I am not ashamed of what I am doing. I feel only an intense sadness for who I have hurt. My family is the most important thing to me, especially since my parent's divorce, and I feel cut off from them for the first time. Even my mom's voice is distant, as if she's on the other side of the world, only giving me half of her attention.

"I'm sorry, Mom…I…" I cannot speak. My voice is cracking too much for her to understand me.

"You're free to talk to me whenever you need to…Tim, I wasn't born yesterday. I'm just trying to understand why you did this."

"I will explain everything when we talk. Just don't say anything to anyone, and I'll call you later."

"I love you," she says.

I hang up the phone and grab my journal from my backpack. The only way I can explain my situation is to show him, to help my brother understand that I had to do this. I want to show him the entry from January first, when I felt so horrible for deceiving him that I went outside and vomited. I need to show him that I did not haphazardly throw him under the bus. I need to heal this wound…or at least patch it up, and fast.

You know that's not going to happen. Be realistic.

My Pharisee looks at me with a searing, almost venomous expression. He looks at me like I am an enemy, and I know I cannot avoid him. I dress as quickly as possible; everything is a blur, everything except the Pharisee. No, he is clear. Too clear. His expression is the expression I hope *not* to see on my brother's face. I cannot avoid it or look away.

This is your *fault. You knew this would happen. Running off to brother's house with your little journal won't accomplish anything, and you know it!*

I have to try! What kind of brother would I be if I didn't try to explain?

The kind of brother who seems to care more for his little experiment than he does for his own flesh and blood.

That's not true! You've been with me this whole time, seen what I've seen, and you can't tell me I'm doing the wrong thing.

The path you're on was always your choice from the beginning—just like every gay man and woman alive has chosen theirs.

Don't feed me that bullshit…

You were never programmed—you just like feeling right. You reveled in the absolutes. It was your pride, not the church, that led to all of this.

Both influenced me. Does that make you happy to hear? I never said I wasn't to blame for how I applied the teachings of my church. But know this: What I'm doing now is the first truly good thing I've done in my life, and I refuse to quit!

The first truly good thing you've done in your life? You are trying to undermine the Bible and what you know is truth. How is that good?

I don't know it's the truth! Would I have done this if I did? Things are not as plain and simple as I once thought. And eventually my brother will understand that, too. He's hurt, but he's a rational guy. If I can show him why I had to do this, he'll listen.

Tim, you lied to him. You betrayed his trust. Don't take my word for it—take his.

I can feel my body shaking. The adrenaline leaves a bitter taste in my mouth as it courses through my blood and brain like liquid speed. The weather outside is sunny, but I see it through a curtain of tears. What if the Pharisee is right? What if my brother disowns me? My world is flooding, and I am losing the only thing I thought I had: control. But maybe that was just another *lie*; maybe that is why I feel the way I do right now.

You are living heresy, and you're the one who will have to deal with the consequences of it. I feel no pity for you.

It is easier to love those who believe the same as us more than those we disagree with. If I am damned for asking questions and testing what old white men have taught me all my life, then so be it!

Late February

It was a dinner party like any other, but I had gotten too confident in being known as Andrew's gay brother, and I was not on guard the way I should have been. Everyone at the party had just finished a raucous game of *Catch Phrase* and I had been pleasantly surprised when, on my brother's turn, his clue for the table was "opposite of Tim." "*Straight!*" everyone shouted in unison. I looked around the table…and felt accepted. It was the first time I did not feel like an outsider around my family and their friends.

After several drinks on an empty stomach, I stood outside my brother's home, smoking with my brother's good friend. "So when did you know you were gay?" he asked.

"For a while, I guess," I said vaguely.

"You know, your brother is doing his best to remember who you are and not make it a big deal."

"Yeah, I know it's probably tough on him." I knew it was probably a great deal more than "tough." After all, there is no room in heaven for homosexuals, at least in our brand of Christianity.

"But, Tim, you've always loved women so much, or at least acted that way…Don't you miss boobs?" He laughed.

"Yes, I do!" I answered without thinking.

"Wait…What?"

"Shit." I belched and tossed my cigarette butt into the yard.

"Tim, what's going on?"

"Follow me."

I took him to the backyard and swore him to secrecy, stumbling over my words and emotions the entire time.

He successfully kept my secret for three months, which was two months and three weeks longer than Josh and Shawn thought he would be able to keep it.

~~~

The drive to my brother's house is a blur. The streets bleed together, and the entire time I try to decide what I am going to say and how I will say it. If things had gone according to plan, I would not be experiencing this for another seven months. I am not prepared for this now! I had hoped to have more to show for my experiment by the time I came out as straight. I am afraid of losing my family—even more so than when I told them I am gay. I wonder if this fear is more characteristic of what my gay friends have talked about when telling their own coming-out stories.

More than anything, I am afraid that this journey is going to end because I slipped and told someone I should not have. The thought scares the hell out of me. I do not want my secret to get out. I want to keep learning and experiencing the things that only the label of gay can ever teach me. I want to experience and live more of this journey, as I have finally become acclimated to my new life. I am not ready to be straight Tim again. I like gay Tim. I like his friends, and I like that he is trying to have an open mind. I like *me*, so much more than I did before. And what would be accomplished having just gotten past the learning curve?

I finally feel the weight of what I am doing, finally understand how essential this is—not just for the sake of experiencing something unique, but because I finally realize that I can and should be better. I can love more. I can change. I can be authentic in my faith for the first time by loving my neighbor as myself. This will just have to be part of the story, I resolve; another chapter in a series of uncomfortable chapters, where nothing is as it should be.

I take a few deep breaths and the panic abates with each exhalation. I think of my new friends, the people whom I finally understand are not the enemy of me, or of God.

I park my car on the street in front of Andrew's house, but I cannot find the courage to get out. Help me, Lord. I do not know what to say.

You can't say anything. You've messed up too badly this time.

The fact that you believe in *too badly's* makes me pity you.

That is the push I need. I get out of the beaten-up Honda and walk to the back yard. As expected, I find my brother, his wife, and the friend who told them, sitting on the back patio. The mood is incredibly tense, and rightly so. They have just found me out. Can they comprehend why I have done what I've done? It is real, now, this moment of this bleak conversation—for the first time I feel the potential for rejection that might cause me irrevocable damage. But thinking about me is selfish. I should be asking instead if I have caused Andrew irrevocable damage, not by coming out, but because I have spent five months lying to him.

"What are you doing here?" Andrew says, beating his wife to the punch.

"I really need to talk to you, to explain."

"Explain what? You lied to us. And for what?" my sister-in-law says. She has a much sharper tone than Andrew.

"That is what I need to explain. I had to do this." I am breathless and overwhelmed.

"This isn't a good time, Tim. We'll talk in a few days."

Andrew's calm worries me. "Why can't we talk now?"

"Because it's not a good time for us. We are with our friends, so just calm down and leave." His tone is unwavering.

"Can't we just talk for a few minutes?" I plead with him.

"No, Tim. We don't want to talk to you! Just leave!" Andrew defers to his wife's remark and gives me a look. It is a vastly different look than the one I saw on his face that cold morning five months ago. "Sunday morning. We'll talk next Sunday morning," he says.

"For whatever it's worth, I'm sorry I put you through this. I will do my best to explain when you talk to me."

"Sunday," he says.

"Sunday."

I walk away feeling defeated. Drained. I feel alone, truly alone. I get into my Honda and turn the key. I need a drink.

Able to patch it up?

You really are a bastard.

Remember what the Bible says about liars? Care for a reminder?

Another time.

~~~

Sunday finally comes. I have been dreading the talk with Andrew. I have no way of knowing how he will respond, if the last week has affected his feelings toward me. I spent most of the night writing down what I want to tell him on 3"X5" note cards, but the last time I rehearsed a speech to give to my brother, I didn't end up saying a word of it. I pace back and forth across the aggregate driveway behind my dad's house, thankful it is not too hot outside. Nashville summers begin mid-spring; today the weather is temperate and clear. But I feel hidden under a dark and ominous cloud.

When my cell rings, my brother's picture appears on my phone. I remember when we took that picture. It was a better time for Andrew and me, a time when all of this would have seemed impossible. I answer the call and my brother says hello.

After making small-talk, my brother gets to the point: "Why did you lie to us?"

"I had to understand for myself what it felt like to come out. I had to feel the apprehension and fear that people face every day when they come out. It may not make sense, but understanding that was essential to this whole thing." My voice is shaking, and my body stutters and quakes as I talk. It shatters my confidence.

"Tim, you threw me under the bus," his says, his tone sharper than before.

"I've been throwing people under the bus for years, people who did nothing to me except believe differently."

"Don't get all self-righteous on me."

"I know you probably won't understand this right now, but this is the first time in my life I'm *not* being self-righteous. I have been a bully and a bigot. What we were taught about these people wasn't right!"

"Don't give me that. We aren't talking about gay, here; we are talking about you lying to me. I never thought you would do that. I trusted you!"

It isn't difficult to see where this conversation is headed, and I brace myself for the crash landing.

"I love you, brother," I say, "but I had to do this. And I don't regret what I have done, not for a second, because it is the first time I've truly understood the path I was headed down. I was wrong all along. I don't know how else to explain it."

"Listen, Tim, you are my little brother and I love you, but you have to understand that I'm not just your brother anymore. I'm a husband, and your actions have hurt my wife." He lets the words sink in. "We need to step back from this whole thing—and from you, for a while. Maybe when you are all done with your year, we can sit down and work things out."

"I understand. I really do. It sucks but I get it," I say, choking back emotion.

"I know you do, Tim. I knew you would."

"I love you, man," I say.

"I love you too," he says.

And then we are disconnected from the call, but more so, from each other. My older brother, my blood, has removed himself from my life. Maybe it was naiveté, but I never thought it would come to this. At least I hoped it wouldn't. I sit in the middle of the driveway, unable to stand. I allow myself to grieve. I wonder if my pain is anything remotely akin to the pain my gay and lesbian friends felt when they were rejected by their family members. Sure, my brother emphasized my "choice" to lie to him—and mine was a choice—but in so many other stories I have heard, parents reacted to the "choice" to be gay. In either case, the sadness and crushing isolation of this moment overwhelms me.

~~~

Shawn finds me, hours later, in the corner of Tribe, four beers in. He sits next to me on the couch and puts his arms around me. My head on his shoulder feels right and comfortable. It is not something I would have done with any man before all of this, but I feel utterly vulnerable and know that with Shawn I am in a safe place. I can fall apart in his arms and trust that his only intention will be to comfort me. He is that type of saint, a hero to me. I begin to cry. No one else is around, so I feel safe to talk.

"What happened? How did they find out?" he asks in a soothing voice.

"Exactly how we thought it would happen. My brother's friend."

"Tim, you aren't perfect, and you slipped—but this project isn't over."

"The whole thing is over now," I say. "I've lost my brother, and my mission."

"Why would you say that? Why would it be over?"

"Because my family knows."

"You barely see your family," he says, rubbing my back.

"But they'll tell people."

"Tim, your project isn't over. It's only just begun. You may not have the same relationship to your brother or your mom that you did before this, but you can't stop what you are doing.

You have to keep going. You have to keep going for me." His eyes express something I have not seen before. "We don't need you to rescue us. We need you to rescue yourself, so you can be the example."

"An example? I don't feel like I could ever be an example." I sound pathetic.

"You already are. I believe in you, but you need to believe in yourself too."

"I'll try," I meekly whisper.

I look across the main room to the bar and see Will wiping down the counter. He is looking at me and smiles as we make eye contact. I feel urgently thankful that he is a part of my life again, and that Shawn is here to comfort me.

"You have a kind heart, but you need to stop beating yourself up. Take advantage of this time while you have it, and keep searching—"

"But I lied to them," I say.

"And I lied to my family about being straight, all those years," he says.

"But that's different. That was your process."

"Maybe. But this is your process. It's unique and messy, but it was meant to be. I know God led you to this. I've always felt your conviction was proof of that." He hesitates before continuing. "I love you, Tim."

"I love you, too, Shawn." I do. But I also feel guilty, knowing that I cannot love Shawn the way he needs to be loved, the way he deserves to be loved.

I feel something else in his words. Does he love me...or is he falling in love with me? I dismiss the thought as soon as I think it. That is the last thing I want to happen right now. Two seasons have passed me by and I know I am past my homophobia, past my irrational fear of gay men. That alone is a small miracle. To be held by Shawn in a gay bar, and to love him as much as I do, this is evidence enough for me. But I know I have to go deeper, despite the consequences. I have a little over six months left and so much yet to discover.

Shawn tries to get my mind off of my brother. He tells me stories, we dance with some of the other guys, he tells me jokes, and when I smile his face lights up. He knows I am in pain, and I know he is in pain because of my pain. How did I get so lucky as to find someone like Shawn to spend time with, someone so intensely empathetic and encouraging? I don't know what I would do without Shawn, but my thoughts stray back to my brother. I don't know what I will do without him in my life, either. I just hope it doesn't come to that.

Part III: The New Testament

"You can safely assume you've created God in your own image when it turns out that God hates all the same people you do."

—Anne Lamott

17 jesus in drag

In the short time I have worked at Revive, the café is living up to its name. I feel more alive, working and talking with people every day. It is freeing. It is convenient. Working as a barista suits me, and I love making coffee in a café that has such a great vibe. It is almost a dream, or at least feels like it. I am fully trained now, and I was even sent to train with a professional barista named EJ at a café in east Nashville. He taught me how to make latte art, hearts and spirals. Inadvertently I even learned how to draw the male anatomy. Steamed sex, 2 percent—it makes the regulars smile.

The other positive side of working at a gay café attached to a gay bookstore is that I get discounts on everything. I even get free movie rentals, all of which have gay themes. Obviously. Last night I watched a movie called *Latter Days*. It is about a Mormon missionary that moves next door to a player. They fall in love, and there is this line where the missionary is talking to a lady on a bench. He tells her that when he used to read the Sunday comics as a kid, he would put his nose up to them, so he could only see thousands of tiny dots. None of it made sense, he says, until he pulled the paper back from his face, and he would see the whole story, and the story was beautiful, and funny, and good. He tells the woman on the bench that life is like the comics. It is a mass of dots that don't seem to make sense, but he likes to think that God looks at us from above, and everything makes sense. From this close we can't expect everything to make sense. The spiritual insight in his words caught me off guard, but then again, things are catching me off guard every day. The credits rolled, and I was sad. I want to share the movie with some of my Christian friends, but they would probably dismiss it out of hand because "homosexuals cannot be Christians." Too bad for them. The movie was great. I returned the movie and clocked in for my shift, and the hours pass in conversation and coffee grounds.

"I'm going to smoke, if that's okay with you," I say to my supervisor, Brent.

"Sure. Take your lunch," Brent says, staring at the computer screen in front of him.

"Bitch, I love you!" I say, walking to the door.

He smiles. "Bitch, I love you!" he says, still fixated on the computer screen.

I walk outside. The cool spring air is refreshing, and I light my cigarette, leaning against the patio's railing. It is nice having a job; in this economy, it is something no one takes for granted. I exhale the smoke and look around, shifting the clove from my right hand to my left. The sunset is beautiful, a tapestry of orange and red, and from my vantage point the view is especially vivid. Cars pass, stirring the leaves and debris of the gutter, and I pull out my phone and text Shawn to ask how his day is going.I have lived with the label of gay for almost six months but am still plagued by questions. I have realized that this whole thing is really just a process, just seeing people for who they are instead of as labels. There is so much more to a person. Take Brent, for example. He is not particularly spiritual, but he told me today that he would love to go back to school for theology. Theology, *really?* Most Christians don't even like studying theology, unless they are trying to justify their own point of view.

I hear music next door. It is karaoke night at the LGBTQ community center, and I am curious if gay karaoke is any different from the karaoke I go to every week. Well, maybe not much is different. Maybe just the song choices are different. One might expect to hear more pop and techno on a gay karaoke night than at the average bar.

Another song starts, replacing the Brittney Spears song before it...and I recognize it. I can't make out the words, and I cannot put my finger on what the song is. The words are muffled by two sets of doors separating me from the other space. But *that song*—that song sounds so familiar. I exhale the smoke and try to figure out the name of the song playing. It is loud, upbeat, and dramatic. I have heard that song a million times! I just do not know what it is.

I look at the Pharisee, and his face betrays worry.

Don't go in there. It's just karaoke night. Stay here.

But I have to. I am drawn, like a moth to a flame. And I am desperately searching my memory for the name of that song.

Nothing is worse than not being able to remember the name of a movie or song you know. It is like my brain has just been struck by an intense, albeit temporary, bout of Alzheimer's. I peek inside the café: a regular is sipping his coffee and reading the newspaper. Brent's face is still angled down at the computer monitor. I am not needed. It is my lunch break, after all, so I shouldn't feel bad about leaving work to go next door for a few minutes.

I open the door to the community center. The music gets louder, but the words are still muffled. Not remembering is like having an unreachable itch.

I look back and see the Pharisee reluctantly following me inside. He does not look happy—but then again he rarely looks happy.

I swing the door open and step into the large meeting room. About thirty people are gathered, all of them singing along with the woman on stage… No, not a woman. A man dressed as a woman. He looks like a young Barbara Bush, wearing a black skirt and blouse, an earthy pink suit jacket adorned with a broach that looks like a shiny leaf, and matching pink heels. His wig is short but feminine, and he is wearing a necklace that looks like a string of fake, gold pearls. His eyes are closed. The crowd is engrossed.

I take a few steps further into the room. The crowd is not acting like a typical karaoke crowd. Their hands lift into the air and their eyes are closed. They are focused, almost trance-like, on the words coming out of their mouths, and all of them seem to know the lyrics to the song. It is magic.

They launch into the chorus. Goose bumps spread over my body, and I am engulfed by shock.

I know this song! I have known it since I was a kid. I have not heard it in years, but I remember it as clearly as ever. The chorus begins and a part of my world collapses.

"Our God is an awesome God. He reigns from Heaven above, with wisdom, power, and love. Our God is an awesome God..."

My jaw feels disconnected from my face. It hangs open as if fixed that way. I am in absolute awe. I cannot move. I cannot think. I cannot do anything but stare: stare at the at the crowd of strangers gathered for a normal karaoke night but frozen in a moment of intense worship. The drag queen on stage repeats the chorus three times before starting the next verse, and all the while, a grand epiphany ripples like electricity through every inch of my body. All my life, I have been taught that gays cannot worship God. Cannot know God. Cannot love God. And I believed it. I believed it so absolutely that I doubted every word I heard this year from Samantha and Matthew, Mel, even Shawn. I sat silently, listening to them but judging them, as if I knew something they could never know. And now this. My pride and my paradigm crumble at the feet of a man dressed like a young Barbara Bush, singing "Our God Is an Awesome God."

A man has noticed me. He sees the shock on my face and walks over to shake my hand and introduce himself, but I can't give him my attention. The song ends and another one begins. Part of me wants to hear Brittney Spears, part of me wants to hear Cher. Those parts of me desperately want that last song to be a fluke, a funny coincidence, so my beliefs do not have to change.

Again my spinning thoughts are brought to a standstill as the crowd begins to sing "Here I Am to Worship," my favorite praise song to sing in church. But this is *not* church! This is a community center in the heart of Nashville's gayborhood. *This is unreal.* I am a lazy bastard, really, and I wonder how I will ever process this moment.

I collect myself enough to nudge the man next to me.

"Does this happen often?" I ask him.

He seems intrigued by my response to the music. "Yeah, actually. Most of us go to church together, so no one really minds when Bill starts in with the Jesus music."

I feel the Pharisee next to me and I see his mouth unhinged, like mine. He looks as if he is in pain, and I put my arm on his shoulder.

The man next to me smiles, and I feel like God is smiling at me.

I am a witness to something that defies everything I held to be truth. I am humbled. Not just humbled. I feel crushed and broken, utterly foolish for insisting this was not possible. The crowd launches into the chorus, and the drag queen on stage really gets into it. He sings the way I sing at church. I know where his heart is. I *know* he is being real, and I can no longer question him, discredit him, or hate him. He is my opposite, but now we are the same. My heart softens, knowing the words that are coming next. I sing with them this time, or at least I try. I mouth the words, half singing, half speaking them under my breath, still too surprised to lift my voice above a whisper, but no one notices. We are all lost in the intensity of the moment.

"Here I am to worship. Here I am to bow down. Here I am to say that You're my God. You're altogether lovely, all together worthy, all together wonderful to me..."

Thirty minutes pass like one minute or a thousand minutes, and for those thirty minutes I sing praise song after praise song. I hear as many praise songs as I would on Sunday mornings at church, and I feel the same spirit, too. I feel a burden lift and a question answered. A Britney Spears song comes on at last, and I walk out of the community center. I have gone a few minutes over my half-hour break. I look inside and see Brent still staring at the computer screen. Our one regular has left, so I know there is no rush. I light up another cigarette and sit.

The Pharisee sits next to me, finally silent. He cannot say anything. He saw what I have seen. I can hear his breath sink deep inside his chest like a stone in water. Or maybe those breaths are my own.

I have been taught that I need to *be* Jesus to the people I meet, that I need to live the love and the faith and the commitment of my God, so that others can see Him, too. If it is true that we can be Jesus to each other, then I will never see Jesus the same way again. Tonight… Well, tonight, I saw Jesus in drag, and now I feel incapable of hate. I know these feelings will lessen and diminish as time passes, that my freedom from hatred is similar to my three-week freedom from masturbation after watching the *Passion of the Christ*, but I hope it is not temporary. I hope I will remember these goose bumps and this shock, and I hope I remember how beautiful it is to live inside this tension.

My clove is almost burned away, an inch of thick ash still clinging to the filter, like my ideologies cling to my heart. I toss the clove into the can by the door. I toss the clove and I toss my ideologies with it. I was wrong. I step into the coffee shop, back to work, but I feel different.

Somehow my year in the closet just got a little bit easier, and all because I saw Jesus in drag.

18 becoming invisible

My mom walks into the restaurant with an expression of relief on her face. No doubt she is relieved to know that her second born is not in fact a gay man. Maybe the simple fact that I am straight is enough to cancel out her frustration and hurt resulting from my having lied to her. Once more, she has a second son who will marry a nice young woman and have cute little babies (I hope). I resent the idea that anyone would be relieved to know that I really am the same heterosexual man they always believed me to be. Would it be the end of the world if I really were gay? Is the crass, bigoted, straight Tim somehow more valuable than the softer, peaceful, more loving gay Tim? Why do we put a higher value on one orientation over the other? Why have I always valued straight people more than gays and lesbians?

When she sits down, she puts her hand on mine on the table, and I tell her all about the how and why behind my drastic experience. She listens and doesn't interrupt, but I am leery of her motives. Maybe my cynicism is the result of the standard responses that I have gotten from the average person when I tell them I'm gay. Maybe I am just becoming more naturally defensive. It could also be the constant paranoia that is present even now. If I was not guarded with people, would I be more wounded by now? But this is my own mother, and I know it is only fair to try to give her the benefit of the doubt.

When I tell my mom about seeing Jesus in drag, her eyes betray a surprise much akin to the surprise I felt that beautifully jarring evening. She apologizes. I ask why, and she says she knows there were times she did not treat me the way she probably should have. "I was just so surprised and shocked, and I needed a lot of time to process what you were telling me," she says.

I know this much is true: It takes longer for individuals who have been inundated with conservative religion to "come around" than others that have not been taught about the "unnatural and abominable" gay lifestyle or "evil gay agenda." Lord knows I cannot judge. It has taken a great deal for me to question and realize that things aren't as I was taught they are, too.

More than anything, my mom is concerned about my relationship with my brother, who told me on the phone that because of my lying to him, he would distance himself from me until my experiment was over.

"He feels thrown under the bus," I tell her, "and all for gay people." I can tell she's distraught. "Mom, I'll tell you what I told him. I *did* throw all of you under the bus for 'gay people,' but only because there isn't a gay man or lesbian woman I've met who hasn't been thrown under the bus just because of the label of their orientation. The only way I could understand was to risk my own relationship with all of you."

"It will all work out," she says. "I just hope it's sooner rather than later. It hurts me to know that my babies aren't speaking."

"It's hurting both of us too. Maybe one day all of you will understand."

The Pharisee smirks at me from a nearby table. He's been fairly silent since the night at karaoke, but his expressions have said the thousands of words they've replace. Right now, his face says, *Maybe one day you'll understand how much it hurts to be lied to by your own sibling.* And he is not too far off base. I don't understand what I have put them through, but it was a price I had to pay.

"For whatever it's worth, I'm sorry."

"I do think I understand, and I really am proud of you." she says. My mom is handling this whole thing much better than I anticipated, and I thankful for it.

Her words are comforting, but I wish that she would have told me she was proud of me while she thought I was gay. I cannot judge her motives, but it seems that because she knows I am straight, she is somehow more open to me than before. My heart aches for the beautiful men and women who are denied something as simple as familial support just because of their orientation. I cannot fathom how painful life must be for them at times. This year is probably a cakewalk by comparison.

After small-talk, food, and iced tea, I leave the restaurant feeling comforted but more isolated from my family than ever. My mom is taking the news well, and the impact of my actions will probably diminish with time, but I have to let go of the idea that I can change their minds. Only they can do that. Only they have the power to attempt to understand or to write me off for what I have done. Worse still are the *what ifs* that I am left with. They never got to meet Shawn or see us together. They never had the opportunity to meet my new friends whom I so desperately wish they could have. With them knowing that I am not really gay, I cannot risk those encounters anymore. I can't risk them slipping, as I slipped with my brother's friend. The news would spread through the community and expose me. Coming clean to everyone is my cross to bear.

The family aspect of my experiment is now tainted, and I have to move forward in the other areas that are still available to me. The chances that my family will tell anyone about my project are slim, and I am not afraid of being outed to anyone else, for now. My family life and my new social life are worlds apart. I am saddened that I have perpetuated this ideological divide for so long, and sadder still now that I have to knowingly live in one world or the other, cut off from one group or the other at any given time. This whole "issue" of homosexuality is only polarizing because conservative religion dictates the standards of religious people. It controls their motives and their reactions. It especially controls their politics. I hope to see the day when my conservative Christian brothers and sisters realize that separation is not the way of Jesus.

I drive to a café to meet my friend Thomas, ill-prepared for my next encounter. I met Thomas at a café a few blocks away from my dad's house, several months ago, and we instantly formed a rapport. His humor and insight into the mundane details of life makes him easy to be around, and since we're from the same neighborhood we know a lot of the same people. We are sitting at a table making small talk and sipping coffee when I see my former pastor, Frank, and his wife, Cindy, walk into the café. The last time I heard from this man, he rebuked my "decision" to be gay in the name of Jesus and told me to get counseling at another church. We haven't spoken since. Thomas sees the visible discomfort on my face but plays it cool. He is friends with these people, too. I hope they don't come over to talk to us.

"You okay?" he asks, sensing my uneasiness.

I nod my head yes but flush red the very next moment when I see Cindy walking over to our table.

I feel as though I've been pinned beneath a magnifying glass. What is she going to say to me? Should I get up and conveniently use the bathroom until they leave? The instantaneous terror I feel is soon replaced by the realization that she does not want to talk to me. She doesn't want to talk to me at all. She's looking only at Thomas, not even acknowledging my existence, speaking only to Thomas, accepting only Thomas as a person. I am invisible to her.

I am angry. No hello? Not even a smile? After three or four minutes of small talk, she politely says goodbye and walks away without have said a single word to me. They leave the café and my heart is racing.

Thomas looks incredulous. "Did that really just happen?"

I smile and sigh.

"That's not the first time this has happened to you, is it?"

"No it's not, but it's the first time with them. I haven't seen them since I came out."

"That wasn't even veiled contempt. It was blatant and abrasive." He shakes his head disapprovingly.

"I hope she doesn't treat the members of their church like that."

"No shit," he says, visibly shaken. "I just can't believe she would be that rude."

"I'm used to it," I say. "I have never felt more alone in my life than I have in the recent months."

"I hope you find peace, my friend. I really do." Thomas is a sincerely empathetic man, especially to those whom mainstream Christianity has turned its back on.

"I do too," I say, trying to shake off the humiliation.

~~~

This has not been the easiest day. I don't feel disconnected from just my family; I feel disconnected from my entire past. But maybe that is a divine parting gift of sorts. Maybe God has blessed me by removing these people from my life—but I don't think I will ever get used to awkward situations like the one I just experienced. What really frustrates me is the rudeness that conservative beliefs seem to engender, more even than the beliefs themselves. It is one thing to hold a literal interpretation of the Bible, and another to treat others as lesser. Shawn and I have talked a lot about this recently. "Believe what you want, but don't oppress me with those beliefs," he said. And admittedly, I have almost always been the oppressor. Only now do I understand that my methods did more harm than good.

With my birthday coming up, I really wonder: Will the friends I haven't heard from finally reach out to me—or will I continue to be ignored? Will my brother reach out? The gravity of everything that the label of gay has changed in my life is being revealed, and the loss of everything that has been robbed from me because of that label is becoming more difficult to process. Part of me is slipping, and with it my ability to cope with the loneliness. For so long, my identity has been wrapped up in the opinions of others, especially those walking the in the same religious circles I always walked. I feel invisible, like I did at the café with Thomas, all the time. While one facet of my social life is thriving, the life I once knew is clearly dying. Only my self is left, praying that the anxiety and depression that are beginning to surface will not take root.

19 the descent

Today is my twenty-second birthday. I am working a fourteen-hour shift at Revive for customer appreciation day. Add the double shift to the emotional turmoil of being at odds with my brother, and I have little to celebrate. Last year, my brother and his wife threw me a party. This year I don't know if he will even text me a happy birthday. Oh, how things have changed. I am serving coffee and food for fourteen hours to hundreds of gays and lesbians, kicking off the two-week-long celebration leading up to Gay Pride Day. I should be more excited about the conversations I'll have and people I'll meet, but I cannot seem to muster any genuine enthusiasm. I am broken. I ache for my family, though it has only been a few weeks since we've spoken.

Last night I drank enough beer that I passed out on the couch at my dad's place, after drunkenly singing "Happy Birthday" to myself about a dozen times. I cried until I couldn't cry any more. It was not one of the prouder moments of my life.

I make lattes by the dozen as customers peruse the attached bookstore. My regulars see though my phony smile and try to cheer me up. Scott and Jason sip sweet tea and flirt with me as usual; when my face betrays the occasional smile, they act like they've won the lottery. Admittedly it is nice to be around friends, even if I am in such a shitty mood. I am not sure how it happened, but these people have become my family...or the closest thing I can have to a family right now. Scott tries to give me twenty-four spankings and promises that the one to grow on will be something I'll "always remember"—but I retreat behind the coffee bar, narrowly avoiding his hand as it whizzes through the air towards my ass. I am so thankful for the counter!

Between every drink I make, I check my cell phone, hoping for at least a text message from my brother. Nothing. No texts, no call, no contact.

Shawn shows up, and I feel my spirits rise. His smile and hug remind me how lucky I am right now. On my break we sit on a couch listening to the live music, and I tell him about the depression I am struggling with. I spill it out, and, as ever, he is kind enough to listen.

"Oh, baby, that's terrible!" He pulls me into a hug, holding me tightly to his chest and rubbing my back reassuringly. It's all I can do not to cry.

I take a deep breath and steady myself. "I'll be okay, really. It's just going to take some getting used to."

"I've been there, hun. A lot of us have. If you need anything, you know I'm here for you."

"Yeah. I know. Thank you," I say, still choking back tears. I check my phone again. Nothing.

Shawn's empathy and genuine concern for my well-being are a beautiful example of his greater grace and masculinity, as he continually plays the role of servant to me on this journey. My guard disappears while Shawn is around, and I realize something inside of me is changing. His friendship is changing me, softening the rough edges. Shawn grabs my hand and holds it as we talk. The physical closeness doesn't bother me anymore. I am lucky to have him. What I have with Shawn might actually be more real than anything I ever had in past relationships. He personifies what I hope to have in a romantic partner one day, and oddly enough, he has become an essential part of my life. His love is so tangible and beautiful that I am beginning to view him not just as a beard, a pretend boyfriend meant to fool those around me, but as a legitimate partner in my life—for a time, at least. Our relationship is limited by the degree to which it can develop, but I try not to think about that. Instead I focus on the moment, on what I can learn from this dear, sweet man whom everyone believes to be my boyfriend.

I love Church Street during the day. I love seeing families emerge and enjoy the gayborhood. A lot of the same families from softball are here. Everyone who knows it's my birthday makes a point to hug me or tips me generously as I make their coffee. The community is as tight-knit a group as I have ever beheld, and I cannot help but wish for a church that was as close in community as this one on Church Street. The Christian communities of which I have been a part could learn a lot about organic fellowship from the gays and lesbians I am lucky to call friends. I never feel pressure to be what I am not, never feel like I am not good enough or unworthy of company and camaraderie. Whether my Christian friends believe it or not, these people are happy and content. They are not more guilt ridden or rebellious than the average Christian. Befriending them has shown me that my projection of morality on others has never been an accurate litmus test of their hearts. I do not quite know what this change of heart will mean for me, after this project ends, but I hope I won't forget.

The hours of my shift pass and my birthday dwindles to a close. Mopping the floor is therapeutic. I watch the dirt tracked inside throughout the day wash away as if it never existed. I wonder what it would be like if the crud and muck in our lives could be washed away as quickly, if we could harness the truth and follow it back and forth in broad strokes, wiping away everything that is undesirable or false. Growing and changing takes effort, and the process is wearing on me. But I feel cleaner, somehow…more pure, even, like a child learning about life for the first time. I hadn't anticipated this return of innocence; but then again, I didn't anticipate a lot that has happened so far.

I did not anticipate having to face my family this early in the year, and, worse, being rejected by some of them. I did not anticipate the loneliness, the bleakness of the average moments that pass more slowly than an episode of "The Old-Time Gospel Hour." I did not anticipate the crushing weight of the closet, the inability to confide in others, the pressure to maintain my cover, or the ever-present paranoia of that cover being compromised. And I hadn't really thought that people would actually reject me because of a three letter word. I mean, who *does* that? I glance at my own reflection in the glass door and laugh.

If perception is reality and our realities dictate our view of life, my life and my brand of religion has been based in a perception that makes the *Twilight Zone* look normal by comparison. The implications of this perception, the unspeakable judgments that were my constant companions, have shown themselves to be more potently evil than anything I was taught to avoid growing up. At least I have nothing to hide behind, anymore. My faith has been stripped to the foundation, and I am not sure of anything I used to "know" to be true.

At 11:25 p.m. I clock out. Still no messages. I drive to my mom's, where I will spend the night, filled with anxiety. A potent fear that tells me that, come midnight, I still will not have heard from my best friend and only sibling. I hope irrationally that I'll pull into my mom's driveway and my brother's truck will be parked there, and my whole family will be inside, waiting to spend time with me—even though it's almost midnight. Then they'll tell me they love me and that everything is going to be okay, and we'll spend the last minutes of my twenty-second birthday eating cake and celebrating together.

But I reach the driveway of my mother's house, and the truck is not there. My last traces of energy leave me. It is only my birthday for another five minutes. Please don't let me down, brother. Don't leave me hanging. I look over to the Pharisee, and his frown is the only confirmation I need.

He didn't leave you hanging. You left yourself hanging. What you sew, you are going to reap. This is your fault.

Our narrow-mindedness left us both hanging. Left us crippled.

Think what you will, but stop lying to yourself. You know what is absolutely true and what isn't. The Bible isn't so hard to understand, and you are deviating from it. What do you really even want?

All I wanted was a text message! The mere acknowledgment that he remembers me. I just wanted a happy birthday from my big brother.

Happy birthday. Happy now?

Fuck you! I open my car door and walk up the stairs to the house.

My mom is waiting with a cake, and beer, even though she never stays up past 9:00 p.m. I am happy to see her, at least, in the waning minutes of my birthday.

"Happy birthday, baby!" She hugs me tightly. Then she sees my face.

I look down at my phone and the display changes from 11:59 p.m. to 12:00 a.m. He didn't even text.

"Are you okay?" she asks, concerned.

"No, mom, I'm not. But at least I understand. At least I get it."

Her eyes begin to water and I realize I am hurting her, so I smile and tell her about my day instead of venting. We eat cake, and my mom walks upstairs to her room, once again believing a lie. First I told her I was gay. Tonight I acted happy. I am tired of playing parts for her—but tonight it is what I had to do.

"Don't drink all of that beer!" she yells down the stairs, her voice laced with concern.

"I won't, Mom!" I yell back in an upbeat voice. Another lie.

I look down at my phone and stare at the empty screen. Nothing. I drink my open beer in a matter of seconds and toss it in the garbage. I open the refrigerator door, see eleven longnecks waiting for me, and grab three of them.

I look at the Pharisee leaning against the entryway to the kitchen. Want one? He doesn't speak. Didn't think so.

The hiss of carbonation escaping the bottle is the only discernible noise I can hear. I am all alone in my mother's living room. I sit on the couch and look one last time at my phone.

Nothing.

Tonight I won't sing to myself, and I will try not to feel sorry for myself, either. Is it really worth it, this pain and heartache? I walk back to the couch and open my messenger bag to get my laptop. Inside I see a wrapped present and a card attached that says *Hotness* in big letters on the front.

Dear Timothy,

You are a beautiful man with a beautiful soul, and we just want you to know how much we adore you. You brighten our days, and for that we love you. Chin up! No matter what, we're here for you... Just remember to bring the sweet tea.

Your patient suitors,

S & J

I open the beautifully wrapped present and find a book I have been eyeing for weeks at the bookstore. It's perfect. I take another drink of my beer and take a deep breath, amazed by the goodness of people and the impact that goodness has on me. I don't feel so alone anymore.

20 happy endings

Alcoholism doesn't run in my family and I don't consider myself to be an alcoholic, but waking up with a splitting headache and a dry mouth makes me question my use of alcohol to numb pain. Starting with the time I took my first drink, years ago, my brother taught me to drink water and take Advil before going to bed—but after drinking the entire twelve-pack last night, I purposely ignored his advice. The light pouring through the living room window in the morning wakes me up, reminding me of that horrible decision. I feel the hangover inside my bones. Every movement elicits the pain of dehydration, but I don't care. I wanted this.

I wanted to feel it so I would wake up remembering everything from the day before. My mom comes downstairs for her morning devotionals and sees me lying on the couch. God only knows what I must look like. She doesn't say anything but silently picks up the eleven empty bottles next to the couch and walks into the kitchen. A minute later, she comes back with a glass of water and two Advil.

My stepdad, Larry, comes down the stairs. "Twelve beers on a nearly empty stomach isn't a good thing to do," he says.

"I feel like I had forty," I say, limping my way upstairs to the guest bedroom.

As I reach the door upstairs I hear my mom and Larry talking about me in the kitchen.

"He's going to be okay. He's got to go through this, and we don't have to understand why," Larry tells her.

"But he's in pain, and I can't stand seeing him in pain," she says. I hear her crying.

"Then you'd better speak to your other son, too," he says.

I reach the bed and collapse.

~~~

For the next two weeks, I live two lives. At work I am trying to learn and engage my new friends, but at home I am quickly becoming the sulking drunk. Admitting that isn't easy, but I am losing myself—and the me I am becoming is not the me I ever wanted to be.

It is Wednesday night at Tribe, and Will puts a second pint of Blue Moon in front of me.

"How's life?" he asks.

"My brother isn't talking to me."

"How long now?"

"Over a month."

"I'm so sorry, Tim." Will does not ask me why my brother and I aren't speaking; he just rests a hand delicately on my back, trying to comfort me. "Let me know if you need anything, even just a shoulder."

"Thank you, Will."

"Love you, bud," he says.

"I love you too, brother."

I look to my left and see two guys kissing in the corner. I used to feel awkward, witnessing that, but now I don't mind. The two guys have been together for several years; I serve them coffee every Tuesday afternoon like clockwork.

I decide to walk down the street to Revive. It is hot, too hot for a Wednesday evening. I miss the cold. I wipe sweat from my forehead and walk inside. My manager, Brent, looks up, surprised to see me.

"Tim, I'm glad you're here. We need to talk about something."

I wonder if I am in trouble, or if somehow my secret has gotten out. "What about?" I ask nervously.

"The café." It's all he can say.

We walk next door to the community center. I look at the stage where I saw Jesus in drag and I smile. This place has memories attached to it that I treasure—but I wonder what other memories it will hold before I leave today.

"So here's what's happening. The owners love the café, and it's been their dream come true to have it. But they just found out last week that their bank is going under because of the economy, and they don't have the cash for the upkeep until it takes off."

"What? You're saying we don't have jobs anymore?" I am shocked. Brent puts a hand on my shoulder, and I feel the burden of unemployment once again.

"We have a week to get things ready for close, or for a new owner to take over."

"A new owner? Who's going to buy the place?"

"The catering business that rents out the back kitchen of the café is interested. But they will be using family to run the place," Brent answers.

"But they're all straight!"

"I know."

"But this is an LGBTQ café! The only one in town!" I feel a deep sense of loss, and anger that Revive won't be Revive anymore.

"We'll have another full week of employment, and a great reference if we need it." Brent looks at the ground, and I am speechless.

"When it rains it pours," Brent says. "It's too bad. We just got this place running smoothly, and we were really enjoying ourselves here."

"This café, this job…is the only thing keeping me from losing it right now." My eyes fill with tears, but I try to compose myself.

"I'll make sure you get a glowing recommendation. This place has been a breath of fresh air, for me, too." Brent seems as upset as I am.

"I understand," I say.

I get up, walk back to the café, open the door, and look inside as if I am seeing it for the first time. The café is beautiful. The waning light of the summer evening casts a brownish glow over the wooden tables and bar. Our merman even looks beautiful, his golden tail and Mardi Gras getup reflecting bright streaks of sunlight in my direction.

I love this place.

I love this job.

I love going to work every day knowing that I'll get to be around people I care about.

I look at the couch and see the Pharisee sitting next to Marco, his arm wrapped nonchalantly over the merman's shoulder.

I'm sorry, Tim, but it's for the best.

No, it isn't!

He doesn't answer, and my mind turns to the faces of my regulars, the guys who've walked the past few months of my life with me and taught me so much about myself—and what it *doesn't* mean to be gay.

Being gay does not mean you are promiscuous or perverted.

Being gay does not mean you are blind to a life of faith. What I witnessed next door proved that. Seeing that drag queen praise God was the most powerful moment I've experienced so far this year—maybe even of my life.

I step behind the counter to make a latte. The hiss of the steamer and the slurping sound of milk as it goes from cold liquid to smooth and silky cream comforts me. I pour the silky froth into the espresso shots and draw a white heart. Being a barista is one of the first things I have ever really been good at. Part of my heart will die when this place closes, but I am thankful for the memories. I have a week left, a single week to take all of this in before it's gone. I take a sip of the latte. I ache. Why does everything good in my life have to fall through like this?

~~~

My last day at Revive comes too quickly. I have savored the experience of this place like a good cigar. Everyone is sad. It is 4:00 p.m. when I clock in for the last time. I see a familiar face. Marshal is one of my favorite regulars because he always stays until closing, keeping me entertained in conversation while I clean.

Marshall is one of the most enlightened guys I have ever met. He wears a black fedora, slacks, and a maroon vest over a black button up, and he's sitting at his usual table with his usual drink: a cinnamon chai with skim milk. Next to his bag I see a wrapped present. When he sees me, he waves and gets up, grabbing the beautifully wrapped present in one hand and his chai in the other.

"Hello, Timothy!"

"Hey, buddy," I answer.

"I got you something that I feel you need to read. It informs the conversations we've been having, and I thought you'd appreciate it, since we won't be able to talk here anymore."

He hands me the gift and I untie the purple lace ribbon and finger the tape open on one end of the gift. I slide off the wrapping and find two books Marshall has talked about for several months. Both are on the topic of AIDS and the spread of the virus across the country. Both are stories of the pain and suffering of those inflicted with the virus, and about the struggle of the gay community to overcome the epidemic.

"I know you've been out of the closet for less than a year, and I'm happy for you…" He hesitates a moment before continuing. "But I want to share these with you because we live in an imperfect world, and I never want you to fall victim to anything harmful. As wonderful as the LGBT folks are, we are still just flawed people. I don't want you to put us on a pedestal the way you used to put your conservative church on one. Be realistic and be honest. And if you ever end up writing a book yourself, like you've talked about, remember that nothing in life is ideal.

You have to be honest about peoples' strengths and weaknesses."

"I don't know what to say."

"The more you know, the less you need," he replies. "Our community, if you can even call it that, is a lot bigger than the label. And like everything else, there's good and bad in it. There's a lot of pain, hurt, and baggage here. I want you to know that I've only ever seen good in you. I pray you stay away from the bad."

"I'll do my best for the rest of my life to stay away from the bad, Marshall. And I'll always treasure our nights on the patio at closing." Part of me wonders if he somehow knows my secret, or if he is just sharing practical wisdom.

"Me, too." He hugs me. I feel a deep sense of sorrow. I don't know if I'll ever see Marshall again. He doesn't frequent any of the gay bars on Church Street. It isn't his scene, he says.

Losing the café means losing more than a job. It means losing members of my family, people I have come to love. Marshall sits back down and I put the books and the wrapping paper in my messenger bag.

Only a few minutes pass before Jason and Scott show up for their last sweet teas, and our last chance for conversation in the café.

"Looking handsome today, boys," I say pouring their drinks.

"Not as handsome as you! Want to come home with us tonight?" Jason asks coyly, his comment half attempt at humor and half attempt to sleep with me.

"We're going to miss you, kiddo," Scott says, putting his hand on mine.

"Not as much as I'm going to miss you guys."

Jason fakes like he is crying . "But, Timmy! Who is going to be my eye-candy now?" His lower lip sticks out as he makes a pouty face.

"I'm sure you'll find someone to charm."

"So what's next for you?" Scott asks. "Are you okay, financially?"

"I guess. Could be better, could be worse."

"Do you need some money?" Jason asks with a smile.

"No strings attached," Scott clarifies. Jason frowns.

"That means a lot, guys, but I think I'll be okay. Thank you."

"Are you sure? We want to make sure you're taken care of. We would be happy to loan you some cash if you need it."

Their generosity reminds me of the first church, in the New Testament book of Acts. There wasn't a need among the community because they shared with each other and provided when there was need. I have never been to a church so willing to meet my needs.

"Well, you can't argue if we tip you a lot tonight, then!" Scott says.

"What kind of tip are we talking about, hun?" Jason asks his partner.

"You guys have been wonderful to know. I'm so thankful for both of you." I look down at the counter and we all sigh. There are no words for our grief.

~~~

The café is empty by the time I pull the chord, turning the sign from *Open* to *Closed*. It is a moment thick with emotion, frustration, and also thankfulness. I found out that the café is indeed being sold to the caterer in back, and my manager will stay on part time to oversee the transition. He will be the only gay employee, and the café will pay the price. The beauty and life of a business is defined by the people who frequent it; Revive's light will inevitably dim with the transition. I have never been more frustrated by straight people in my life as when I think about the changes that will kill this business.

Brent mops the floor while I do dishes, but we don't speak. We are both too sad to talk. I never thought I would enjoy a job so much. I never anticipated the emotional imprint a gay café in a small gay district in the Bible Belt would leave on me.

I count the money in the tip jar and laugh at the obscene amount waiting for me. Scott and Jason took care of me. Everyone took care of me tonight. Even though they do not know about my experiment, I feel comforted that every single one of them knows *me*. After we finish cleaning, Brent and I take one last look at our little café.

Behind us, the manager of the bookstore is deep-cleaning behind the appliances. The café has to pass some sort of health inspection for the new owners to take over. He tells us that we are free to go, but I don't want to go. I want to enjoy the place a little longer. Brent seems just as frustrated.

Brent and I walk to the back gravel parking lot, and he hugs me.

"It's been a pleasure working with you…" he says softly.

"I owe you a lot for hiring me. It's been great," I reply.

We walk to our cars. Before I close my door, Brent rolls down his passenger window.

"Bitch, I love you!" he says, smiling.

"Bitch, I love you, too!" I reply.

21 pride and prejudice

It is nearing late June, the season for celebrating Gay Pride Day. I have never been to a Gay Pride celebration, but I've got an idea what it's like, hearing so much this month from friends. Everyone at Tribe and Play has been preparing, the way one usually prepares for a holiday like Christmas, with parties and presents and drag shows. I park my car several blocks away from the festivities and make my way to Riverfront Park. It is 10:00 in the morning, but the weather application on my phone says it's already over a hundred degrees. Sweat pours down my neck and chest, and my purple t-shirt clings to my body like saran wrap. I look awful—but then again, so does everyone else out in the heat. I think of the drag queens, of their makeup that must be melting off of their faces, poor girls! Sindy (Ian by day), a regular at Tribe, told me yesterday she was planning on wearing black, but I hope she changed her mind.

By 10:45, the park is crowded with people. To my left is a group of drag queens, to my right a group of drag nuns, representatives of the order of the Sisters of Perpetual Indulgence. This group of Nashville sisters is a non-profit that raises money for the underprivileged—and they wear rather shocking outfits. The impression they give is a combination of the *Sound of Music* and *Beetle Juice*. The Sisters do a lot for the community.

I walk up and down the waterfront, surrounded by more shirtless men than I have ever seen in one place. Shirtless men and rainbow flags, *everywhere*. Shawn told me heat plus homosexuals equal skin, and he wasn't lying. I wish some of the lesbians would follow suit...

The closet is killing me.

There is really only one day a year that everyone can get together like this, and everywhere I look, I see reunions. People are hugging, kissing, laughing, and talking with each other. I am surrounded by thousands of people, and for the first time in my life, I am in the minority.

That's when I see him: a guy standing on a bucket, street preaching, noisily proclaiming his message of "absolute truth." The young man reminds me of my former Liberty University schoolmate, Patrick, who has since become one of the most vocal street preachers in Virginia. I feel bad for his community—or any community that has to listen to him on a regular basis.

This man is in his early twenties and is sweating as much as I am. I hand him a bottle of water. Instead of thanking me, he yells down at me, asking if I want to repent of my sins and turn to Jesus.

"Jesus knows my heart," I say, repeating something Samantha said in New York. I bet she would treat this guy with grace, but I feel angry. I feel violated by his assumptions and proclamations. He is another reminder of who I was…what I am coming out of.

"Are you a homosexual?" he asks, eyes locked on mine.

"I'm gay, if that's what you are asking." It has never been so easy to answer the question as it is right now. I am proud to be thought of as gay. Someone behind me laughs.

"I implore you, turn away from your sin and repent!" He punctuates the word *repent* through his small megaphone, and I cringe. *Implore?* Even his vocabulary is self-righteous. I feel his prejudice in his tone. If I feel that, I know everyone else does, too.

"Jesus knows my heart," I repeat.

"Then when you reach the gates, He'll say, 'Depart from me, I knew you not,' and you'll be damned. Do you really want that?"

I look to my right and see the Pharisee frowning at the man.

"Why do you stand on a bucket and put yourself higher than the people you are shouting at?" I ask. "Why do you exalt yourself so arrogantly? 'For everyone who exalts himself will be humbled, and he who humbles himself will be exalted.'"

"Luke 14?" he asks.

"You tell me, preacher. You seem to think you know enough for the both of us," I say.

"I am exalting Jesus, not myself," the man says. "'God opposes the *proud*, but gives grace to the humble.' What are you celebrating today, again?" he asks.

I ignore his question. He is baiting me.

"'The aim of our charge is love that issues from a pure heart and a good conscience and a sincere faith,'" I say. "'Certain persons, by swerving from these, have wandered away into vain discussion, desiring to be teachers of the law, without understanding either what they are saying or the things about which they make confident assertions.'" I quote I Timothy as if I wrote it, and I feel ownership of it. It is the first time I feel like I am using the Bible justly, like I am using the passages I've committed to memory to defend instead of attack. It is fulfilling and empowering. The street preacher stares at me in silence. "Or to put it more simply," I continue, "we can either throw scripture back and forth at each other, which serves no one, least of all God, or you can back off, before you do more damage. Brother, you have no idea what you are doing."

"You are not my bro—"

"Yeah, yeah, I've heard it all. *Pax vobiscum.*" I turn around and walk away.

I don't wait around to see if the street preacher stays and preaches on or if he leaves. I can't hear him anymore as I walk away. Either way, I had to get away from the man on the bucket. The spectacle of the gospel being brutally twisted and manipulated by people addicted to telling others that they are going to hell is more than I can stomach anymore.

"I tried," I say under my breath.

"We know." A young woman behind me smiles. Her eyes are gentle and the sun reflects brightly off her hot-pink hair. "We heard, and we appreciate what you said." She reaches out and squeezes my shoulder.

Over the next four hours, I spend time with my softball team, grab a Coke with Jason and Scott, and sit under the Vitamin Water tent with friends, trying to stay cool in the oppressive June heat. Things feel right, and I am having fun…but I still feel angry about the street preacher.

Conservative Christianity teaches us to love everyone; however, that love can take many different forms. It seems to stem from an "I'm right, you're wrong" biblical perspective, which imposes only two rather limited options: Insist others conform to your spiritual world view, or ignore those who don't. A friend of mine calls it the "brother's keeper" method.

If I have learned anything this year, it's this: Condemning people from a soapbox doesn't work, nor do attempts to modify the behavior of others. It is not the words of scripture that change an individual's heart; it is the Spirit in and behind those words. That same Spirit teaches us to leave the finger-pointing to someone far more capable, and to love sacrificially and completely, without motive or thought of personal gain.

I quoted I Timothy to the street preacher because it seems like something he was never taught. The aim of our charge is *love.* and certain persons, by swerving away from that aim, have been caught up in vain discussions, desiring to be teachers of something they don't understand. Unfortunately, modern-day Christianity has created more than a few of these "certain persons." For the longest time, I was one of them.

When Christians begin to question whether options one and two might both be false and consider the possibility of a third, or even fourth option, they are often swiftly labeled by their fellow church members as *heretics*—or *emergents*, if you prefer the religious lingo—and are told to either accept "in faith" one of the first two options; or they are pressured, like splinters, out of the church body. More and more, these splinters are leaving organized religion, and now I just might be one of them.

These believers are beginning to question things as I am questioning things, not content to stay in the religious bubbles of their youth. Social justice and acceptance of differing world-views is, for many, replacing the "turn or burn" interpretation of the gospel. I see this even in the Bible-Belt culture of Nashville, and it gives me hope as I move forward on my journey.

It pains me to think that my life will be forced in so many different directions when this year is up. When I started, I did not know that once I set out on this path I would never be able to go back. I am changing. And my community won't accept those changes in me. They rejected me because of a label, because I didn't hide my "sin" like they do and keep a smile on my face while we sing our hymns and hide our true selves from one another. No, we won't bring up their addictions, their gossip, or their infidelity. Instead, we'll mark my "sin" with a capital S— maybe it'll even be scarlet—and count me as lost to the enemy. I really do have it better now, having made my exodus from the churches of my youth.

I wonder what would happen if…instead of preaching from soap-boxes and shouting through megaphones, or spending millions on political campaigns meant to hinder the rights of the gay and lesbian community…what would happen if we pointed the finger at ourselves? What if we chose to live intentionally in community with everyone, regardless of our differences? What would happen if we shut our mouths and simply served the people in our neighborhoods and cities, without an agenda? Would the message of Jesus survive? Would the gospel still be as powerful and applicable, in our modern context, if our methodology evolved?

I think so.

22 rescued

I am in the second act of this story now, and the novelty, like new-car smell, has worn off. The novelty of the closet wore off a long time ago, but I'm still inside it, alone. I cannot imagine living this way for much longer. It's crushing my spirits to a degree I never anticipated. We were not created to be alone, you and I. We were created with a need for otherness, a need for community, and I am just beginning to realize how much the closet hinders community   and even more than community, how it hinders love.

Two weeks have passed since Gay Pride Day, and boredom is killing me. No job and no money makes my time on Church Street less enjoyable. I am sitting on the back patio of my father's with a case of piss beer, listening to "The Best of Puccini" and the sound of cicadas trying to mate with each other. I miss my friends, the regulars, and all of the conversation and laughter we shared at the café. Loneliness and desperation are growing as my social life deteriorates into nonexistence. I'm still living at my dad's house, and I often resort to drinking alone. The realization hits me that this year is more than half over.

Losing my job at the café has turned my black cloud into a tropical depression. I haven't felt this bogged down, this *trapped*, in years. The combination of pretending to be someone I'm not and the emotional distance between me and my family are taking a toll. I wonder, is this plunge into the melancholy unique to me, or is it a natural byproduct of the closet?

The green of the grass is topped with the light frosting of the freshly cut grass that lies atop it, and it has a distinctly Southern smell that I have never found anywhere other than Tennessee. I love Nashville…but even the city itself is starting to feel oppressive. The claustrophobia of my life is shattering any semblance of stability I've found.

And then the phone rings with a distinctive ring, and I know I might just be okay. It's my good friend Connie, who could more aptly be described as a guardian angel or a second mom than just another peer. I met Connie through our mutual friend Jay from New York, but until recently, I was always put off by her brand of faith. She lives several hours away, in Memphis, so we rarely get to see one another. Jay told her about my experiment and she reached out. Connie is a very liberal United Methodist pastor; throughout her ministry, gay and lesbian issues have been a passion. Lately she has been calling me daily, and I wonder how she knows, or always seems to know, when I am struggling. I wonder how she knows just the right time to call and check up on me. Every time I hear that ringtone I know that at least for a moment, I'm not completely alone.

"Hey, kiddo. How're you holding up?"

A few seconds pass and I don't respond. I hiccup. "I was just smelling the grass. My dad mowed the lawn, and it smells great out here!"

"That bad?"

I can't hide anything from her. "No, no! Everything is good. I was thinking about going to Tribe tonight to spend some time with the guys."

"Sounds like you've already brought the party home. How much have you had to drink?"

"Not enough."

"Oh, hun…Have you seen Shawn lately?"

She doesn't press me for details I don't want to give. I like that about her.

"Not much. He's been really busy." Another hiccup. "I miss Shawn!" Everything comes to me like an epiphany when I've been drinking, even the smallest things.

"Sounds like you could really use a friend."

"I'm okay, really. I've only got five more months of this thing, and then I'll get my life back!"

I try to focus but I see a small yellow butterfly several feet away. I like the way it floats, bobbing up and down on the air like a kite, only more graceful. Part of me wishes I could float like that. I wonder if it will ever be possible. I would probably have to lose a lot of weight…but then again bumblebees have a body mass higher than any other flying bug and somehow it seems to work for them. Why aren't there any bumblebees out here right now? It is summer, after all. I wipe my face with a wet rag.

"Hello? You there?" she asks.

"Connie, I'm not well." Another drunken epiphany.

"Tim, just come here."

"Where?"

"Memphis! God, I hate it when you're drunk!"

"That makes one of us."

"So is that a yes?"

"Can we visit Graceland?"

"Does that mean you're coming?"

"I don't know. I need to find a job. And what about softball?"

"You sent me your schedule months ago. After tomorrow, you've got the next three weeks off before your tournaments. Just come stay with my family and I'll help you with your project."

"How can you help?"

"Well, for one, Charlie and I are the only ones who will know about your project. We won't even tell our kids, or anyone else for that matter. You'll get to see what it's like to go somewhere new, where the label of *gay* is connected to you from the first impression."

"That sounds like a great plan! I'll be there in two hours!" I stand up and start walking to my car. I don't even have my keys.

"Hell, no, Tim! Are you crazy? Sober up, play your games tomorrow, and then come down   *sober*!" She yells that last part and I have to pull the phone away from my ear.

"Okay, okay! I'll stop drinking."

"That a boy!"

I can hear her smiling on the other end of the line. I open another beer and hope the hiss of the carbonation escaping is not loud enough for Connie to hear. I have never felt so low.

~~~

After a little over two hours of driving, I pull into Connie's driveway, barely able to park on the steep incline. I pull my backpack and duffel bag from the back seat and see a furry cat jump onto my hood. The cat turns in two quick circles before curling up and closing his eyes. What an oddly charming little creature. And then I feel it. For the first time in years, I feel *home*.

I see Connie through my driver's side window, standing on the porch. It is an odd thing to leave Nashville without any plan or itinerary, awkward, but somehow good and comfortable. Connie gives me a huge hug and tells me it's great to see me. She has the warmest spirit, and I feel instantly at ease.

"How was the drive?"

"As good as can be expected. Got to think a lot…and sing opera at the top of my lungs."

"Glad I wasn't there!" She smiles.

"You know, this is the first time this year I've done anything with *me* in mind. To get away and just breathe."

"Don't get too comfortable. My daughters are beyond excited to have a guy to talk boys with!"

"Thanks for this."

"I believe in you, Tim. Just count the past month as a hiccup and keep moving forward. You know I'm here for ya."

We sit in Connie's study, and I put my feet up on the ottoman, exhausted, drained, paper thin. I look over and see myself in a mirror. I look like I have aged several years in a matter of months; the creases in my forehead are a preview of what's to come. I've even lost twenty pounds. Between a softball and dancing diet, I have spent most of my summer running from bar to bar, and ball field to ball field. I sigh and Connie tilts her head, a look of curiosity on her face.

"What's wrong, hun?"

"I'm just so tired."

"You want to take a nap?"

"Not that kind of tired," I say, taking a deep breath. "My soul is tired, and my heart has broken so many times this year for so many people, and for myself, that I feel like I've got nothing left."

Connie smiles.

"Tim, you're growing, and that's never easy. Don't put so much pressure on yourself. It's not your job to save the world."

"No, but it's my responsibility to make amends for my life. I feel so much guilt for who I've been all this time and how I've treated these people."

"What's going on with your brother?"

"Still no word, but I can't push it. I'm just going to give him the space he asked for and hope things work out." I retrieve the letter he wrote me before his wedding out of my bag, and I hand it to Connie. "This is what I've lost. I can't believe it's been less than a year since he wrote this."

She reads the letter and I see tears in her eyes. Then she looks up and smiles.

"Trust me: your brother will be your best friend again before too long. He feels like he's been played for a fool and that he didn't have a choice," she says, echoing the guilt that exists inside of me. She sees my face. "Tim, you're doing the right thing, but you've got to follow through with respecting his wishes."

She thumbs the letter and looks down at it thoughtfully. "What you're doing is important, but you already know that. What's left to doubt?" she asks.

"I think the reason I haven't loved other people has just as much to do with not loving myself as if does with what I've learned growing up."

"What do you mean?"

"If I've realized anything this year about myself, it's that I am a pretty insecure guy. I used my religion to bully people, to feel superior to them. If I loved myself, I probably would've known better." I lean my head back against the top of the leather chair and sigh.

"I'm so proud of you. You are getting to the point that you aren't just carelessly pointing the finger. You're looking inside first, and you need to keep following that path."

"Someone else I know told me to start within. Why am I the last to figure these things out?"

"Don't worry. Eventually your eyes will adjust to the gradient of colors that the black and white's have cheated you from."

Ana•s Nin once said, "We don't see things as they are, we see them as we are." Connie's words confirm that. As my perspective continues to be challenged, my view of others is changing. I look back on who I was before and feel humbled. All we really have in this life is each other, and I think that was God's intention. The gospel really is simple: loving Him means loving each other.

Hours later, after running errands and eating dinner, Connie and I sit on her back porch. Before I arrived, she stocked the fridge with foods she knows I like and even purchased Captain Morgan and Coke for mixed drinks. So we sit, talking about God, and life, and faith, and otherness, and I feel…at home. I feel free to melt into my wicker chair and free to release every thought I have kept so tightly locked away from people in the past seven months. I release it. I share stories of all the people I have met and about the downward spiral I've fallen into since the beginning of summer. Connie does not respond; she just sits, listening while I talk, crying with me when I cry. And I know she accepts me for who I am. For the first time in my life, I feel a true sense of safety. This unexpected haven in Memphis has restored something I thought I had lost   my hope   and I know that Connie is right. Everything really will be okay, and I am doing the right thing. I just have to keep trusting God to direct my path. And this experiment is my cross to bear, my opportunity to learn empathy. Everyone has a calling in life, a cross to bear. I never anticipated that I would find my cross in the closet.

23 don't tread on me

I wake up and stretch, trying to remember the last time I slept through the night without waking up in a cold sweat. Tossing and turning and dreams have been the bane of my nights for the past few months. I feel like I am in emotional rehab and Connie is my sponsor. I look down at my phone and see no missed calls or texts. I haven't spoken with my parents in a week, and I wonder how long it will be before they call. I have all but disappeared. When will they notice?

Lying back on the bed, I pull out a book I got from the bookstore attached to the Revive. I long for the little café like a lost friend and wonder what all of the boys are up to. The book, *Thou Shalt Not Love,* is a compelling read. I feel fortunate to have been directed to so many books and movies that challenged my old ways of thinking and continue to challenge me as I question and re-question the assumptions that I clutched with white-knuckled pride.

I hear a tapping on the door, and Connie tells me that breakfast ready. *Breakfast?* How on earth could I have gotten so lucky? Two nights ago I was alone in my dad's house, eating expired ramen. Now I am in a house with a family and Connie has made breakfast.

I throw a t-shirt on and walk to the kitchen, where I see eggs, sausage, and biscuits. The smell curls its way to my nose, drawing me as though two cartoon fingers were pulling me by my nostrils. Julia, Connie's oldest daughter, just shy of seventeen, laughs at the expression on my face and the rabbit-like twitch of my nose as I smell real, home-cooked food.

"What's wrong? Haven't eaten breakfast before?"

"It's been way too long," I reply.

"You better leave some of that sausage for Becca, or she'll eat *you* for breakfast!" Connie yells from the next room.

"We will!" Julie and I yell in unison.

"Have you ever been to a drag show?" Julie's question catches me off guard.

"Are you really asking me that? Of course I have!"

"Have you ever been *in* one?" she asks.

"No! I would never want to subject anyone to that sight!"

"That's too funny!" Connie laughs from the other room.

"Well, we're all girlfriends here!" I say, leaning back far enough in my seat to wink at Connie in the other room.

After breakfast Connie tells me that she's taking me to an LGBTQ potluck at a nearby Catholic church. I feel uncomfortable and picture the Catholic embassy in Lower Manhattan.

"Who knows, Tim, you might meet a boy." Julie laughs, her smile infectious.

"I don't think my boyfriend would like that too much, but there's nothing wrong with flirting. Besides, I'm pretty picky about the boys I go out with." I wrap my arm around Julie's neck and pull her into a hug. I feel like I have a little sister, and it makes me feel warm inside, like I am needed.

"You should be picky," Connie says. "All of you kids should be picky!"

~~~

The Catholic church is called Immaculate Conception. As we walk inside we hear a hundred voices deep in conversation. This is the first support group I have attended this year. Go figure, it's at a church attached to the organization I protested against a few months ago. I know that not all Catholics are the same, that, like Protestants, there is a huge variety of paradigms contained within the whole, and that is okay. We set our food down on the table with the other potluck dishes, and a petite woman runs over to Connie. Her name is Beth and she is another deeply entrenched United Methodist. Her hair is short and brown, and her glasses fit snugly on the bridge of her nose.

"You must be Tim!" she says, pulling me into a tight hug.

"And you're Beth?"

"That's me. Now, I've heard through the grapevine that you just came out recently? Congratulations!"

"Thank you. It wasn't easy but I'm making it." I take a sip of the coffee Connie hands me.

"I'm not completely out yet," she says, "but the time is coming." She looks down at her shoes and takes a deep, calming breath.

In her tone there are hints of deep pain. Even though she puts on a brave face, I sense that her pain may only have just begun. She stands next to me with her arm around my shoulder, and it isn't the embrace of a stranger or acquaintance; it is the gentle touch of an aunt or a sister. The immediacy of our connection catches me off guard, but not in a bad way. I feel a soul connection to this petite woman, this closeted UMC minister in training. I cannot imagine what it would be like to spend so much time training for a ministry, all the while knowing that if I came out, I would be expelled from that training and barred from ordination. Beth reminds me once again that to live a life in the closet is to walk on egg shells, especially if one is part of a religious institution. I look over at Connie, who smiles as she watches Beth and I talk.

I spend the next half hour mingling, eating, enjoying the company of a wide variety of people. I meet a guy named Mark who is pushing seventy and has been with his partner for just under thirty-eight years. I can tell he has spent the majority of his life navigating others' opinions. Having been openly gay long before it was considered normal by anyone, his somewhat cautious demeanor is understandable. After our talk, he kisses me on the cheek and tells me that he is happy I have so many years ahead of me where happiness and safety are mine for the taking. I am fixated on what his words really mean. How many years did this good man spend afraid? How many years was happiness an unattainable dream? How many tears has he shed in loneliness and isolation, because the world hated him?

As Mark and I talk, a young man walks into the room. Mark waves the young man over and insists I meet him. "His name is John, and he's a good kid."

John introduces himself. He is extremely well built and his hair is cropped short, typical of a soldier.

"Military man?" I ask after he introduces himself.

"I was," he replies.

"Is your contract up?"

"I was dishonorably discharged, actually." A sullen look of frustration replaces his smile.

"What? Why?"

Mark sighs and puts his hand on John's shoulder. He squeezes knowingly, and I catch a telling look on Mark's face. And then it hits me. This young man is the first I have met that suffered at the hands of Don't Ask, Don't Tell (DADT).

"One of my commanding officers attends my church. A few weeks after I confided in my pastor that I'm gay, he told my C.O. ...and it didn't take long for Uncle Sam to get rid of me. It's been the hardest year of my life." His expression is pained. "After two tours in Afghanistan, I am kicked out for being queer."

"I've seen it happen too many times," Mark says. "But times are changing. I'm excited for you youngin's."

"John," I say, "you didn't hook up with anyone while you were in the military or do anything to draw their attention?"

"I never so much as flirted with another person after I enlisted. That was my career, man! I was going to be in the Marines for the rest of my life. I loved it, and trained for it, and was good at what I did. The part that makes me want to scream is that my discharge was dishonorable. I didn't do a single fucking *thing* that was dishonorable as a soldier!" John takes a deep breath and puts his hand on Mark's, which is still perched on his shoulder. "Mark has heard my story too many times. Bet he's sick of it by now," John says as lightheartedly as possible.

"Never, my boy. Telling that story is part of your journey, and believe it or not, I'm more proud of you every time you share it." Mark looks at me. "Tim, you wouldn't believe how much more calm John is now. The first time we met, not long after it happened, I was almost afraid of him. He was so angry."

"I can imagine," I say, even though I don't really have a clue.

"Yeah it was pretty rough," John says, regaining his composure.

"All that danger and all that sacrifice, and we aren't even able to marry our partners," Mark says, his words betraying his own struggle.

"It isn't fair," I say. "So what are you doing, now that you are out of the military?"

"I'm just trying to put my life back together. I am trying to find something new for a career."

I feel compelled to hug John, so I let my body close the distance between us and I wrap my arms around his torso. He leans his head on my shoulder and sighs.

"The United States government is just like the church."

"How so?" I ask.

"They shoot their wounded," John says. Mark snorts his assent.

"Thank you for your service, John. Even if it was cut short, you are a hero to me."

"To both of us!" Mark agrees.

His arms wrap around me tighter than before. I feel the strength in his arms. He hugs like a Paris-Island trained Marine. "Thank you, guys," John whispers. "I really needed to hear that." Over John's shoulder, a few feet behind Mark, I see Connie looking. Her expression is grim, and she nods slowly that she understands. She knows John, or at least his story. This LGBT potluck is a support group, a tight-knit community of people, and probably a very necessary part of everyone's life. I wish I could be a part of it regularly.

Like many, I have spent my life believing a lie. It is the lie that there are no longer second-class citizens in this country. There are. John and Mark are second-class citizens, and I am a second-class citizen now; and anyone sympathizing with us, like Jay Bakker when he came out as an ally of the community, is crushed underfoot just for their association to us, and they are assigned second-class status, too.

Here's another lie: *America is a Christian nation.* If we were, thousands wouldn't die every year from starvation, poverty, murder, or war. If America was a Christian nation, there wouldn't be second-class citizens. All men and women would be equal. No, we are no more a "Christian nation" than anywhere else. While our country has been blessed, we have tainted our blessings by our cruelty to those who are different. This year has proven it to me. John is proof, and so is Mark.

I walk over to Connie after John, Mark, and I part ways.

"They're sweet, aren't they?" Connie asks.

"They're more than sweet. Mark is a testament to same-sex relationships, and John is a hero," I say. "I just can't imagine why this country wouldn't let John serve. It really makes no sense."

My imagination plays a scene like a movie in my mind: John is in Afghanistan holding a black M16, dressed in his desert camouflage. I see him moving with his squad, mortars and shrapnel flying mere inches above his head. He fights for our country willingly, accepting of the possibility of sacrifice, all the while knowing that our great country doesn't understand, accept, or even like him. He knows this, and still he risks his life. I see him hunkering down in the dirt, praying for safety as he and his fellow Marines slowly advance on a site rumored to be the meeting place of a terrorist cell, and I see him breathe a sigh of relief as the house is cleared and the mission ends. I let this scene play through my mind, and the reality of his dishonorable discharge pierces my heart like a piece of shrapnel in the desert. He is a better man than I am, stronger and more courageous and just because he's gay, his experience and talents count for less than his comrades' with the "proper" orientation.

Their loss.

The rest of the night, I meet people who have experienced all forms of rejection from the mainstream, and I sit silently while they tell me their stories. A few feet away, Mark and his husband hold hands, their love as vibrant and strong as it ever has been thirty-eight years and counting. I wonder how many straight couples could boast that number of years.

Before we leave Mark walks over to say goodbye. "It was a pleasure meeting you, Tim. I hope you come back!"

"Me too. It's hard to get down here much, living in Nashville, but I will do my best."

"He's a good kid," Mark says to Connie.

"Yes he is," she agrees.

Mark gives me a hug and a kiss on the forehead. The kiss reminds me of the way my grandpa used to kiss me.

"It was a pleasure to meet you," I say, waving goodbye.

Connie and I walk outside, and I take one back look towards the church. Just outside the door, John waves goodbye. He turns and walks back inside, and I see the back of his shirt for the first time. The white letters on the black t-shirt read *Don't Tread on Me*. I watch him inside until he moves out of sight, and soberness washes over me. I am sorry for treading on you, John. I am sorry for marginalizing your bravery.

"So what did you think?" Connie asks as I fasten my seatbelt.

"That was great. Really great, actually."

"I know you're depressed, and I know you feel isolated and alone, but don't let that pain blind you. You are the main character in the story of your life, but other people are the main characters of their own lives. And sometimes you can find healing just by playing a supporting role in someone else's experience," Connie says as she backs the white suburban out of the parking space and pulls out onto the road that will take us home.

"That's true," I say.

"I know I'm preaching to the choir, but I want to remind you of that. I've battled depression before, and I understand how easy it is to lose sight of the big picture."

I feel reinvigorated, almost a restoration of my purpose. This whole year is about listening to others and understanding how diverse people really are. It occurs to me that the reason for my progression away from who I was and toward who I am becoming, is people. In listening to others and allowing them to share their hearts with me, I have finally conquered my irrational fear of *different*.

"So what's next?" I ask Connie.

"I have cupcakes baking at home, and you haven't lived until you've tried my cupcakes!" Connie says as we pull into her subdivision.

"I can't wait." I can't wait for the cupcakes and I can't wait for everything else this year still has to offer.

Two years later, on September 20, 2011, Don't Ask, Don't Tell was repealed. I heard the news and thought of John, hoping that wherever he was, he felt some small measure of peace.

24 new bridge

A month passes in Memphis and I feel rejuvenated. I had forgotten what it felt like to be part of a family. Even though I am struggling as much as ever, Connie has filled a unique role in my life. She is a counselor, a teacher of sorts, encouraging me to question my beliefs in a way no one else has before. One of the more recent topics of conversation is gay marriage; the more we talk, the more I feel my eyes opening to the arguments of equality. Why do I believe I have the right to marry a woman, but individuals involved in same-sex relationships don't have the same access to sanctioned lifetime commitment? Is the concept of gay marriage at its core really even a moral one?

I am less and less sure of the things I used to think were black and white, especially in light of the beautiful, long-lasting relationships I have witnessed this year. I think of Mark and his partner, who have been together for much longer than I've been alive. I wonder what it must be like to be told by the government and the church that my relationship holds no more validity than that of two boyfriends going against the social and biological norm. Their relationship convicts me of narrow-mindedness. Similarly, my softball coaches have been together for twenty-five years, and the way they are together is inspirational.

One of the things I love about Connie's house is that I am free to spend time by myself in the guest room, and her family does not consider me anti-social for taking that time. Connie encourages me daily to spend time in thought, prayer, and writing in my journal. I sit on the bed, stretch, and flex my hand after writing three pages in the black notebook on my lap. It feels good to process my thoughts on paper, to argue back and forth with myself. The endless debates I wage have filled two notebooks in the month I've been here. It is the most productive way for me to process. I stretch my arms above my head and yawn, trying to ignore the Pharisee sitting at the desk.

You're taking your doubt too far. Marriage? An obviously sacred, heterosexual covenant? Don't spit on that sacrament.

Sacrament? So you're a Catholic now? We live in a country where politics and religion are supposed to be separate, yet the conservative Christians get to withhold rights and privileges from people outside their faith?

You can't separate politics from morality. People vote the way they believe.

But our country is not run by the Southern Baptist denomination…or at least it shouldn't be.

God created marriage for man and wife. Why didn't the Bible have examples of homosexual marriage, if it is okay to be gay?

The Bible doesn't talk about a lot of things. That doesn't mean they don't exist.

Adam and Steve, was it? Oh wait, that's right   it was Adam and Eve.

Doesn't the Bible also say it's better that a man not be alone? So that excludes gay men? That excludes lesbian women?

Weak argument!

Not really. You throw out scripture passages with no regard for historical context or logic.

So you've made up your mind, then?

We'll see.

~~~

A result of the back and forth of the equal marriage debate is an event Connie decided to put on several months ago. "New Bridge" will be a night of comedy, speaking, and conversation in downtown Memphis. Beale Street is renowned for its bars, its blues and its barbeque, but Connie hopes to bring the marriage equality conversation into that public forum, too…and if nothing else, to entertain. The event's keynote speaker is our mutual friend, Jay Bakker. Who better to speak on the issue than a man who has held both beliefs and was cast out from the mainstream church like an outlaw? Jay *is* an outlaw, an outlaw preacher…and as I continue to question the dogma I have been force-fed most my life, I think I may just be one, too.

I stand on Beale Street on the afternoon of the event and pass out fliers to anyone willing to take one. It is almost a hundred degrees outside. And then time runs out and I walk back to the theater, hopeful that a crowd of people will participate. Only a handful have shown up. The theater seats seven hundred and we have maybe seventeen people there to participate in the conversation. But the show must go on, and so Connie nods her head for everything to begin. I know she is disappointed with the turnout. Months of planning and hard work have gone into tonight. Marriage equality is an issue Connie feels very strongly about. I wish more people had come.

The lights in the spacious theater dim, and multi-colored spotlights illuminate the stage in plethora of colors. It wasn't planned, but the lights reflecting off of Connie's shirt as she goes on stage are reminiscent of a gay pride flag. She announces a local improvisation group, and they perform *Proposition 8, the Musical.* I laugh, but am simultaneously frustrated. The writers of the satirical tribute seem to understand Jesus more than I ever have, and that really unnerves me. Jesus fulfilled and freed us from the law, yet I have lived most of my life a slave to law. Addicted, even. The conflict elicits a dilemma for me. Am I supposed to love everyone unconditionally and model the teachings of Jesus without forcing my beliefs on others   or is it my moral imperative to force-feed my interpretation of the Bible on everyone that disagrees with me? What is my interpretation now?

Pharisee stares at me knowingly. *You know the problem I see? You have consistently thrown the baby out with the bathwater, compromising your beliefs on a whim.*

No, I haven't. I'm just beginning to understand that I have to look at the world through a bigger lens than my own personal faith.

This musical is blasphemous.

It's satire.

My Jesus is holy, he's not a comedian. My Jesus is God.

Mine is too, but he was also a man. Don't take that away from him. He laughed and cried and told jokes, just like the rest of us.

I don't think you'd recognize Jesus if he was sitting next to you.

Because I don't believe my faith in him gives me license to ruin peoples' lives?

The Pharisee doesn't respond. The commotion on stage has ended and I hear a single voice. I look up and see Jay on stage, talking about his late mother with tears in his eyes. I feel for my friend. So much pain in his life, yet he uses his faith as a tool to alleviate pain in others. Maybe that is his way of healing.

At the end of the night, as we walk back to the car, my suspicions are confirmed: Connie is depressed. She is sad that the event did not reach as many people as she had hoped it would. I want to comfort her, but I don't know how. I want to celebrate with her that she pulled it off, but the numbers were not what we had hoped for.

I pull her aside and hug her. And all I can say is "Thank you." She looks into my eyes, her emotion more palpable than I have seen before, but she makes her best effort to smile.

"Why?" she asks, voice stuttering in her sadness.

"Because this entire night has made me think more deeply about marriage equality than I ever have before, and you gave me that opportunity. Even the absence of people showed me how important this issue is. My eyes and heart are open."

"Really?" Connie begins to cry, and hold her tight.

"Yes, Connie. Mission accomplished."

~~~

How can anyone hate another human being with such a passion? That is the question I ask myself the morning after the *New Bridge* event, as Connie, Jay, our friend Tim, and I tour the National Civil Rights Museum. Martin Luther King, Jr. was shot and killed in this place, and I feel the prejudice and hatred in the air as I study the exhibit. We look at pictures, read the posted newspaper articles, and tour the timeline of the movement that changed the history of our nation for the better.

Like any war, any struggle, there were casualties. There were many casualties. The most noticeable at the exhibit was the sacrifice of Dr. King, whose life gave hope to the second-class citizens of his day. I reach the site of his hotel room and see the place where a great man made a great sacrifice. Emotionally, it is almost more than I can handle. Twenty feet away, Jay stares solemnly into the small viewing area where a single pane of glass separates viewers from the hotel room. Dr. King is one of Jay's heroes, and as I tour this museum he is quickly becoming one of mine, too. Jay breathes heavily, tears running down the length of his cheeks as he seemingly memorizes every detail. It is almost too difficult to watch.

For me, humility is what makes a man or woman a leader, and the humility of Dr. King is what impresses me so greatly. Even the motel room is humble   it is a hole in the wall, not a suite at the Hilton. Jesus was born in a small cave that probably reeked of sheep shit, and he lived in poverty during his three-year ministry. Gandhi also modeled humility, walking around in paper-thin sandals and barely any clothing, surviving on the generosity and kindness of others. Jesus and Gandhi brought powerful empires to their knees, and so did King. These are three of the most radical leaders in history, and none of them held the power of titles or money. They didn't need to. They served their convictions and the people, and in so doing changed the world.

Touring the Lorraine Motel reminds me of the Soulforce pledge to non-violence. It also makes the book *Black Like Me* come alive. I wonder how long it will be before a comparable museum is dedicated to the LGBTQ struggle for equality?

Walking back through the exhibit, a sign catches my eye. It was posted in a white neighborhood cautioning parents not to leave their children unattended, lest black pedophiles kidnap and rape them. It is a striking sign: It is the same rhetoric anti-gay bigots used in California when Proposition 6 was on the ticket. Proposition 6, also known as the Brigg's Initiative, would have made firing gay and lesbian school teachers   and those in support of gays and lesbians   mandatory. Why? Because "all gays are sexual deviants and pedophiles." Thank God for Harvey Milk, who fought and helped defeat Proposition 6.

The sign in the museum stirs something within me. How many of my beliefs are linked to the fear I see in these signs, and how much of what I was taught growing up was actually based in the Bible? Not much, it seems. Every day my conservative views on homosexuality are revealed to be less spiritual and more based on stereotype.

I re-read the sign and sigh. Apparently we have only shifted our prejudice to another group of people we can safely call *outcasts*. Second-class citizens. Unnatural. *Abominations*.

I point to the sign and Connie reads it and shakes her head.

"Hate won't ever disappear," she says. "As long as there are people there will be hate, and these lies will be shifted to the next group of undesirables as soon as gays and lesbians win their equality like the African Americans did."

A few seconds pass.

"Do you think that's why so few people came last night?"

"Maybe. It wasn't planned as well as it should have been, but I think hate was a factor."

"If it makes any difference, *I* learned something."

"What's that?" she asks.

"I don't think I can tell two men or two women that their love is less legitimate because they're gay. I'm for monogamous, loving relationships. For marriage."

My five weeks in Memphis has succeeded in pulling me outside of my depression   but not because things have been magically repaired between me and my family or because I feel more stable than I was in Nashville. My five weeks in Memphis have shown me that as things have become more difficult, I've become less experiment-focused and much more me-focused. Connie reminded me of that.

Conservative Christianity taught me that Christians are the oppressed, that because we follow Christ and the Bible, we are condemned by society...but it isn't that simple. I wonder how much of the persecution we face is the result of our own inability to coexist without being jerks. This year I have been on the receiving end of needless abuse, and this experience has shown me that love should never be coupled with an agenda. Sure, stereotypes exist about Christians that aren't true. Sure, just like gays and lesbians, we Christians are known by the most radical among us...but at least we have the freedoms to live our lives as we see fit. We have freedoms that my gay brothers and sisters have been fighting for and will have to fight for for a long time to come. The ability to express affection in public without being sneered at, to marry who we love and want to marry, to build families and pass on the experiences and life lessons that we've learned to our children...these are things that I have always taken for granted. These beautiful rights are being withheld unjustly from so many of our citizens.

I feel myself softening daily, cleaning out the closets in my own mind as I make room for my experiences. I'm sick of the little voice in my head disagreeing with someone's story because his opinion doesn't line up with my personal views of holiness. I want to believe that God is faithful in His mercy, and that He isn't lying when He says my only job is to love. That's it.

That's the only desire left in me: To love my God with my heart, soul, and mind, and to love my neighbor as myself.

25 another season ends

Softball ends today. It is my last game, and I don't know what to feel. On the one hand, I will have my Sundays back…but on the other, I am going to miss my team. There is something healing about going to the ball field on Sundays instead of the sanctuary. Maybe it is the feeling of the grass beneath my feet, or the *crack* of the oversized ball slamming against the aluminum body of the bat. It is therapeutic. I've played sports most of my life, but I have never had so much fun playing a sport or been so humbled by the athleticism of my fellow teammates.

I kneel behind home plate and know I finally found my position. Playing catcher came out of nowhere, but for some reason my clumsiness is less obvious here. The only down side is that I can't smoke in right field like I used to, but I would rather be in a position where I do my part instead of aimlessly tripping over my own feet as I run after a fly ball.

The batter standing in front of me is a man named Julio. We've had drinks together at Tribe a few times, but he remains a mystery to me. A friend told me that he is HIV positive and that his partner just passed away. I feel sad for Julio, even though he seems to be moving on with his life. He uses the bat to knock the dirt from his heels and takes a few swings before the pitcher throws the ball.

"Nice form!" I say, whistling at Julio before the first pitch is thrown.

"Don't get any ideas back there. I'm *always* the pitcher in my relationships!" he jokes. The pitch is thrown and Julio's bat connects with the ball with a sharp crack. He drops the bat and takes off towards first base.

"That's very selfish of you!" I yell after him as he runs.

"I *know*!" he yells back.

I turn my attention to the runner rounding third base and I know she isn't going to stop. "Give me the ball! Ball! *Ball*! *BALL*!" I scream. The softball hits my glove a split second before the runner slides home and I tag her out.

"*Yes*! Good job, Tim!" Drew shouts from the dugout. The hoots and hollers from my teammates make me feel good. I toss the ball back to the pitcher and kneel, happy that I finally feel like part of the team. I'm going to miss this. This is so much more enjoyable than playing sports in high school. This is about fun and community.

The game ends and we lose by two runs, but I've stopped caring whether we win or lose. The ability to play and the effect of the environment on my senses is rewarding enough. I love the smell of grass and dirt as the hot, wet blanket of heat from the summer sun reigns over me. I love the feeling of the baseball glove on my hand and sweat soaking through my team shirt. I love the sounds of laughter, happiness, and community from the people I have finally learned to love. All of it combines into something fulfilling.

At the beginning of the season, in between our first doubleheader, I was reading a book on the bleachers. The book was called *Finding the Boyfriend Within*, and my teammates were merciless in their teasing. Every weekend I was asked, "Have you found him yet?" and I always answered "Yes! His name is Eduardo and he's a bouncer at a club in Atlanta!" Every week I added to the story. While the joking always a source of entertainment, there is something to be said for finding that peace within ourselves. And I *have* found him, my inner boyfriend but his name isn't Eduardo. His name is Me, and this year has given me my first chance to leave behind the expectations of society and religion, so I can find myself. I think I have found myself.

The summer season draws to a close and I look towards fall and winter, and the end of my experiment. So much has happened, and so much has changed within me, but it isn't over. I still have a lot to learn. Incidentally, I won the award for most improved player on the team. (I wasn't able to go to the end-of-season party because I was out of town, but Drew made sure I got the news.) I can only hope I improve as a person as much as I did in softball.

Part IV: Revelations

"Progress is impossible without change, and those who cannot change their minds cannot change anything."

—George Bernard Shaw

26 the other side of the rainbow

Change is a funny thing. It can creep up on you unnoticed, or it can paint itself as vividly as the bright lights of the Vegas strip, illuminating your steps in a tapestry of reds and blues and purples, impossible to ignore. I walk into the gay bars now like I am walking into my home, and I greet the boys like I greet family. For months I walked into Tribe consciously, but now it all seems subconscious, thoughtless, and beautiful. It seems normal.

Every night is the same. I walk into the bar and make my rounds from regular to regular. Will gives me a kiss on the cheek and asks me how I'm doing, and when I answer that things are great, I feel warmth radiating from inside, from knowing that I am being honest. Things that used to bother me, like seeing two guys kissing, aren't a big deal anymore; nor is the flirtatious banter from the men I would have recoiled from only a few months ago. I feel a deep and calming peace; I still have questions and concerns, but I no longer see these men as my enemy or the enemy of God. They are just people, like me, as unique and gifted as any other individual made in the image of God.

On the other hand, walking into a church feels about as natural as walking into oncoming traffic.

It is Sunday morning, and I am attempting to visit the same local mega-church I went to in spring. Not long after the service begins, something horrible in me is confirmed. The band plays their cheesy music, and with every strum of the guitar or head-dip from the drummer "getting into the spirit," I snicker and sneer and wonder how many of them are living in the closet. I laugh at the keyboard player as he plays the same three ambient notes while the praise leader gives us fortune-cookie thoughts for worship. I smile as he reads scripture passages from his iphone and drinks his coffee—a true hipster wannabe. I laugh at the lighting and the décor. Why are all of these churches decorated in the same cookie-cutter way?

Then the pastor gets up to speak, and I analyze the sermon promo video like a snobby film critic. As he speaks, I listen for trigger words so that I can discredit him; I make a mental list of possible topics or phases that will piss me off enough to leave in protest. If he talks about gays, tithing, or politics, I resolve to walk out...not because I would be genuinely offended, but because I *want* to dislike what he has to say. I *want* to dislike him...even though he has never been anything but kind to me. I dole out judgments indiscriminately. I feel like I am better than these people. My heart is hard. It is bitter. I feel judgment welling up inside of me. I view this church the way I would have viewed a gay pride parade before any of this happened.

And then the pastor begins speaking about fear. He talks about how there are times in our lives we pass up opportunities for relationship because we do not know how to accept someone who is different. He asks whether or not we are versatile in our adaptability with the people God places in our lives. I can say that my acceptance of gays and lesbians feels somehow full, but this new inability to tolerate Christians suggests that I may have strayed into yet another unhealthy extreme. The pastor says that hate is not the root of the ever-widening gap between Christians and those outside our bubble, but fear is. Fear. Pure, unhealthy, destructive fear. He's right. I have spent most of my life afraid, and even now I'm afraid.

Why am I so afraid?

Why can't I just love people?

Why can't I just accept people?

I feel angry. I am overwhelmed and disgusted, overcome by frustration. I look at the Pharisee, and his face betrays a twisted measure of triumph.

Now who's the Pharisee?

Me.

At least you can finally admit that.

Don't even start! These people hurt me. They've hurt my friends. Damn them!

Really? Who? Which ones have hurt you? Point them out to me.

You know what I mean.

Do I? You just said "these people." What's that supposed to mean?

All of them, and what they believe; It is hate masking itself as relationship. They want to change people and make everyone religious robots who vote red and believe the earth is only six thousand years old.

I feel sick, and nausea brings me back to that night with Liz. I feel the same kick in the gut, the same exasperation, the same feelings of guilt. I am on a path that will end in the same betrayal, but this betrayal will be wrapped in a different skin. A single thought squeezes into my conscience.

I am still a bigot, just a different kind this time.

My experiment seemed to have been drawing itself to a tidy close, and now…well, now I see that I have only just reached the next step in my journey. I stand up and walk of the sanctuary, but for the first time the Pharisee doesn't follow. He doesn't need to. I just proved him right.

~~~

Until this morning I thought I had come a long way since the first days and weeks of my experiment, but now I feel somewhat defeated on the opposite extreme. Instead of loving Christians and hating gays, I realize that I've only succeeded in flipping the object of my prejudice. I feel at home in the gay bars and uncomfortable at church. I feel safe with my gay and lesbian friends, but I feel a constant, nagging irritation and discomfort around other Christians. This morning was an unholy confirmation of that. I know this reversal is partially due to the negative experiences I have either had or witnessed this year—but it is also a sign of bitterness.

Prejudice is at the root of these polarized communities, I think. We embrace those whom we feel safety with and reject those that believe differently; and in so doing we miss the big picture. We live together on this planet and share the everyday places we inhabit, yet we are unable to see each other as we should. And right now, I am having a hard time recognizing Bible-Belt Christians as my brothers and sisters. I feel like I've failed. I do not want to flip from extreme to extreme. I want to be a man of peace and reason, and a man who loves everyone without prejudice. But how? I am a bigot, and I just don't know how to be anything else.

I am sitting at a café by my dad's house in Nashville, reading the Sunday *New York Times*, drinking coffee, trying not to dwell on the fact that I am back at square one…when I see someone from my past. My old pastor, the man who wrote me a devastating email the day after I came out, the man whose wife completely ignored me the last time I was here, walks over to the counter a dozen or so steps away and orders coffee. I hide myself from view. I see him, but I don't want to be seen by him. As I hide, adrenaline begins to pump through my body and a barrage of emotions resurface after months of trying to bury them. I feel anger and hurt…but mostly I feel fear. Why am I afraid of him?

Is it because the last time I saw him and his wife, she completely ignored me? Is it still the email he sent? I remember his email as if I read it yesterday. I think it was one of the most hurtful things that happened to me in the first weeks of my experiment, something I still haven't allowed myself to process. I have been too busy to process it. And now here he is, only a few feet away, and alone. I feel bitterness as I watch him joke around with the barista, and I feel—I *know*—that my bitterness isn't right, even if I do feel hurt by him.

I look at my Pharisee and his expression telling.

You've wanted an opportunity to be a man of peace, and here it is. What are you going to do?

Hope he doesn't see me...

That's it?

That's it.

And there you go, proving once again that you don't get it, proving that you're just as much a hypocrite as ever.

But I looked up to him!

And he let you down?

More than let me down, he made me feel alone. I knew he wouldn't be *happy* I was coming out...but did he really have to be so impersonal?

Ah! Now I understand! You love those who don't hurt you, but you don't have to love those who do...

That's not the way it is. But I'm not going to talk to him right now. It's not the right time.

Excuses. I thought you were "better than this"—"enlightened," even.

Maybe I'm not.

Is it possible that you want to have a grudge against him because it gives you a villain? You're wearing your hurt like a badge of honor, as if it gives you credibility in this experiment to have faced persecution.

Doesn't it give me credibility?

No, it doesn't. But how you respond to it does.

I look back towards the counter and see him signing his credit card slip. Without seeing me, he turns and walks out the door, fumbling in his pocket for his car keys. I watch him walk away as if in slow motion, each step he takes an abundant opportunity to run after him and talk. No. I refuse to talk to him. He's the last person I want to talk to right now.

One step forward, two steps back.

Shut *up!*

But the Pharisee is right, and I don't like what he's saying. I want to hate him, too, but I can't. I want to discredit everything he says, so I do not have to step farther outside my comfort zone—which, ironically, now excludes the church I was a part of—because if I have learned anything this year, it is that leaving my comfort zone is the last thing I want to do.

Life has a funny way of teaching us things. I think the obstacles I will face tackling my bitterness against conservative Christians will be more difficult, even, than tackling my hatred of gays. Why? Because the way a lot of Christians practice their beliefs, the way I always practiced my beliefs, hurts people. It hurts me now. Maybe I never truly did leave my comfort zone. Maybe this year is more about conquering my prejudice than accepting and affirming gays and lesbians. And if that is true, maybe my religious programming alone is not to blame.

Maybe all of the questions I've been asking have been too small all along.

Once again I feel as though I'm standing at the foot of an Everest-sized dilemma. I just hope the rest of this year provides enough time to resolve some of these realizations. I put my headphones back into my ears. My coffee is lukewarm now, and I feel the urge to smoke a clove. I stand up and look around, making sure no one else I know is around. I walk outside and look at the Pharisee.

You should go to church tonight.

What? Are you crazy?

If you want the answers to your questions, maybe you should go back to the beginning. Maybe you should go see what happens if you take his advice and go back to church, but…

But what?

But instead of going somewhere else, go back to his church.

~~~

Several hours pass before I allow myself to get dressed and ready for church. I do not want to go. Even the thought of going scares me. My hesitancy runs much deeper than mere hurt; I really don't want to be around people who believe I am unnatural and vile because they think I am gay. Who would want to purposely surround oneself with people who vote against equality and think that just because you are interested in only the same gender means you are also, at best, a pervert? I know gays and lesbians who attend conservative churches. But those people are, in my experience, the minority; and they usually have a deep attachment to their church because of family or friends.

Maybe I would be less vexed if somebody in the church had noticed my prolonged absence and sent me an email or text message…But that is the past now, and even though I would rather do anything else, I know I am supposed to confront this anger inside of me.

The drive to the church is a short one, not nearly long enough for me to mentally prepare. I park and lean against my car and smoke a cigarette, and I pray. *Lord, help me love these people, too. Help me love everyone.* I feel conflicted. I don't want to go inside even though I know I need to. I have had these feelings before, this apprehension: It was the first night I went into a gay bar. I was so nervous my body was shaking. Now I feel as if I am in some bizarre alternate reality that is somehow opposite but the same. I look up and see the steeple of the church. It looks as foreign as the club lights did back in January; the church clothes people wear as they walk into the sanctuary seem as alien as the drag queens were, that first night. I am a different person, that much is clear; but I still seem to build my comfort zone on the extremes, and the exclusion of the other side is unacceptable. Is it possible to readjust again?

An old friend sees me standing by my car and runs over to greet me. The smile on his face is enormous, and it warms my heart. "Tim Kurek! How are you doing?" He ignores my outstretched hand and pulls me into a hug. "I've missed you, brother. How are you?"

"I'm doing well. How are you?" I say, somewhat shocked by his genuine greeting.

"I'm doing great. I've missed you, man." He's always been a good guy, my friend, and standing with him makes me realize how much I have missed him, too. It feels odd, though…wrong, somehow. How can I miss someone who hasn't tried to reach out to me? How can I feel a connection to someone who thinks of me as an abomination?

"Yeah, I've missed you, too. It's been too long," I say, feeling awkward.

"Let's go inside! Everyone will be happy to see you."

"Sounds like a plan." I toss my cigarette and reluctantly follow my old friend.

Walking inside the small building is painful. My heart feels stressed and it aches with each breath. I feel guilty for being here, like I am betraying my new friends. By re-entering this place, I feel like I am condoning the attitudes and beliefs that have hurt so many. But I have to go inside, I have to understand why I feel so angry at these people. Until I took my first two steps inside the church, I didn't understand just how hard my heart has become; but as I confront my own bitterness and feel it tangibly for the first time all year, I am overwhelmed. I look around like a stranger and feel like one even more. Very little has changed here.

I walk forward through the sanctuary and set my messenger bag on a pew. I wait for my old pastor to see me. And when he does, the look on his face is one of shock. He looks happy to see me…but pained at the same time. I memorize that look. It burns into my memory.

"Tim, it's good to see you."

"It's been a long time."

"Yes, it has. How are you?" he asks, still surprised by my sudden reappearance in his church.

"Never better, actually. This year has been a good one."

"Well, I'm happy you are here. We'll have to talk after the service."

"I look forward to it." I shake his hand and feel mixed emotions. I am happy to see one of my old mentors—but I cannot forget his email and how much it hurt me. I sit down in the pew after saying hello to several other parishioners. Everyone seems to be looking at me. How many of them know I came out? How many understand why I left the church in the first place? Maybe the pastor didn't tell them, but surely word got around. I sit in the pew uncomfortably, praying that I can make it through the service.

During worship I think back to that room of people in the community center being led in worship by the drag queen—Jesus in drag—singing the same songs we are singing now. I sing with them in mind, and it makes things easier. It is easier because I feel more mindful of my faith. The "body of Christ" has gotten a lot bigger for me this year. I know I can't discredit others' faith the way I used to. I wish the people here could see what I have seen, and I wish they knew how much in common they have with people they refuse to acknowledge.

The music ends, we sit down, and the pastor gets up and starts preaching. My old life becomes real again and the glimpses I get into my past are healing. The Pharisee is right. I have thrown the baby out with the bathwater, and it is humbling to think that not everything I was part of before all of this was bad. I had forgotten how at home I always felt here, with these people, and I wish I could combine both my lives...impossible as that would be.

The sermon ends and the pastor explains communion. I sit as everyone walks forward and participates in it. I don't. I know the church disagrees with what they think my lifestyle is, and I don't want to participate for multiple reasons. I don't want to disrespect their beliefs while I am here. That's not why I came. More than anything, I don't want to participate in communion in a church that would not be okay with my gay and lesbian brothers and sisters partaking. It is a non-violent protest of sorts. Several parishioners look at me questioningly, probably wondering why I am not going forward, but eventually they move on and I keep my seat.

After the service, people line up to hug me. All of them are cordial, and all of them treat me with kindness. Once again I am convicted, remembering what I have thought of these people since I came out. Assigning blame to those who haven't reached out and being honest about how certain people have directly hurt me are two different things. I have perceived and assumed what these people have been thinking about me for months, and I have used those assumptions against them without giving them an opportunity to prove me wrong. Maybe I was afraid to. Maybe my instincts were to push them away because *I* felt pushed away. For better or worse, these people are my brothers and sisters, and all of them are a part of me. Even the pastor is a part of me. While it may take me a while to overcome the emotions attached to his words, I am hopeful that in the future I will be able to reconcile my frustrations with him. Life is so much richer when we can acknowledge everyone without bias. It is more beautiful when we can see each other as beautiful—in spite of their hurtful words or actions. Maybe this is what being a peacemaker is all about.

And then the moment comes when my reason for being here tonight presents itself.

The pastor and I are at the front of the sanctuary, alone.

My nervousness returns, but I'm ready for it. "You know," I say, "I've missed being here. I feel like I left a part of myself here when I left."

"You did, and we've missed having you."

"Thank you for saying that. It's been an interesting year, but a good one. I'm a lot happier now."

"That's good, Tim, really. You know, I've thought a lot about you since you left, and I want you to know that if I had it to do over, I wouldn't have just written you. I would have talked to you more about your choice. Granted, my position wouldn't have been much different, but I would have approached it more personally."

"You mean that?"

"Yes," he says thoughtfully.

"I don't need you to agree with me," I say, "but I do need you to respect that it's my life, and our involvement in each other's lives is a privilege, not a right. We need to be more mindful of that privilege when we are sharing our beliefs."

"I wish I had it to do over. I'm sorry if you were hurt by my message." He puts his hand on my shoulder, and I know he means what he's saying. Even though I don't agree anymore with his theological approach to his faith, I feel a certain measure of perspective regarding how he and I are supposed to relate as humans.

"I was hurt by a lot more than your message. A lot of people have hurt me this year, but I guess that's okay with me now."

"Why's that?"

"Because for the first time in my life, my beliefs are my own. They aren't hinged on anyone else."

"That's always a good thing. The church has gone through a lot of changes and lost several people. I didn't know if we were going to make it…I know what it's like to face criticism, and the question of how to respond, more now than ever."

"And I've been watching how you handle it, from a distance," I add. "I think you are doing a good job. The church really seems to be more like a family since I left."

"Believe me, we are. It's been a humbling thing to experience." The emotion in his voice and on his face is the most authentic I've ever seen from him. He really has changed. I just wish he knew how damaging his beliefs can be, especially when spoken so carelessly.

We make more small talk and eventually make our way back to the parking lot. Before I leave, he hugs me.

"You know I love you, right?" he says.

"I love you too, brother."

I get into my car and turn the key in the ignition. The engine comes to life and I put the car in reverse, waving to him as I pull out of the driveway. The Pharisee sits next to me.

I'm proud of you.

Why?

Because you'd forgotten that Christians are people too, and now you remember.

They are people—but I won't forget how much pain they can bring by carelessly judging other people.

Everyone causes pain. Everyone hurts everyone else. It's a fact of life, a sad one.

I can see that, I guess.

Think you'll ever go back?

Not this one, my friend. Unfortunately, I was only meant to be here for a season. It'll probably be a long time before I'm comfortable at any church again. I will always do my best to follow God with my life, but being part of a brick and mortar church doesn't appeal to me at all.

Fair enough.

I drive back to my dad's and sit in my car for an hour. The sheer number of thoughts and emotions I feel make going inside impossible. I sit, captive to the dialogue playing out inside my head, and I know it will probably take years for me to process all of this. But tonight was a good first step. Tonight I got to confront hurt and encourage a brother. I am starting to believe my past was necessary, so that I can be the man I am becoming. Everything really does happen for a reason, even if we don't understand it until years later.

27 the walk

I have never been one for causes, never thrown myself behind any cause other than the church. I looked at organizations as crooked, misdirecting money, cheating the people they claim to serve. I have been skeptical. But when a friend asked me to walk in the Nashville Cares AIDS walk, I thought back to New York and the homeless man I saw covered in lesions indicative of the virus. He was a skeleton covered in paper-thin skin, barely able to hold his cardboard sign that read simply, *Please help me eat. I have AIDS.* I thought back to this man, sitting in a stairwell covered in pigeon shit, this man created in the image of God, and I told my friend I would most definitely join him for the walk.

When Nashville Cares emailed me the information about the walk, I scanned through the materials looking for the "gay message." Years in the church had taught me that AIDS was a definitively "gay issue" and some went so far as to say that it was a terrible punishment from God for men engaging in anal intercourse. But when I looked through the packet, LGBTQ folks were hardly mentioned. What was highlighted were the many ways that AIDS can be contracted. While I read, I began to see the big picture. AIDS a devastating virus that kills people, gay and straight, every single day. *AIDS* is the enemy, not the people with AIDS; I feel guilty for avoiding the epidemic by turning it into a "gay issue."

I drive downtown to the site of the walk, park, and people-watch as rain turns the grounds into a thick pit of soft mud. Even though I was only able to raise $100 the week of the walk, I feel good for having been able to raise anything, and I feel good about this walk and this cause. I'm a tiny piece of a much larger puzzle here, and as I stare at the people walking back and forth, families and friends, all smiling, I realize how beautiful the puzzle is. It feels beautiful, like life feels beautiful. To see so many come together for a cause, and to know that this whole thing is still just one city doing what so many others across this country are doing today as well, makes me feel hope.

By the time I reach the registration tent my shoes are caked with mud. It is a thick Southern mud left by the thick Southern rain, and even though everywhere I look I see cold, wet faces, everyone looks happy.

"Name?" the man asks me as I reach the tent.

"Tim Kurek," I say.

"Hello, Tim!" He is very welcoming. "It says here that you raised $100 for the walk. That's great! Are you excited?"

"Very. It's my first time here."

"Well, thank you for helping us out. Without you and everyone else, we'd be even further from finding a cure." He hands me a bag with bumper stickers and AIDS ribbons, and also a t-shirt.

"A t-shirt? Wow, that's cool."

"Yep. You also get a water bottle with the ribbon on it. Have a great walk!" He smiles, and before I step away he's greeted the next person in line. What a nice guy.

I reach the main stage area and look around. Everywhere I see tents from local businesses and organizations. It's eye-opening to see how many groups in the community came out to support the cause. I make my rounds from tent to tent and see the many businesses present. The *Tennessean* and every bank in the area are here, and numerous restaurants and other small businesses are selling their goods—their profits, of course, going towards AIDS research. I even stumble across two churches...but neither of them are mainstream. And then I am struck by a realization that leaves me immobile, shaking my head. I look over at the Pharisee, angered by the epiphany.

Why aren't they here?

Why isn't who here?

Who do you think? Nashville has multiple multi-million-dollar mega-churches, and none of them are here! Why? There isn't a single mainstream church represented here! Don't they care enough about the community to participate?

Be fair.

Fair? Be fair? Are you kidding me?

Don't judge them for not being here. They probably don't even know this is happening.

I *know* they do.

How's that?

The information is plastered all over every Starbucks in town—and every non-denominational pastor I know is addicted to Starbucks.

Still, don't dismiss them. The church does its part for people with AIDS. Think about Africa.

Maybe little orphans in Africa…but how about people in our own backyard? Why does the church send millions of dollars and thousands of people across the globe, when there are men and women dying every day within walking distance, completely alone?

You also have to look at AIDS as a symptom of a bigger heart problem. By preaching the gospel, the church is helping to prevent the spread of the virus.

Are you serious? So we ignore the people who already have it? Sounds like a cop-out to me. In fact, what you just said offends me. The church can teach abstinence or the dangers of using illegal drugs and needles, but it all seems like talk without action.

Don't write off an entire religion because Nashville churches didn't show up.

Look around you, for Christ's sake! Everyone is wearing a "Nashville Cares" t-shirt, but I don't think it's a stretch to say that maybe, just maybe, some of Nashville doesn't give a shit.

Believing is seeing. When I see a non-affirming church show up to an AIDS walk, I'll apologize.

This is your *first AIDS walk.*

It was a tad off my radar until recently. But I won't make that mistake again.

I walk to another booth and see some friends from Tribe. They smile and wave me over, but I hesitate. They are stretching for the walk under a covered area. I would join them, but I need to process all of this. What would I do if I ever found out I had HIV or AIDS? Would I lose hope?

~~~

After stretching I see an old friend, my former manager from Revive Café, Brent. As soon as I see him I feel a deep sadness that Revive was taken from us so abruptly. I miss that little café more than I have ever missed a job before. I only had a few months there, but they were a few of the best months I've ever had. I remember the smell of a perfectly timed espresso shot poured into silky steamed milk. I wonder if Brent misses it too. He's walking with his partner and their puppy, and he probably has a new job by now. I wonder if working with me was as pleasant an experience for him as working with him was for me.

Brent and I walk together and catch up on life, and he is not the only one I'm reunited with. Most of the regulars from the café are also here. It's funny how much more we can appreciate the good things when they're getting lost in the rearview mirror. Everyone agrees that what we shared in that little shop on Church Street was a truly profound blessing.

The Nashville Cares AIDS walk is three miles long, but it feels like a hundred yards. The rain actually provides a peaceful ambience to the walk, and though it is getting cool outside, the warmth of the crowd somehow makes up for it. It is a profound experience: we aren't just walking in a big circle, we are walking towards a goal, and with every step we are closing the gap on finding a cure for an epidemic I never knew existed.

"I'm going to go see the boyfriend," Brent says.

"It was great seeing you!" I say.

"Bitch, I love you," he says as he walks away.

"Bitch, I love you…"

Brent rejoins his partner, and I see another regular from the café and decide to walk with him.

"Jonathon! It's so good to see you." I haven't seen Jonathon since opening day of softball. He was on the travel team this year, so we never had the opportunity to play each other. I give him a tight hug, and he pop-kisses me on the cheek.

"Tim! How are you?"

"I'm good. And you?"

"Been better."

"What? Why?" I ask.

"A friend of mine just found out he contracted HIV from a needle he used a few years ago before he got clean. His whole family is here walking with him today," Jonathon says, breathing deeply. "Oh, look, the finish line!" Jonathon always had a short attention span, with conversation and with men, but I cannot help dwelling on his friend's situation.

"I know. It went so quick. Your friend, is he going to be okay?"

"We hope so. HIV can be monitored and managed, sometimes for decades. But it's still a battle."

"I can't even comprehend it."

"He's not my first friend with HIV. I've known several men who didn't take care of themselves and were a lot less lucky. Every time one of them passes, I feel like a part of me dies with them…But listen to me—I'm probably depressing the hell out of you! You're young. You won't have to see what I've seen. The '80s and '90s were tough."

"At least we're raising money for the research."

"Yeah, but we could be raising a lot more," he says as we walk past the finish line and high-five volunteers to the left and right.

"How so?" I ask, taking a bottle of water and an orange slice from another volunteer.

"Look who *isn't* here. No one from my church, or any of the major churches, for that matter. Do you know how efficiently churches can raise money? Could you imagine how much we could raise if we were committed to finding a cure, together?"

"So you noticed."

"It's hard not to notice. I guess they won't be passionate about the AIDS research till they find out their kids, or brothers, or parents have it. Then just try to stop them!"

"I thought the same thing."

"Well, I'm going to go meet up with my friend's family. Pray for him, okay? I know you're one of the Jesus people." He hugs me and kisses me on the cheek again.

"Will do. See you later."

Jonathon walks away and I feel the same anger from earlier, just worse. It is worse because it's not just me that has noticed the absence of my old community…other people noticed it, too, and those people have less reason than me to defend the church. I am frustrated. I didn't know that loving your neighbor as yourself was contingent on the neighbor being a white Christian male, between ages eighteen and forty-nine—and straight.

I walk back to my car and try to kick the mud from my shoes before getting in. The rain has picked up, and it is getting cooler outside. But before starting my car, I grab my bag of stickers and peel the back off one of the little red ribbons. I stick it on my dashboard and flatten it to the surface with my thumb. I do not want to forget any of this. I look at the little raised ribbon, lightly touch it with my finger, and I wonder just how long it will be before we actually do find a cure. I hope that in the meantime, someone will have given that homeless man in New York a blanket and some food. I refuse to let myself think of him be-ing gone.

28 i kissed a boy and i didn't like it

Moving through the packed karaoke night at Springwater is like moving through a heard of zebra on the plains of Africa. The smoke takes some getting used to (even if you are a smoker), as does the ever-present stench of cheap beer. The Tuesday-night crowd is a diverse mixture of punks, bums, hippies, and drunks. Mix in the oddball Christian, and you've got a recipe for something truly unique.

Josh and I are waiting for our song. We put in our infamous Tenacious D standard, and Chris, the DJ, nods his approval. He is one of those guys who does what he does simply for the love of it. The combination of a regular bar family, beer, and the lesser-known gems the musical world has produced over the past three decades, reveals a side of Chris I wish everyone could see.

On stage, Cara, known to the superstar karaoke crowd at Springwater as Lucky, sings "Bridge over Troubled Water" better than any rendition I've ever heard. My boyfriend Shawn is up next. He is going to sing his traditional Boyz2Men song…the one during which his voice melts the underwear off every man and woman in the place. On stage, Shane, AKA Pimp Daddy Supreme, toggles the lights between red, green, and blue, adding to Lucky's performance, and the crowd goes wild. This is the only real way to spend a Tuesday night.

I am on my first pitcher of beer when Shawn comes over and gives me a kiss on the cheek and a hug. It has been a while since we have been able to spend time together, much less go on a date…but as I have grown more comfortable in my life as a gay man, I've been less and less in need of rescue by my knight in shining armor.

"How are you doing, handsome?"

I can tell by his voice that he has had a few beers and seems to be feeling the effects.

"I'm doing well. I've missed you!"

"I've missed you, too," he says, his hand rubbing my back as we hug. His physicality is normal enough, and I'm completely comfortable with him, but something feels different. His usual restraint that comes from knowing that I'm a straight man seems to be waning, and for the first time I wonder how flirtatious he'll get.

Earlier this year, before I spent significant time in a gay bar or club, I would have reacted very negatively to any sort of physical flirtation; it wasn't until Shawn and I started spending time together that I became comfortable. Even the provocative humor from men like Scott and Jason, my two favorite regulars from Revive, would've been enough to send me into a place of extreme discomfort. And there were situations as recently as early summer where I would revert back into a place of revulsion. Thankfully that was always fleeting.

Ultimately, I had to recognize flirtation for what it is—a compliment—and not as some sort of literal play to get me into bed. Even flirtation rooted in that desire became easy to deal with, because I began to recognize it as part of a unique individual's sense of humor. I can't judge. I used to make the same kinds of jokes, speak with the same edge of suggestive humor towards women. It feels like lifetimes ago.

Shawn holds me for what seems to be ten minutes before being called up on stage to sing. As he walks towards the microphone, Josh meanders through the packed dive bar to my side. "He's drunk," Josh says and I nod in agreement. But even drunk, Shawn can sing. He belts out his Boys2Men tune with the precision of a professional, and everyone in the bar is on their feet.

"He sure is on his game tonight."

"Yes, he is," I reply.

"He isn't hiding his attraction tonight, is he?" Josh asks me quietly.

"You noticed? It's okay. Shawn and I always flirt. He is the only one who gets to be that way with me."

"But what about me, bubba?" Josh says.

"You're a given!" I laugh.

After Shawn finishes, he walks back over to the table and retrieves his beer.

"You were fantastic!"

"Ah, really? Thank you!" Shawn pulls me into another hug…but it's not just a hug this time. Something strange begins to happen. I am pulled into something I am not remotely ready for.

I see Shawn's lips pucker, and seconds tick by like calendar pages flying off their binding, one by one by one. The real possibility that I would have to kiss a man at some point this year flashes through my mind, and I weigh my options. Kiss a man who I know loves me and has selflessly been there for me—or a stranger who surprises me on the dance floor? It seems like an easy answer, but either way, it means I am kissing a dude, and that is not something that any part of me really wants to do. I feel guilty for my near-constant flirtation with Shawn; I can't imagine what it must be like to have someone you're attracted to flirt with you, just for show. Do I owe it to him? He has gotten nothing from me, physically; maybe a kiss is a way to show him how much he means to me.

I debate, but it isn't an easy argument.

"Am I really this drunk?" one side wonders.

"You knew this would happen at some point, and it really should be with Shawn!" the other yells.

"But I'm not really gay."

"If an actor can do it, you can too!"

"What will everyone think?"

"Who gives a shit what they think?"

"He's not just doing this because he's horny. He cares for me."

"And that matters?"

"But…But…"

"Just let him do it!"

I see Shawn drunkenly measuring my response. I haven't turned my head yet and forced an awkward kiss on the cheek, and that has not escaped his notice. Now I know I'm in for it. His face lights up and his lips move toward my own.

This is it! I'm done for!

The warm flesh of his lips collides with my own like two shape-shifters melting and contorting together, and it takes me a second to compute exactly what's happening. I'm kissing a man—not with the full vigor I'd kiss a woman, mind you, but with the meek, guilt-ridden resignation that this is something I have to do. Shawn puts his hand on my cheek. His gentleness, even while drunk, even now, is something that I admire in him. I try to think of anything but what is happening. I feel burning hatred for the seemingly sluggish passing of time, as if each second is trying to karmically spite me. But I cannot get over this scene. I am kissing a man! I am actually allowing myself to be kissed by another guy. What the hell am I *thinking*?

I feel the tip of Shawn's tongue slide across my upper lip…

Enough! I can't do it! I'm not gay. The desire for physical anything with a guy will never be there.

I pull away as unassumingly as possible and look up at Shawn. He is smiling…no, not just smiling; his face has broken out into a full-blown grin. He is thrilled, and all I feel is guilt.

Shawn really wasn't kissing me because he was horny and wanted to kiss someone. He wanted to kiss *me*. Something else is happening between us, and I do not want to think about what it means. I am a straight male. I have always known it, but never more than right now. I feel uncomfortable and totally put off. I don't like this feeling. But is violation by something you allowed to happen valid or appropriate?

beautiful tradition that has filled in the many holes where my dogma once resided.

Billy Graham once said, "It's God's job to judge, the Spirit's job to convict, and it's my job to love." I wish I had believed this all along and just loved people. It is so much easier, and so much more rewarding, than creating clones that we teach to go out and create more clones. The whole process shows we *don't* get it, that we do not understand how much bigger God is than the box we have created and tried to stuff Him into. I think of that box now and realize it isn't holy or righteous or true. The box is evil. It cripples the Good News.

I am at the café again a few days later, but this time I am alone. The clamor of latte mugs and the hiss from the espresso machine seems constant, providing just enough background noise for me to slip inside myself to think. On October first, the inevitable end of my experiment became real. The finish line lies just ahead of the most difficult aspect of the year: my second coming out. I've begun to wrestle with the idea almost constantly. How can I tell all of my new friends that I am not actually gay? Will they hate me for having lied to them? Before I did this experiment, I had no understanding of *safe spaces*, had no idea that in coming out I would be trespassing into a sacred place. By the time I understood, it was too late and the only thing left to do was finish this journey as sensitively as possible. Being a straight man in the closet, living in and around the gayborhood of Nashville, has made me feel like a bull in a china shop. I sit and ponder these things, and I pray I haven't damaged anyone in the process. Only with the passing of time will I be able to see with clarity what this entire thing means—not only for me, but for my gay friends. I know people will judge my intentions and the nuances of how my theology has changed, but I expected that. I will face the objections, the doubt, and the cynicism with as much grace as I can muster.

Love never fails.

A finger taps me on the shoulder and I look up. Angela smiles at me and puts her bag on the table, only to walk back to the counter to retrieve her non-fat latte with caramel sauce dribbled over the velvet surface of the steamed milk. She is wearing designer jeans, a beautiful sweater, and a white pea-coat, and she looks like someone out of a magazine. Her posture, even in a state of relaxation, is perfect. I have never been more impressed by someone, or more intimidated. Even more puzzling is the odd feeling I have that she and I are destined to be friends. I've never had a friend like her, and I hope I don't screw it up. My inner Pharisee has been quiet lately, but I know he's still there, and the prospect of a repeat of that night with Lizzy still scares me. I never want to hurt anyone like that again. As I wait for Angela, I pray that God will show me how to love everyone, no matter how similar or different they are.

"So I've been thinking lately: You are really a handsome man!" Angela says from halfway across the room, walking back to the table.

"Really?" I've had my share of men flirt with me this year, but I've never taken it as a sincere compliment. My insecurity and interpretation of their motives always seems to hinder me.

"Yes. And I want you to learn how to model!" she says.

"Excuse me?" I choke on my coffee. "What do you mean, *model?*"

"Model...Like this!" Angela sets her latte on the table and walks the length of the café as if it's a catwalk, ignoring every stare, finger-point, and laugh along the way. Her confidence is alarming, but what really shocks me is how oblivious she seems to be of the people around her.

She sits down, demurely crossing her legs with a feline like grace, and sips her drink. "You see? It's as simple as walking."

"But did you see all those people pointing and laughing, Angela? Geez!"

"Let me teach you an important lesson about life. If people are pointing or laughing, you win, because that means that their attention is on you, and attention is a commodity that all celebrities possess."

"I just don't think I can do it. Look at me. I don't have a six pack, I have a keg!" I say.

"You can do it and you will do it…Right now. Call this a lesson of self-confidence." Angela snaps her fingers and I reluctantly stand up.

"How am I supposed to do this?" I whine.

"It's as easy as walking with an attitude. Just keep your back straight, your eyes focused on one specific point, and no matter how you move your head, never take your eyes off that spot. And suck in that beer gut!" She waits a few seconds, but I don't move. "Go on, Timothy. You can do it."

It is difficult to describe the range of emotions I feel as I face the open space between the tables, knowing I am about to strut in front of a thirty-plus college kids. I feel self-conscious, insecure, and ridiculous. But I trust Angela, and so I put my right foot forward, and going against everything inside me, I begin to walk. I pick a point on the far wall to stare at. I know that the looks from my critics will easily dissuade me if I acknowledge them, so I don't. As I make my turn and staring back at Angela, I am walking on a cloud. I feel invincible! Damn the people laughing at me. Damn the frat boy who just whistled at me from across the room as his friends roar in laughter. Each step feels liberating. As I reach Angela, I realize that I didn't walk for her, I walked for myself. She throws her arms around my neck, hugging me tightly.

"I'm so proud of you! That was fantastic! Your posture needs work, but you looked masculine and raw. How do you feel?"

"That felt great, especially when I heard those guys laughing! I felt like every step I took was a giant 'fuck you for judging me'!"

The corner of Angela's mouth turns in a provocative way and she makes a kissy face and winks at me.

"You are a beautiful man, and you have nothing to be self conscious about. Don't you ever doubt yourself! Never ever doubt yourself!"

Taking compliments from Angela is easier than from other people. It is easier because I know she is telling the truth. There is no pretense or fa?ade, there is only the softened heart of someone who has experienced enough cruelty for a dozen lifetimes, has learned to fully accept herself, and in so doing, has learned to accept others. And in that way she's achieved a certain kind of enlightenment, a sublime state of being that seems lifetimes away from me.

I have always been taught that we learn because of, or in spite of—and regarding people outside "the faith," it would only ever be in spite of. Lessons like community, loving my neighbor, and confidence are not things I anticipated encountering while outside my church...but the secular community seems to generally grasp these concepts without an organized church body—and I cannot discredit them, no matter how much I have been taught to. Am I trying to discredit the vast amount of good one can learn *inside* the church? Of course not. But I am facing an even more substantial truth that, even as a self-professed Christ-follower, I do not have a monopoly on truth.

After making me treat my favorite café like a runway, Angela finds us a quiet table on the patio to talk. She refers to herself as a spiritualist but doesn't ascribe to any one belief. I tell her I'm a Christian, and I can see that she is put off by the word. It is depressing to think that people across the divide, on the other side of the so-called culture war, think of my faith tradition so negatively. I don't think it's the actual Christian faith that bothers them so much as the people who claim to follow Christ. In fact, I've never gotten a negative response when referencing Jesus in any situation this year. If only professed Christ-followers, myself especially, would align "Christianity" with Christ by removing the politics, pomp, and arrogance from our everyday expressions of faith. Maybe then we could begin undoing the vast amounts of personal damage we have inflicted upon the very people Jesus has called us to love, people who are just as much the children of God as we believe ourselves to be. We Christians may be unaware of the effects of our words and actions, but in any case, damage is done.

Angela's apprehension is convicting. I am learning the unfortunate lesson that most of us in the church have lulled ourselves into a false sense of spiritual competence, where we feel infallible—no matter how fallible we claim to be—and see others as too ignorant to teach us anything about our God that we don't already know. But maybe that is the point: to be humble enough to learn from those whom we do not want to acknowledge as credible sources of wisdom. Maybe that is why God honors the "least of these," blesses the meek, comforts those who mourn, and calls peacemakers the sons of God. Until this year, I was proud enough to have missed this, but it helps to know that I still have time to rectify this paramount mistake and reconcile myself to a much bigger God than the one I've kept so neatly in my little box.

"Angela, could you just answer me one question?"

"Darling, I'll answer you a million questions if you ask them." She bats her eyelashes playfully, and I chuckle.

"Who are you? I mean, you walk into my life—a true dame—and now you're sitting here telling me you want to teach me how to model. What's your story?"

"My story?" she says, sighing.

For a second I fear I've put her off by prying into her life before she's ready.

"My story isn't probably much like your story, Tim."

"I figured as much. You don't have to tell me if you don't want to."

"It's okay, handsome…it's just hard to relive. But I'll try." She takes a sip of her coffee and stares at her polished nails, lost in thought.

Albert was six years old when he realized the house was empty. The absence of his mother triggered a range of emotions that would challenge even the strongest of adults, much more a young boy. The reason for her disappearance was a mystery, confused by loneliness. Nothing made sense.

Every day Albert would wander the modest Victorian house while his father was away at work, always careful to avoid the room that once belonged to his mother. It was a room that had inspired so much warmth, so much hope…but since her disappearance it had become a shell of a former life. The shivers that ran down Albert's spine when he saw the door to this room elicited panic attacks and tears, which dripped on to his unkempt clothing that was badly in need of a wash.

"Normally, when one parent is taken out of the familial equation, the other attempts to pick up the slack…but not my father." Angela pauses to sip her latte. "My father acted as if she were still around, like shit was still getting done. But it wasn't! Dishes were piling up in the kitchen to a point that our neighbor, Mrs. Thompson, could see them through the window and would come over while my father was away to take care of the mess. She had been a close friend of my mom's, but didn't seem surprised that she wasn't around anymore—which always made me wonder. She ignored me, but I didn't mind. I was just happy to hear someone else in the house. It made things better for me."

By the age of seven, Albert had begun to conquer his fear of his mother's room. When he wasn't at school, he would sit in the hallway with his back to the door and do his homework, trying to remember any little detail of his mother that he could hold. He'd write these details down, but there weren't enough. He needed to go inside, to see her things and touch them, smell them. Surely that would help him remember.

"Easier said than done!" Angela says, taking a deep breath, looking off to my left like she is watching himself in that hallway. "It took me weeks to put my hand on the doorknob, and another month to turn the damned thing. I don't even remember what I was afraid of. So I just stood there. I can still feel the cold brass against the sweaty palm of my hand, still feel the numbness in my wrist that kept me from turning it. And then one afternoon it just happened. I turned the knob and went inside."

The room was darker than he remembered. The shades were pulled shut and the air was stale, but it was still the place he remembered. Lying on his mother's bed was a deep red sundress, the hanger still looped through the sleeves. Albert reverently approached the dress and pulled the fabric to his nose, inhaling deeply. He could smell traces of her perfume clinging to the fabric, and it was all that he needed to feel his mom's presence. It was the beginning, the tears and the memories stirred something deep within the motherless boy that could only be described as *hope*, a single ember that, like a drug, brought Albert to a place of peace.

"I can still remember that smell," Angela says, tears running down her face. She takes a deep breath and lights a cigarette. "I still remember the lavender. It was bright, and warm. It smelled like the home I'd lost. I remember sitting on the edge of that bed, just clutching that dress to my chest, sobbing into it, holding it as if it was more than a piece of fabric. I held onto it like it was my mother. I think I may have even talked to it, but I don't remember. All that mattered was that it was my mother's favorite, and that it smelled like her."

I don't know why Angela is sharing all of this with me. I feel honored, and crippled with empathy. I realize I'm wiping tears out of my eyes.

"I remember not being able to sleep that night. I felt like I'd just won something, or was going somewhere fun the next day, like a theme park or something. The excitement gave me a high. I spent damn near three hours writing in my notebook that night, writing memories that felt like they'd just happened. I could hear my mother's laugh, see her looking in the mirror while she applied her makeup. I remembered the pearls she wore, one white and one pinkish that hung from two ends of a silver chain that wrapped around her neck. I got to see again how beautiful she was, and how gentle. I got to taste her home-made bread, got to remember running on the beaches of Long Island. I stood next to her in church again, singing hymns that I loved only because I got to listen to her singing them. And it was all beautiful." Angela exhales a puff of smoke through her nose and smiles. "It was the beginning of a powerful time in my life, a time when I accepted who I am and first had the courage to act on that acceptance."

"How so?" I say, using a napkin to dry my eyes.

"It was when I first acknowledged that I was my mother's daughter, not her little boy. I had always wanted to grow up and be a beautiful woman. The idea of growing up a man felt foreign and wrong, and felt like a lie. A few weeks after holding that dress in my hands, I was back in my mother's room for the hundredth time. The deep red sundress that I always put back in its proper spot on the bed was there looking at me, and something inside of me said that I was supposed to wear it. So I stripped down to my underwear, delicately took the hanger off the dress, slipped it over my head, and for the first time in my life, felt whole. I was *Angela*. You see, my mom always called me her angel, so it just felt right for me. Perfect, even. I looked at myself in the mirror for a while and thought, *You, Angela, you are a beautiful woman. You take after your mother.*

Albert had always struggled with the realization that he was different. On the playground he would sit in the swing and stare at the other boys, never once feeling like he was one of them. He was isolated and it didn't take long for the other kids to notice. Albert suffered bullying from elementary school through high school.

"Oh, believe me, honey, it only got worse after I started dressing in my mother's clothing, even though it was in private. No one knew I was doing it, but as I sat in class, I'd imagine that

I was a beautiful woman, like Joan Collins in *Dynasty*. Alexis Carrington, my hero, the ultimate diva!"

But Angela's secret was discovered when she was eleven. One afternoon, as she walked around her house in one of her mother's black dinner gowns and heels, she turned around and found her father staring at her.

"He was an old-fashioned Sicilian, hardened by a culture that said you couldn't show emotion and still be a man. It wasn't uncommon for him to beat me for little or no reason. He hit my mom every once in a while, too. Gave her a black eye once, on Christmas Eve. But hell, I was *Angela*, and I *knew* he wouldn't understand!"

"It happened so fast. 'What in the hell are you doing, you little fuck?' he asked me. I told him I was being me, and he actually laughed. 'You want to be a cunt? I'll treat you like a cunt!' And then he grabbed me and threw me on the ground and forced me to perform oral sex on him. He was so violent…I remember thinking I was going to die. I couldn't breathe. That was the first moment I allowed myself to hate my father." I hand Angela a tissue and she wipes running makeup off of her cheek. "I left as soon as I was able. I moved to New York City and became a runway model, which was a dream come true!"

"Wow…I don't know what to say." I think of the violation, and anger courses through my body. Why would he do that to his own child? This is evil—not Angela.

"You don't have to say anything. The molestation happened several more times over the next few years. But I've forgiven my father. I even still call to check up on him."

"You still *talk* to him?" I ask.

"I call him long enough for him to answer, and that's how I know he's alive. One day I'll call and he won't answer, and I'll know he's gone. Then I'll hop a bus back home and wear the hell out of a slinky black dress, and pay my last respects."

"You are a recipe for disaster Angela, the product of so much chaos and tragedy. But you're more beautiful for that, and I'm humbled you'd share your story with me." I choke back tears, still trying to process everything she's just said, trying to put myself into her size nines.

"That's why I told you, Timothy. Because I know you think I'm beautiful, and that's what separates you from almost everyone else I've met here, so far." Angela smiles and puts her hand on my shoulder and squeezes.

That is when I lose it. I excuse myself to go to the restroom, and I look in the mirror, weeping at for the pain Angela has experienced. Nearby, the Pharisee leans against the wall, listening as I cry. The look on his face is snide.

I don't mean to be rude, but it's pretty clear that the reason he is transgendered is because of his father.

The Pharisee's tone and words offend me so greatly that I hit the sink with both fists as the last word is uttered. The porcelain shutters against the tile wall behind it. Hatred swells inside my body.

Damn you for saying that! And damn *me* for ever having thought those kinds of things.

I'm not judging him.

She's *her,* you son of a bitch, and she was *her* long before *she* was molested. Why is it that you have to take everyone's story and pervert it according to your limited understanding of things? Why do you have to control and dominate every difference, reduce people down to this sin or that, this person is wrong, this person is right? How dare you!"

So I'm not allowed to have an opinion?

Not when you try to sell your *opinions* as gospel truth! Right now you can shut the hell up and butt out of my life! I have to get back to my sister.

I walk away angry, but feel like I am being cured of a disease. It is the worst kind of disease, a plague, even; the kind of sickness that has always fueled my inherited spiritual narcissism and kept me from truly being in relationship with someone I never would have known, or wanted to know, otherwise.

I know that all of this may seem like common sense to anyone raised in other parts of the country, or to other parents: that embracing someone different—or, much harder, allowing oneself to be embraced by them—seems like a no-brainer. But conservative Christianity doesn't allow for such things. It does not make room for the advancement of communion with someone like Angela. Instead it calls for something else, something much more insidious. It teaches us to manipulate that person's emotions, so that we can change them into our image. I would never wish to change Angela. Being changed myself because of her is enough for me to feel that I have listened to my Jesus, been willing to admit I do not have the answers to her past pain and scars. Singing a few hymns and reading a few verses cannot undo the damage done to her in her life for being transgendered.

A few minutes pass and I walk back to the table. Josh has finally made it to the café and is sitting at the table with Angela. Both are laughing, and I know that means she is back in entertainer mode. For a few brief minutes, I got to see so much deeper, and for a few minutes she honored me with her story. I reach the table and sit down. Josh sees my puffy eyes and gives me a questioning look.

"You okay, buddy?"

"Yes I am, actually."

Angela smiles at me, and I breathe. For the first time in years, I'm able to breathe.

We banter back and forth, tell stories, and share jokes. We drink coffee and make obscene comments about cute guys, and we laugh. We laugh like we have never laughed before, enjoying every second, care-free and uninhibited. Every so often I look over at Angela and she smiles at me. She is definitely right about one thing: she is beautiful to me, so very beautiful; and I know she looks at me the same way. I am because she is. *Ubuntu*.

30 a reunion

It has been several months since I was in New York, protesting with Soulforce, but Mel White and I have kept in touch. A few days ago he emailed me and said he would be in Nashville to give a talk at a nearby college for National Coming Out Day. I jumped at the chance to go, knowing this may be my last opportunity to see Mel for quite some time. It is not often one gets the opportunity to sit and learn at the feet of a man who has been a figure in the civil rights movement for so many years.

I drive the fifteen minutes from my home to the college, all the while praying my car will make it. The break light, check-engine light, and fasten-seatbelt lights are permanently lit, now. They remind me of a dashboard version of the Vegas strip. I wish I had the money to pay for repairs. I have yet to find a new job, and I am getting by doing odd jobs for friends. I hate yard work!

As I reach the college and park, I say a silent prayer of thanks and walk into the building. The room is the size of a small theater with maybe two hundred chairs lined up on either side. My eyes scan the room for Mel. He is talking to a student and his back is to me. He is wearing a navy blue sport coat, tie, and khakis. And he looks to be in good spirits as he turns. Mel's smile is a small miracle. I say that because if you have read his story and know all that he has endured in his life, the fact that he is able to smile at all is surprising. Granted, he has enjoyed many happy memories, but walking in his shoes during the several decades of reparative therapy would wipe a smile from anyone's face. Electroshock therapy, isolation therapy…Mel is a testament, not just to the human spirit but also to the Holy Spirit. His humility in itself has inspired me this year, as it convicted me as I look back to my freshman year of college at Liberty University.

Mel sees me and lights up. He gives me a big hug and welcomes me with such warmth that I am at a loss for what to say.

"Looking good, Mel!"

"You're looking good yourself!" he says, ever the charmer. I've dropped a few pounds since New York. "So, how is your year going?" Mel asks excitedly.

"It has been the most eye-opening and life-changing thing I have ever done!"

He smiles. "From bigot to ally in under twelve months...I must say, I'm impressed."

And I think he *is* impressed. When we first talked last October I was a different person. I had made it a goal to accept and love the LGBTQ community, but I never thought I would become an advocate or ally. I tell Mel about being outed to my family, and he puts his hand on my shoulder in sympathy.

"Tim, you're going to face a lot of opposition from both sides, but when they see your heart, that will go a long way in calming those fears. But, hey, we'll talk more later. I've got to get up there soon to talk." Mel hugs me again and then walks away, and I look for a place to set my stuff down and find a seat.

There are moments in one's life where the unexpected becomes an all too tangible reality, when things one never expected to happen, happen. One second I'm meandering through a room of people to find an empty seat, and the next I hear a voice. It is a voice from my past, but how long past I can't figure out.

I turn around and see someone I thought I would never see again. It is Elizabeth, the daughter of one of my childhood pastors, from a church that I have always jokingly blamed as responsible for "ruining me." The things I learned there set me on a path that led me where I'm at now...but then again, maybe that isn't such a bad thing. The sight is more than surprising. Not only is she sitting there, she is holding the hand of another

young woman and looks rather in love. The irony of the situation is not lost on me.

"Oh, my God! Elizabeth?"

She laughs at my shock. "It's me. How are you Tim?"

"I'm doing well...but at a loss for words at the moment.
You're gay? Really?"

"Takes one to know one." She laughs again.

"And who is this?" I look over at the young woman whose
hand Elizabeth is holding, and she smiles warmly.

"This is Nicole."

"Pleasure to meet you, Nicole!" I am completely and utterly
dumbfounded, and the look on my face probably gives me away.
How can this be?

Nicole turns to Elizabeth and smiles. "Is this the guy you
knew from your old church who came out earlier this year?"

"Yes it is," she replies sweetly.

"Wow, it's nice to meet you, finally." Her tone is feminine
and soft, and she reminds me of a movie star from the old black
and whites: very classic-looking in her features, and very beautiful.

"It's nice to meet you too." I look over at Elizabeth, still
shocked. "You're really gay? Are you serious?"

"Hey, now, I could ask the same about you! My sister told
me you'd come out, and I was surprised. You'll have to tell me
all about it."

"You will, too!" I say. "After Mel gives his talk, we'll have to
catch up! Mind if I sit next to you?"

"Well, why wouldn't you?" Elizabeth says playfully.

I try my best to focus on Mel's speech at the front of the
room, but my heart races at the implications of what is happening next to me. My conservative pastor's daughter, sitting
next to her girlfriend, holding hands...Don't let anyone ever tell
you that God doesn't have a brilliant sense of humor, or that
He doesn't know how to put you in the exact situation needed
to help you conquer your prejudice. Elizabeth must have gone

through hardships that no one will ever know, navigating those waters with her family.

Elizabeth was never just my pastor's daughter. She was my babysitter from time to time and even helped lead our small youth group. We were in the same church until I experienced my first church split at age thirteen. The split was my first taste of the black-or-white, my-way-or-the-highway mentality. Until that point, I thought everyone outside our denomination was bad, and that we were all bonded in our ownership of the truth. When the church split, I saw our small church divided, and saw people that claimed to be a family virulently severing relationships and friendships in a way that scared me, even as a young child. Elizabeth's family was on the other side of the divide from my own. Since we left, I have not seen her...Except once.

Jacob was the oldest brother in the family, only slightly younger than Elizabeth. He was like a big brother to me, the one who taught me how to play basketball and throw a spiral. He was my friend. When our church split and splintered off in different directions, I missed Jacob dearly. A year or two after leaving that church, I got home from school and found my mom sitting on our back steps. She had a look on her face that I hadn't seen before, and I knew something was wrong. When I asked her why she looked upset, she told me that Jacob had contracted bacterial meningitis and passed away. For several minutes, my world went numb. I couldn't see or hear. I stumbled to my room and began to sob. Why had God allowed this to happen? Why had someone so young been taken in such a random and cruel way? His poor family, a larger family than my own...five children. What must they be going through? I ripped a box out of my closet and dumped the contents onto my bed. Within seconds I found what I was looking for: a small photo album with pictures of all of my old friends from church. I found the picture of Jacob. Seeing that picture, knowing that I would never see him again, pushed me over the edge.

Two days later, Andrew and I went to the funeral, picked up by another family that had stayed in the church. My dad didn't like that we were riding with people from the other side of the divide. It was one of the first seeds of resentment spouted in me towards our belief system, towards the churches we attended. My friend had died, and still the drama of the church was the focus of conversation.

Walking up to the casket, I saw the first body I'd ever seen. I looked at Jacob, his body resting peacefully, and I felt a part of my innocence leave me. This was what people talked about when they talked about death. Jacob was there, but he wasn't, at the same time. It was a shell of who he was. The light was gone from his face in a way I hadn't imagined I'd ever see. Not now, not this soon. I looked down at his face and remembered how he had taught me to shoot a basket. *Put your fingers right here, buddy, over the lines, here and here. Steady your feet, and when the ball leaves your hands, snap your wrist like* this, *so the ball gets a good spin. Aim for the top of the square above the hoop, and you'll be draining them all day long! Got it, little man?* I remember how Jacob made me feel. I wasn't just a little kid to him, I was an equal. It was that empowering attitude and encouragement that I remember most.

I saw Elizabeth that day, but we didn't speak. She waved at me with a half smile, and I waved back, lost in grief. She was playing the part of the host, helping family and friends find their seats, making sure the music playing was appropriate for the audience. I couldn't have imagined someone could be so busy at a memorial service. If Andrew died, God forbid, I would have hidden in a hole. I would not have had the strength to help my family the way Elizabeth was helping hers.

Mel finishes his talk and I look over at Elizabeth and Nicole. They look happy, and I am happy for them. I still cannot believe we are sitting here together, celebrating National Coming Out

Day together. It feels right, and I am in awe of the randomness of it all. Is this really happening?

I introduce Mel to Elizabeth, and she introduces Nicole, and I tell him how we know each. He gets the irony, understands the randomness, and I know he understands what this means to me. It is a game-changer to re-imagine my childhood in light of this revelation. Mel hugs me goodbye, and I feel blessed to have seen him again. I wonder when our paths will cross again. I wonder if they will ever cross again. I hope so. Mel has taught me so much, mostly through the example he has set as we have interacted. I am lucky to count him as a friend. I came here tonight to hear him speak, but now I know that there was a deeper purpose to it all.

Elizabeth and Nicole bring a plate of cookies to the table, and I think back on this year and how everything has woven together so intricately. Of all the people I have known, and all the revelations I have had, this one has caught me off guard the most.

"So how long has it been?" Nicole asks us as we scoot our chairs closer to the table. Elizabeth and I lock eyes and exchange a knowing look before either of us explains.

"Well…The last time we saw each other was at Jacob's funeral," I say.

"Yeah, that was it. So it's been quite a while," Elizabeth says, remembering as I have remembered tonight.

"He really was a great guy…Do you remember the time we broke the table trying to dunk the basketball?"

Elizabeth laughs, her smile happily replacing the more emotionally severe look of loss from only seconds before.

"And then all of you blamed it on the one girl in the choir!" she says.

"Yes, yes we did." I take a bite of a cookie and look down at my hands. "You know…if he was here, I think he would be happy for you, Elizabeth."

She smiles. "I've wondered that for a long time…No one else in my family is, but I like to think you're right. I think he would be."

"I was wondering how your family felt about you coming out."

"They didn't take the news well. Remember that girl that I was roommates with before Jacob passed?" she asks me.

"More than roommates?"

"Yep."

"So how did you two meet?" I ask, looking at Nicole.

"Funny story! Elizabeth and I met at an ex-gay ministry group. I was one of the leaders and she came to it because her family would 'take her back,' so to speak, if she changed her ways." I can already tell Nicole is a sweetheart. She grabs Elizabeth's hand as she speaks, and I can see the love in her eyes.

"We started hanging out a lot, and the ministry group caught on that things were happening between us. They ordered us to stay apart, said we couldn't be friends, or we would have to leave the ministry. We had to choose between our church group and each other. Even though it sucked to be given the ultimatum, it wasn't a hard decision to make."

"So are you back out to your family yet?" I ask Elizabeth. She shakes her head no, and I can see that the closet has been weighing on her. The mere mention of her family, and she looks tired.

"I was disowned once, and I just don't want to lose them again." I hear the pain and conflict in her voice, and I feel the gravity of her situation. I also understand that apprehension, and fear, that still small voice of fear that tells you that you will lose the people you love if you come out.

"I just told myself that if my family disowned me for coming out, then I never really had their love and support from the beginning," I say.

Nicole nods her head in agreement and I know I've voiced her sentiment.

"But then again, I don't have nephews or nieces that I would have lost…so your situation is much different from my own," I add.

"The thing that hurts the worst is that when I was 'out,' every time they saw me, they would act so sad. They treated me as though I were dead and they were talking to my ghost. Every time they saw me, I wanted to shake them and say, 'It's me! It's Elizabeth, your daughter, your sister, and I'm still here!' It broke my heart. They already lost one child…" Elizabeth looks down at her hands, and I feel overwhelmed with frustration. She said it best when she said that they had already lost a child. Why lose another because of prejudice?

"Elizabeth…weren't you with your first girlfriend about the same time Jacob passed away?" I ask.

Her face goes a pale, and I can tell I have inadvertently struck a nerve. I feel terrible seeing that look of angst on her face, knowing that I am responsible for drudging up old memories, old wounds that might be best left unopened. "I'm sorry. I didn't mean to pry."

"It's okay, really. It's just the darkest time of my life, and every time I think about it I feel a little overwhelmed." She takes a sip of her iced tea before continuing.

"When Jacob passed away, I had just decided to act on my feelings for the first time. I had chosen to be true to myself, and to be happy. It was the first relationship where I actually felt honest, where I felt like I was being me. And then I got the phone call about Jacob—and my world crumbled, and everything fell apart. I felt overwhelmingly *guilty*. I felt like God was punishing me for being a lesbian and for choosing to act on my feelings. I just knew it. And it wasn't just me He punished…it was my family, and my poor brother. I was to blame for Jacob's death. I was the reason he died. I fell into a depression worse than any I'd ever experienced, and instead of allowing myself to process and grieve, I forced myself not just to withdraw from my family and friends, but to watch my family from a distance, in their pain…" She pauses to choke back tears and takes another sip of tea. Nicole's expression says it all. When Elizabeth is upset, she is, too.

"The last time you and I saw each other was the funeral. I remember that day especially because I felt like I had to hold the family together. I didn't have the right to grieve, so I ran around playing host and making sure everything went smoothly, because I didn't want to hurt my family any more than I already had. It has been the single greatest struggle I have ever experienced…I am still trying to process all of it."

"But you don't still think it was your fault, do you?"

"No. But that is the problem with what you and I have always been raised to believe. We were taught that if you didn't live up to a certain set of guidelines and standards, that God was out to *get* you. That He hated you, and His vengeance would be swift. At the time, blaming myself was the only thing that made sense." Elizabeth speaks, and I know that no amount of words could ever hope to capture the intensity of the pain and heartache she felt over the past thirteen years. I cannot really ever understand, but I feel sick as she pours out her heart. And as she tells me her story, part of me is overcome with shame because I have said to so many people, so many times: If you don't follow the letter of the law, God will punish you. Elizabeth's face shows me the consequences of that mentality.

I wonder how many people have experienced what Elizabeth experienced and felt that their orientation was the reason something bad happened. I wonder how many parents have told their children is was their fault and forced guilt and shame upon them. I wonder how many times I have used those same tactics to try and "save" someone.

"It has taken years of counseling and therapy to get past that guilt and self-blame. And it doesn't help that I have to hide who I am to my family. I love them so much, and I just wish I could be in their lives authentically. I wish I could be honest with them," she says.

"For whatever it's worth, I know Jacob didn't die because you are a lesbian. He died from a rare strain of a virus that has taken many before him and will probably take many more before it's all said and done. Never, never, never think that God works so maniacally. You were fearfully and wonderfully made, and I hope you'll always remember that."

Elizabeth reaches across the table and grabs my hand, and for a moment I feel like a small child again, like she is my pastor's daughter who comes over and orders pizza and watches movies with me. I feel that childhood connection and that bond and know that she is the same person now that she was then. Yes, she is older and wiser, but she is the same. She was always so kind, and I am happy that she hasn't lost that trait. I am happy that she is not bitter and jaded and hard-hearted...that through all of the years and all of the pain, she is still the beautiful person I knew as a boy.

The three of us walk to our cars and spend another hour in conversation. I know this is the start of a beautiful friendship, and, more, I know that in seeing each other, part of us both is finally able to heal. We have been given a rare gift. We have witnessed each other as functioning, healthy adults: two people who have made it through an upbringing of faith that teaches works above faith and guilt above love. And we are stronger for it, I think. Elizabeth is strong. I know because she overcame her dark night of the soul, but instead of running away from her faith, she ran to it honestly. I hug my friend and her partner, and we say our goodbyes.

I feel profoundly blessed as I navigate this crazy journey that will soon be coming to a close. Elizabeth has confirmed the powerful truth that our God is not vindictive. When He acts in our lives, guilt is not His medium. Love is. Love is the conqueror of guilt and shame. I get into my car and wave to Elizabeth and Nicole. I hope they enjoy a long and happy life together, and that my old pastor comes around. I hope he understands how precious life is, and that Elizabeth is not a ghost. She is a vibrant and loving young woman, and he is lucky to have her for a daughter.

31 baby human

My brother and I were inseparable as children. When I was two or three, Andrew invented a game called "Baby Human." In this game, I was baby human, but for some reason I always acted like a dog. I think it was Andrew's attempt to show our parents that he wanted a puppy, but my only motivation was making my big brother happy. And I loved it when he laughed, especially when I was the one that made him laugh. He was my hero and has remained my hero for most of my life.

I was always the less athletic one. When Andrew and I played football in high school, I remember his devotion in teaching me the plays and helping me work on my three-point stance. We would stand in the yard and practice together, and in true big-brother fashion, he was always there for me when I needed him. I remember one grueling practice in particular. We were running extra laps as punishment for having lost a game the previous weekend, and when I was two laps away from finishing, I fell to my knees, exhausted. I wanted to pass out, to throw up, and I wanted water. I wanted to quit. Andrew had already finished his laps but saw me from the other side of the field. And so, in the ways befitting a big brother and team captain, he ran around the track and helped pick me up. He ran those last two laps with me and pushed me forward with words of encouragement. He wouldn't let me quit. He wouldn't let me lose hope. He wanted me to succeed. It was a pinnacle moment in my young life, because it was the moment I saw my brother as a man instead of just a boy. He had grown up. I hoped when I grew up, I would be at least half the man and half the leader he was.

Two months before my experiment began, I was the best man in my brother's wedding, and with the help of his friends, we threw him an incredible two-day bachelor party. I knew what was about to happen with my life, and he had no clue, but at least I got that moment with him before I leapt into the unknown. The morning of his wedding, we sat and drank coffee on the porch of the farmhouse and talked about what he thought being a husband would be like. I told him he was going to be a great husband for the same reasons he is a great brother. He is faithful, and he is a servant. That's really all there is to it.

I think about my brother often—every day, in fact—and my heart aches, knowing it has been a little over five months since we last spoke. Only a few weeks ago, I heard from my mom that my brother and his wife are trying to have a baby. The thought of this silence between us lasting longer than it already has is crushing. The endless depression, knowing that my family is splintered, has weighed heavily on me. I did what I had to do, and I would do it again, but I hate myself for having lied to Andrew and Maren. I remember that first morning after I came out, when I came out to them while we stood in the kitchen, and I remember the feeling of my nerves boiling over. I remember throwing up and crying at the same time, and how Maren brought me the can of Sprite and asked me to come back inside. It was the first true act of kindness during my experiment, a lesson in humility, and a realization that I really am lucky. So many others aren't. Liz surely wasn't as lucky. Nor was Will, or Shawn, or so many others. I was lucky.

To have a brother is to have a second self, a companion during the formative years and beyond. Having a brother means having a co-conspirator, and someone else that understands your frustration with your parents. It truly is a beautiful relationship, being brothers, and when Andrew and I stopped talking unexpectedly, part of my being vanished.

It is time to drive to my brother's house. I decide to go under the guise of delivering a a book that I think Andrew will like, and

I write him a letter and tuck it inside the front cover. I do not know what to expect from this encounter, but I hope that he will at least read the letter and know that I miss him.

I turn the keys to the ignition, take a deep breath, and pull out of the driveway. The burden of reconciliation belongs to me. My year is winding down, and this is another thing I know I have to do. A part of me is thankful, though, that he found out when he did. Where would I be and what would I do, if I was just about to tell him the truth? I'd be emotionally unstable, like I was that morning before I told him I was gay in the first place. And while my second coming out still looms with others, I feel a small measure of peace knowing that with my family, all that's left is communicating the lessons this year has taught me, and praying that those lessons are as eye-opening for them as they have been for me.

As I drive to my brother's house, I think about other areas in my life where the burden of reconciliation belongs to me. I used to believe that it was the responsibility of gays and lesbians to come to me and to the church, but now I see it has always been the opposite. The damage done by the mainstream church is vast, and the burden rests on our shoulders to apologize without expectations or reservation. It is not come be who I am; it's I'm truly and deeply sorry; and, please, let me be in relationship with you.

I park on the street in front of the house like I did that day five months before, and I sit. My brother's truck is in the driveway, so the inevitability of seeing him becomes real, and I am so overcome with fear that my body shakes in response. Apologizing for the pain I have caused is one thing, but not knowing how he will respond is almost more than I can bear. I grab the brown paper bag, take a few deep breaths, and walk down the driveway and onto the walkway leading to the door. Every step makes me feel like I am wearing an old diver's suit, the ones that weigh hundreds of pounds, and I feel constricted. With each breath I am acutely aware of every rib inside my chest, and by the time

I reach the door my palms are sweaty and I feel dizzy. If I hyperventilate, at least I have the brown paper bag the book is in. Always be prepared: a lesson my brother and I learned in Cub Scouts.

After taking one last deep breath, I make a fist and knock. I knock and then I wait, and when my brother doesn't answer, I knock again.

What if my sister-in-law opens the door?

What if he opens the door and tells me to leave?

What if he's here and purposely ignoring me because he doesn't want to see me?

I live in these doubts, trying to convince myself to leave. Instead I knock again, more loudly. A minute passes and still no answer.

My breaths come shallow and in rapid succession. I have to close my eyes and just focus on breathing. With the exception of coming out, I have never been so nervous. The possibility of rejection has never seemed so real. Why won't he answer?

I knock again to the same result, and so I sit on the top step and light a cigarette, looking out onto the familiar scene of their yard, wondering where the past five months have gone. Has it really been almost half a year since I sat and smoked in this very spot? Andrew's truck is parked in the driveway, so he must be ignoring me. I decide to leave the book and the letter and go, so I walk to his truck and put it in the passenger seat for him. Walking back to my car, I feel defeated and cold...but more than anything, I feel hopeless.

For months I have felt an overwhelming burden to share stories with Andrew. Not to speak in broad concepts or theological terms; just to tell him stories from my year that helped me understand. I want to tell him about Jason and Scott, Will, Shawn, and my trip to New York, and I want to tell him about Jesus in drag. I want him to hear about these people that our church wouldn't let us know before. I want to share the epiphanies, and the stereotypes that my experience has proven to be myth, and

I want to humanize these beautiful people so that he doesn't see labels, just people. I think it is the only way for him to understand why I did this. It may just be the only way for anyone to overcome their aversion to labels.

An hour later I am sitting at a café by my home, having already made plans to hang out at Tribe. I need a good beer. My phone rings. I look down in time to see my brother's picture flash onto the screen. *What?* He's calling me? *He's calling me!* I answer nervously, hoping for a positive moment, something I can hold onto to feel better about this schism.

"Hello!"

"Hey, Tim." His tone is more even than mine.

"How are you?"

"I'm good. I just got the book and your letter. Thank you."

"No problem. I just hope you enjoy it."

"I'm sure I will." He pauses, and I wonder what he's about to say. "I'm just calling because I wanted to see if you wanted to go grab a beer or something. Maren is out of town…and it's been a long time."

"You're telling me. Five months. I'd love to grab a beer with you, but I made some plans and I can't break them with these friends."

"What plans?"

"I'm going down to Tribe to see meet some people I met back in Memphis who are passing through."

He knows what Tribe is. I tried convincing him to go with me when he thought I was gay.

"Oh, that's fine…" He seems disappointed.

"How about tomorrow afternoon?"

"That works too."

"Great! I'll see you tomorrow, then!"

"See you then." He sounds positive.

We hang up the phone, and elation overtakes me. Could I really be getting my brother back?

~~~

I knock on the door and the doorknob turns. This is it, the moment I've imagined for months. The door opens and I see a huge dog, and my brother holding him back. Andrew looks the same as ever, but the dog looks like he's going to pee, he is so excited.

"Jack, *down!*" Andrew yells. Jack obeys and sits, and Andrew opens the screen.

"Brother!" I say, smiling. Before he can say anything, I pull him into a hug and I hold him tightly.

"I've missed you, man," I say, trying not to cry. Like always I kiss the top of his head and he laughs.

"I've missed you too," he replies.

We move to the couches and while Jack sniffs me and licks my face, Andrew goes to the refrigerator and grabs two long-necks.

"How's life?" he asks as he sits in his usual spot on the couch.

"Life is great, actually. I'm very happy." I take a sip of the seasonal ale and read the label nervously.

"That's good to hear! Mom says you've been traveling a lot."

"Yes. I spent some time in Memphis, and I'm going to Kansas City for Christmas. It's been a busy year."

"Sounds like fun." He takes a sip of his beer. "Maren is out of town right now at a wedding. I'm just trying to get stuff done around the house while she's gone."

"The house looks great!"

"Yeah. We've been doing a lot of work on it lately."

"I hope I own a house someday. I'll have to find a woman with great credit, though!" Andrew laughs, and I feel good just talking to him.

"How's your project going?" He broaches the topic diplomatically, and I can understand why. My project is what created the need for this "reunion" in the first place. I think for a moment before answering. I want to be as thoughtful and intentional with my response as I can be.

"It has changed me and my life—and my faith. This year has taught me more than I could have ever anticipated, and the whole thing has been humbling. To say the least."

"What do you think is the biggest change this year?"

"So far, the thing I've learned is that this experiment has less to do with being gay than it does with people in general. I always felt superior to anyone who didn't believe as I did, but now I'm seeing that that mindset really is dangerous. I've learned that gays and lesbians aren't anything like what we've always been taught. They are every bit our equals. For instance, I have friends here who have deep, fruitful relationships with God. Before, I didn't think it was possible."

"You've met gay Christians?" He seems puzzled.

"Let me tell you about a few of them, and about the night that really changed my life." I pull out my laptop and open up the file that has all of my pictures of the year. He moves next to me on the couch and I start telling him about some of the people I've met.

And he listens. He sits and looks at the pictures and asks the occasional question, and he listens. I show him the picture of Jesus in drag, and he seems fairly shocked. I pat his back and tell him I understand. My brother may never agree with the things I tell him about my friends and their impact on my life, but he doesn't discount any of my stories. He just asks questions and listens as I tell him story after story after story.

"You know, the hardest part of coming out was lying to you." I look at him in the eyes and take a deep breath. "I vomited outside, after telling you."

"I just wish you'd told me the truth all along."

"I couldn't, though, man. I had to try to understand the fear that people feel when they come out to their families. I had to open myself to the possibility of rejection from *my* family. But you've got nothing to worry about. If I were really gay, I would've been blessed by your response. You loved me through it, and it meant a lot to me."

"I'm sorry we haven't talked, but you've got to understand where I'm coming from. Maren has been a part of the family for two months and her brother-in-law comes out, and then several months later she finds out it's a lie and sees how it hurts me. She was angry, and I was angry, and we needed time to process things."

"I get it. I really do. I can't apologize for my experiment, but I am truly sorry you were hurt."

"And I'm sorry if I made you feel like I didn't care about you when I thought you were gay. I really didn't know how to process your coming out. I don't think any of us knew how to process your coming out."

"I know you may not want to hear this, but that is because of the religious system we've been captive to for so long. I'm not trying to preach to you, but I have gotten to see things, to witness firsthand how violent and hypocritical it is to claim to follow a God of love—and then treat family, friends, and strangers the way we do, because of our religion. It reminds me of the words of St. Augustine," I add: "'The Church is a whore, but she is my mother.'"

Andrew smiles at me. "You're growing up, Tim. You're really growing up."

"I couldn't be 'baby human' forever." Andrew and I laugh and raise a toast to Baby Human.

"I'm glad you came over," Andrew says, looking over at me. I can see the same relief in his eyes that I feel in my heart, and the burden lifts off of my shoulders.

"Me too, brother. Me too."

32 love never fails

I walk into the restaurant, excited to see Shawn. Reconciling with my brother was a paramount experience, and there isn't anyone I want to share the news with more than the man who has been there for me throughout this entire unorthodox journey. When I think of Shawn, I think of goodness. I see a beautiful man who has shared his life with me more than anyone else has this year—I daresay more than anyone in my life has—and I am thankful for him. Shawn has been my shoulder to cry on, an endless well of encouragement as I have struggled to overcome years of dogma and make sense of the chaos. He has been my protector and my teacher. He's been my pastor and my family, my dance partner and my drinking buddy. He has been more than a friend. In every way possible, Shawn has been my better half.

A few days ago I had another epiphany: My relationship with Shawn has been the most stable, functional, and healthy relationship I have ever had. And as I've considered that fact, part of me wishes that things were different and that I could be with him legitimately. It will never be a reality; this relationship evolving into something more, for very obvious reasons. No matter my esteem, I cannot look at Shawn in the way that would be essential for us to be together, in the way he so deserves. I was born straight. He wasn't. It is a given…but somehow that still hurts, still gnaws at the spaces of my heart. If anyone has ever deserved happiness, it is this man who has sacrificed and served me as a friend, while I sought the answers to my prejudice. I would have been lost without him on this journey.

I see Shawn sitting at a table, looking at a menu, his gentle posture and relaxed demeanor a trademark of his being. He's wearing a dark blue button-up shirt, nice jeans, and an unassuming gold chain around his neck. His hair has been cut, and he is freshly shaved. As I get closer to the table I can smell his cologne, which is somewhere between a masculine citrus and an outdoor, earthy pine. He looks at me. He looks at me and recognizes *me*—in a way so few ever have. I feel a heaviness in my soul, heaviness that I do not understand.

"Hey there, beautiful!" Shawn stands and hugs me, wrapping his arms around my shoulders, enveloping me. He holds me with more purpose than usual, as though he's trying to hold onto this moment, as though it might be the last time for us.

"You smell good," I say, my cheek pressed against his upper chest.

"I wore it just for you," he says flirtatiously.

I look into Shawn's eyes and something feels *off.* His expression, outwardly positive, masks something else, and it unnerves me as I sit down and scoot my chair in closer to the table. It is not the look a friend gives another friend. It is the forlorn look of a lover. It's a look hinting at the unrequited, hinting at something hidden but about to boil to the surface. I feel unsure, like I know what's about to happen yet naively hope for something else.

Shawn reaches across the table and grabs my hand. He has reached out this way a thousand times before, but I feel an urge to pull away. I have never felt the urge to pull away before. There has always been the agreement, the understanding that what we can be is limited. But the line of understanding dividing us feels muddled and broken now, and I know everything between us is shifting off track. I have had this same feeling before, this same prediction of loss…but never with a man. Never with someone like Shawn.

"Are you okay?" I almost mouth the words because I know something is very wrong, that my dear, sweet friend is struggling.

"Of course…Do I seem like I'm not fine?" Shawn's voice betrays a soft frustration.

"Something just feels different, off somehow."

He looks at me, and I see emotion welling up in his expression. He looks like he's in pain, and I so want to help him with that pain—except I can't. Deep inside, I know I am the root of his pain. I do not know why, or how, or what has led us to this point, but I can feel the wrongness inside of me, and the guilt. Earth-shattering, life-changing guilt. I may not have lied to Shawn about my orientation, but honesty has not prevented pain. His face…I see it in his face, in his eyes, I see it in every bit of soul behind those eyes. I am to blame for this.

Shawn doesn't speak. He doesn't need to.

"It's me isn't it? It's our arrangement…It has gotten too real." I hold back a tear from falling and feel shame. It is the first time in my life that I have felt this kind of shame, because, I think, it is the first time that I have hurt someone so pure and so dear as the man sitting across from me. But Shawn knows me too well. He reads my expressions as I have read his. He squeezes my hand and cuts me off before I say anything else.

"It isn't you, Tim. You were always up front with me, always honest about this thing. I guess I just let myself get carried away. This has honestly been the best relationship I've ever had…and go figure, it's with someone that I've known all along I can't have."

I shutter and let out a breath. His words confirm every fear inside of me.

"Tim, it isn't your fault. Don't ever blame yourself for this. What you are doing is brave, and I have been so happy to be a part of it. I am so blessed to have been a part of it. Really and truly."

"I don't know what to say." I don't. I do not have a clue how to put words to the feelings of sadness and gratitude I feel. I want to tell him so many things, but it isn't the right time. Right now, no words would do justice to the pain Shawn feels. I fidget with my free hand, thumbing the black rolled napkin that holds the silverware. "What's next?" I ask, voice shaking.

"Well, I think we should enjoy our last dinner. And then I need to take some time. I have to protect my heart and figure all of this out. We'll still see each other around, I'm sure…just not like this. Not like this." His words trail off into a whisper, and we are both left in silence, him holding my hand, and me wishing, for the first time in my life, that I could make him happy.

After dinner I struggle to say the words, to speak the truth. I have to. I can barely even say them for fear of making things worse, but I want Shawn to know he wasn't alone in this. I want him to know that this was real for me, too—just not in the ways that would make us possible.

"Do you remember that first night at the bar when I told you about my experiment?" I ask, my tone solemn.

"Yes, I do."

"That was the first time I looked at the men around me as *men*, not as gay men. I don't know how you did it or why it happened the way it did, but yours was the heart that showed me how backwards I was. In the entire time we've known each other, I would have never been able to predict that the best relationship I've ever had would be with a guy. I'm fucking straight, for Christ's sake! I guess what I'm trying to say is that it takes a pretty special guy to make a straight guy wish he was actually gay. You have no idea how much I wish I could be that for you. It breaks my heart knowing you're hurting."

Shawn doesn't respond with words. Instead he wraps his arms around me, like before, with a sense of urgency and purpose. In our embrace, we both struggle to let go. I feel a tear slip down my cheek, and I know I am not the only one. We are stuck in this moment, stuck in the raw emotion of it. We are stuck in future nostalgia, knowing that we will both look back on this and smile, and not just smile but feel the deep melancholy when we remember that this faux relationship grew beyond anything we could have foreseen. This is not the end of a fake relationship. This is as deep a breakup as I have ever experienced.

I have finally learned a lesson. I would do this entire experiment again just to stand in the presence of this man, my friend, and to feel the warmth radiating through me because of his overwhelming love. I have never felt such love from another human being. There is a stirring of thanks within my soul that softens the parts of my heart that religion made so callous. Shawn has been Jesus to me. He has proven that love is something I cannot limit to an orientation, and that sex is not really the ultimate goal of anyone with a pulse. *Love is. Otherness.* And while we all have our baggage and our pain, and love may seem impossible or out of the question, the need for it is still always there, that irresistible need makes us human. Maybe that is the reason why I Corinthians 13 ends the way it does, with three simple but divine words. Three words that are the answer to most of our problems on this beautiful blue planet. Three words that make faith so beautiful. Three words that I understand now—because of Shawn.

Love never fails.

Period. End of story.

Love. Never. Fails.

Shawn's arms relax, and as I am released from his embrace I feel parts of me falling away. It is an avalanche of the soul that I owe to this one man, this lone angel of goodness whom God has brought into my life to make me a better person. I feel born again yet vulnerable, and better because of him. I am more myself than ever before, more confident in my life's journey. I have always believed in higher callings, divine journeys that we are given to undertake so that we can learn or unlearn whatever will be essential for us to reach our potential. This calling of empathy is the highest I have ever known. To empathize is to understand intimately; and what could be more profound than understanding, even if only in a small way, the hurts, joys, victories, and defeats of another? This is why Jesus is my hero, and this is why Shawn is now too. Shawn taught me how to do this. I owe him for it.

Shawn says a simple goodbye and kisses me on the cheek. And as he pulls away and turns to walk from the restaurant and from me, I feel a wholeness in this experience. I feel a small measure of peace that I didn't before tonight. While it is only a small piece of a much larger puzzle, it is an important piece. I take a deep breath, turn away, and walk towards the park. I need to sit on the bench by my favorite statue, look up at the lights of the Parthenon, and process this entire experience. Even though I am alone, I know now that I'm not. I possess a part of Shawn's heart, the most intimate gift he could give—and it will always be with me, because love never fails.

Love never fails.

Love never, ever fails.

33 freddy, please

Spending the holidays in Missouri isn't my first choice, even though it has presented me with the blessing of seeing extended family I haven't seen in several years. But I have to do it. I have to do it because one of the last pieces of this beautiful puzzle is an opportunity I never thought I would have: Visiting Westboro Baptist Church in Topeka, Kansas.

Westboro Baptist has become notorious in recent years for its outspoken protests at the funerals of soldiers and spiritual leaders. Even more deplorable than the act of protesting a funeral are the methods they use to do it. "God Hates Fags" and "God Hates America" are the two most recognizable slogans one sees Westboros carrying as they exercise their First Amendment right. Even though they've been featured on news programs, documentaries, and movies, I need to see if they will speak with me.

In March I found the church's phone number online. It was on a list of organizations most likely to be prank-called, and I decided I'd see if the number was legit. The voice that answered was a young man's, and before I could even say hello, I was met with the most defensive tone I've ever heard. Go figure. The number of phone calls they receive in a day probably trumps the number most mega churches receive in a month. And almost all of them are combative, I'd imagine.

"Is Fred there?" I asked meekly.

"No, he's not, but we wouldn't let you talk to him even if he was," the young man snapped.

"Okay. Who could I talk to about visiting your church?"

"Why do you want to visit?"

"Because I would like to learn more about what you believe."
I spoke as respectfully as I could, blocking out the images flashing through my brain of their signs. It took focus.

"Oh, well, you'd want to talk to Shirley, then."

"Is she in?"

"No she's at the hospital right now."

"That's not good. Is she ill?"

"No, she's fine. She's there because a family member is in labor."

"Oh, wow! Congratulations. Could you leave a message for her?"

"Sure." He seemed surprised by my sudden burst of positivity. "What do you want it to say?"

"If you could just tell her a guy named Timothy called to get info about the church, I'd appreciate it."

"Okay. I'll make sure she gets this." His tone was friendlier.

"Thank you, bro. I appreciate it."

"No problem. Have a great day!" he said.

"You do the same, my friend."

The change in the young man's tone from the beginning of our conversation to end was dramatic, an evolution more than an attitude change, and the interaction was convicting. It was convicting because even though Westboro's congregation is looked at as the most evil the Christian religion has to offer, they're still people. They still grieve, suffer, and celebrate joy as much as anyone else. My decision of whether to call back was a no-brainer after that conversation. If the young man playing secretary treated me decently, even if only in small talk, maybe the older members of the Phelps clan could do the same.

The next day I call back, and a woman's voice answered. From the interviews I listened to, I recognized it as Shirley Phelps, Fred's daughter; and just as the young man had been defensive, Shirley was even more so.

"Who's this?" she asked sharply after I said hello.

"My name is Timothy, and I called yesterday. Did you get my message?"

"Yes, I did—"

"Congratulations on the baby! Is he or she healthy?" I spoke in the most upbeat voice I had inside of me, hoping to break the ice like I had with the young man.

"Oh, he's healthy, and he's going to be another powerful voice for God!" She sounded combative but also conflicted, like she was trying to decide if my call was a prank or if I was genuinely interested in speaking with her.

"That's awesome! What's the little guy's name?" The silence on the other end of the phone lasted a few seconds, and I waited, hoping she hadn't hung up.

"His name is Ezra Joel, after the Old Testament prophet who knew the law like the back of his hand!" She held his name up, proclaiming it like the baboon in the *Lion King* presented Simba to the rest of the animals from atop Pride Rock.

"That's a great name! My mom named me Timothy, but I think I was named after a family friend instead of the Bible character…" I said. And then something both unexpected and beautiful happened. Shirley began laughing.

"Well, we can't all be as lucky as little Ezra!" Her laugh, albeit brief, was filled with something beautifully human. It revealed a heart that I never thought I would see—and it gave me hope that I might have made a good impression.

"No, we can't," I said with a laugh.

"So you wanted to get some information about the church?" Her tone became less personal and more business-like, and the brief window into Shirley Phelps' psyche closed.

"Yeah! I'd love to visit, if you guys are okay with that."

"Why do you want to visit?"

"I'm writing a book, and you guys present a pretty extreme view. I was hoping to hear more about why you believe what you believe."

"Because the Bible preaches God's wrath and God's hate as much as his love and grace! Why do you need to visit?"

"I'd just really like to, if that's okay with you."

"Well, I guess that'd be okay. You've got to understand, we have to be careful. People have tried to blow up the church in the past few years."

"What? Are you serious? That's awful!"

"The children of Satan outnumber the children of God." Her responses seemed rehearsed, as if from a script written from Levitical law. "When are you planning on coming?"

"Honestly, I don't have a clue; I am just hoping before the end of the year I'd get the

chance to come visit."

"Just let us know when you are coming, and we'll see you then!" Her voice became pleasant again, catching me completely off guard.

"Thank you, Shirley. I appreciate your time. Looking forward to meeting you in person!"

And as odd as it may sound, I actually was. I would love to have a conversation with the daughter of Fred Phelps. I would love to see if showing her even a small measure of respect would take the edge out of her voice for an entire conversation. I would love to see if showing her the love of Jesus will soften her heart towards me.

It probably won't make a difference, but it's worth a try.

~~~

So now I'm driving, crossing the state line from Missouri into Kansas, listening to Christmas music as I make my way to Topeka. It is an odd feeling to be driving into the heart of a church so many people deplore—and that I myself feel so strongly against. They have caused so much pain. The Phelps protested the funeral of Tammy Faye, the mother of my friend Jay, and the hurt and anger on his face when WBC is mentioned is eye-opening.

They poured salt in the wounds of a life-shattering moment, and Jay still feels the burn.

A few short months ago I realized I had become a Pharisee towards believers, and while I feel more balanced now than before, I need to know whether I am able to love everyone. *Everyone.* If I can't, this whole year is a wash. I think the thing I have learned best is that I really don't have a choice in who or not to love…even if they are the Phelps. This year has taught me that extreme hate is almost always born out of extreme fear, and fear is the product of insecurity and abuse at the hands of cruelty. And if that is true, then Fred and Shirley are either beyond crazy or just beyond terrified.

I told my friends and family I was going to visit Westboro, and all of them seemed afraid, their apprehension apparent in their responses. My mom asked me not to go, and my friends asked me to take someone with me: "If those people are audacious enough to wave signs like that around a bunch of soldiers' families, they're audacious enough to hurt you."

I declined both suggestions.

And as I pull into Topeka, I notice something on the directions that I missed when I printed it. The zip code of Westboro Baptist Church is 66604. Some might call this a coincidence, some an omen, but I call it divine irony.

The Pharisee looks over at me and smiles. Even he disagrees with Westboro. The Phelps are the furthest extreme on the religious spectrum, and their theology of God's hate and wrath are disgusting to even the most ardent fundamentalists.

Do you honestly think they are going to let you inside? You've got earrings, and you are a big guy. They are going to see you as a threat.

I hope not. I'm coming in peace.

They don't know that.

I've got to try.

Do as you must, but don't say I didn't warn you.

I drive down the street and park my aunt's car. The church is bigger than I expected, much bigger. I see a huge banner advertising their new website: *Godhatesamerica.com* it reads, in huge bold, red letters.

I make my way to the corner of the sidewalk to get a better look, and I see a traditional church sign that would usually announce service times and church updates. With the exception of the name, it's empty. It is empty because it has been vandalized, and the message written with red spray-paint reminds me of the banner on the front of the church. It shows me that there is a little Phelps inside us all, because it reads *God hates the Phelps!*

If I believe that God is a God of love, I cannot pick and choose the objects of that love. God *even* loves Fred Phelps. I wish I had paint thinner and a scrubber. I wish I could take down the *God Hates America* banner too. All of it makes me sick because both messages are untrue, equally untrue. I do not care how closed off Westboro is; the iron gates and wood fencing are nothing more than a piece of the image they want to portray.

Making my way back towards the side of the building, I find and opening in the gate, walk to the door, and attempt to open it. It's closed. I push the bell and knock a few times. No one answers. I knock on the door again and ring the bell next to the frame and listen. Nothing. I hear nothing and feel a sense of defeat. I have driven the hour and a half from Kansas City for no reason, and won't get the chance to talk to anyone. And then I hear muffled voices, arguing inside the door, and it opens, revealing a woman. She is not like any women I have ever seen in church growing up. She is dressed in old-fashioned clothing, and her head is covered.

"Hello!" I say, grinning from the excitement that I am finally face-to-face with someone at the church.

"What are you doing here?" the woman asks sharply.

"I spoke with Shirley and told her I would be visiting. Is she here?"

"Go away! You aren't wanted here!" She snaps at me like a dog snaps at an intruder.

"I love your head covering. Very traditional!"

"Get out of here, you little shit!"

"So you cover your head but you curse at visitors? Not as traditional as I thought." I take a step back and turn sideways, trying to speak through my body language. "Shirley said it was okay for me to visit. I spoke to her after Ezra was born." I drop the name, hoping it'll give me some credibility.

Another door to my right opens. It's the door to the sanctuary. Another woman pokes her covered head outside. "Leave, or we are going to call the police!"

Her words surprise and amuse me. "I was invited here. Could you please let me talk to Shirley?"

"Listen, you child of Satan…Go away!" says the woman in front of me.

"My mom always used to call me that. She'll be pleased to hear it confirmed by someone else." I don't think she appreciates my attempt at humor.

"Fine, have your way. You can talk to the police about it," says the woman to my right.

"I just want you to know, even though you guys are speaking to me this way, I love you. And that vandalism on the sign outside isn't true. God loves you too."

I notice the Pharisee is watching both women as I speak, shaking his head in frustration.

"We know he loves *us*! It is *you* he doesn't love."

"I've been told that before"—I think of my old hall-mate Patrick. These women said exactly what he said to me when I came out—"and I know it's not true."

"Get out of here, you little bastard! We are having a meeting, and you aren't allowed in."

"Why didn't you say so?" I smile and speak lightheartedly again.

"We've called the police. Repent of your evil! Are you a fag?"

"As a matter of fact, I guess I am." I've never been so proud to be associated as gay.

"Your deplorable sin is going to damn you to hell for an eternity. Repent and accept the fire," says the woman to my right.

"So even if I repent, I'm damned? Your God kinda seems like a dick." My response is emotional and reactionary. I have lost my objectivity and my grace, but it really is hard not to be a smartass in the face of such ignorance.

"You're the dick, kid!" The woman in front of me sneers.

"Can you just answer me one question?" I ask.

"What?" she asks.

"Why do you embrace hatred the way you do?"

"That's easy. Because the mighty and holy God of the word says that He hates sin and sinners alike. This nation is an abomination, and his wrath will pour out upon it in holy judgment."

"Well, I guess a visit may not really be the most appropriate thing for me at this point, but I want to tell you something. You represent everything I am against, but I do love you, and I hope that the Lord opens your eyes to the true message of the gospel. I hope it saturates your hearts and that you find peace…because you will need supernatural peace when you realize how many people you have hurt. Merry Christmas."

"Don't presume to teach us about God, faggot."

And just like that, both doors slam shut, and I am left in the quiet winter morning once more. I walk back to the car, slowly. The Pharisee is in front of me.

Those women were scary—like Kathy Bates from Misery *scary!*

No. Those women weren't scary, they were *scared.* God be with them.

I feel my heart breaking as I reach the car, and I turn to take one last look at the church.

I drive past the old church sign, the one that was vandalized, and I feel calm. God may hate sin, but God does not hate the Phelps. God does not hate anyone, for that matter. I drive away from the city with something inside of me missing. I have left a piece of my heart at Westboro Baptist Church, and I *will* pray God changes their hearts.

34 the ball drops

It is New Years Eve today, and I am sitting at the bookstore, formerly attached to what was Revive Café. I'm trying to capture and write down a few of the thousands of thoughts running through my head. It is comforting to be back here, to enjoy the vibe of the bookstore. Although this may be the last day of my year, it is the beginning to something else completely, something new and exciting and real.

My experiment has led me around the country and taught me to appreciate the people in my own backyard. Although I will miss my ability to blend into the community, it will be nice to be myself. Fortunately, "myself" has changed a lot this year. How could I not have? Every day I was confronted with new questions and new answers. I was inspired and encouraged, and as I look out at the bookstore and see people perusing the shelves, I am hopeful that I will be able to show these beautiful people just how much they mean to me.

I look over to the registers and see some of my old bosses. They are in good spirits, and I wonder how their view of me will change when they learn that I am not really gay. Will they be angry...or will they feel as though they have contributed to changing the life of someone, even though they weren't aware of it at the time? I hope they feel part of something special.

The couch I'm sitting on faces the back window, but I hear the small bell attached to the door ring as someone opens it, announcing arrival. The bell hasn't rung much since I've been here, but it's New Years Eve, so I doubt it will much at all today.

I wish you could see this place. I wish you could experience it the way I have experienced it. I wish you could understand the impact that this little establishment has had on me, and all that

I've learned while I was here. It is fitting that I am spending my last hours before the party tonight writing at this little store on Church Street. It is a stone's throw away from the places I spent countless nights, from this little gayborhood that I have called home for a year now.

The bell on the door rings again and I hear the familiar voices of Scott and Jason. They are in the middle of a conversation, but they stop and greet me as soon as they see me.

"Looking sexy, handsome!" Jason says, pinching my butt while he hugs me. Scott laughs at him and ignores the flirtation.

"How've you guys been?" I ask.

"We've been doing well. We're here with some friends from out of town who have been staying with us. Our house is clothing-optional…" Scott winks at me.

"You really should come over!" Jason says.

"Alas, I've already got plans, but we'll have to hang out soon. I have a lot to tell you two," I say, dreading the thought of what they might think of me when it's all over.

"Sounds like a plan," Scott says giving me a kiss on the cheek. "Sure you don't want to ring in the New Year with us?"

I kiss his cheek and smile. "Would that I could. Would that I could."

"Okay, kid. We love you!" Scott says, sighing.

"And we miss you terribly!" Jason adds.

"I've missed you guys too…a lot. You have no idea what you two mean to me." I feel teary-eyed and nostalgic. "Just know that no matter what, I love you both!"

"I love you too, Tim," Scott says thoughtfully.

"And I love you more!" Jason hugs me, and I smack his butt as we separate. "Ooh! Saucy!" he says, winking.

I sit back down on the couch and take a deep breath. Is this moment *possible*? Am I really going to miss being thought of as gay as much as I think I will this moment? I think I will, but only because of the relationships I have been able to have because of it. The sad fact in life is that labels really *do* divide us. They seem to dictate, in no uncertain terms, how we relate to each other as people. Labels serve as a barometer of sorts, how comfortable we will be in each others' presence…and I do not think I'll ever be as comfortably received again as I have been this year. I may be an ally. But that is just another label.

After another hour of writing I pack my things and put on my coat. I say goodbye to my old managers and make my way to the door. It's a moment I have thought about for a long time, a moment I have pondered as I walked under the blue-grey sky of Nashville, and it is every bit surreal as I dreamed it would be. I look back around the bookstore and take a deep breath. The door's opening rings the bell, and I feel content. I did all that I could here, and I let the place change me.

Cold air meets my skin and I shiver.

See you later, Church Street. You've been a wonderful teacher.

~~~

An hour passes before I arrive at the party at my brother and sister-in-law's home. It is the first party of theirs I am attending since we reconciled in October, and it seems fitting to know that as clock strikes midnight, I will be with the same people I was last year at this time. Everything has come full circle. I am happy that my brother and I are a part of each others' lives again. I park the car and look over at the Pharisee, who shows no sign of leaving.

It's been a year since you started this crazy thing.

It's been life-changing.

You've successfully become an apostate.

Oh, no. I've finally become a Christ-follower. But things aren't ending the way they should be ending.

Why is that?

Because of you. You're still here.

Yes, I am. You want me to leave?

I want you out of my life forever. And after seeing the things we've seen…How can you still be here?

That's a good question. I'll be here until I can't be here anymore.

I get out of the car and grab my things. This year has left me feeling emotionally constipated. Will things be different, come midnight? Will anything be different tomorrow, or the next day? I hope so, but I cannot say for certain.

The walkway to the front door is slick, but I make it to the door without slipping. Before I even knock, Maren answers. She hugs me, and I see two glasses of wine on the table. "How are you?" she asks.

"Good. I'm ready for midnight!"

"I bet."

Andrew comes out of the bathroom and gives me a big hug. "How's your day been?"

"It was good, really very good. I spent the last few hours on Church Street. It wasn't easy."

He nods his understanding. Things with my brother have gotten better lately. It was encouraging that he allowed me to share my pictures of the past twelve months with him. It showed me that he was trying to understand, and trying is all I can ever ask of anyone.

"What's the next step?" he asks casually.

"I've got to come out of the closet."

"How do you think people will take it?"

"I think most of my friends will react positively. There are a few I'm worried about…well, three people, specifically."

"You scared?" Maren says.

"Definitely afraid of hurting someone. I'm afraid of hurting someone and losing my friends."

As the hour passes, people begin showing up. They are the typical eclectic bunch that usually appear at my brother's parties. High school friends, college friends, church friends, couples, singles, family. And while spirits are high, everyone looks at me hesitantly, knowing that my relationship with my brother has been strained. Does it bother me? No. I've been in more stressful situations in the past eighteen months than these people can fathom. This is a party, and nothing stands a chance of flustering me more than the prospect of my re-entry into the label of straight.

I haven't written about it, but my first day at Revive Café, I purchased a necklace and have been wearing it ever since. It is a silver dog tag with the pride flag on it and a second tag with the Bear Organization's darker-colored pride flag. The Bears are an organization of burley gay men that socialize and raise money for charity. While I was a barista, I became a Bear Cub, and I got the second tag to add to the necklace. I have been wearing both silver dog tags around my neck all year, and they feel like part of my body. While I stand at my brother's side and talk with the various people coming and going, every few seconds I trace the outline of the necklace around my neck and think fondly of all the memories I've made this year.

The clock strikes 11:00, and I am taking everything in. I want to be present every second I have left. I want to know the feel of turning the key to my inner closet and letting straight Tim out again. I want to celebrate the ability to be who I am. As I think about how life will change, I hope it never goes back to how it was before. I am acutely aware and thankful for everything that being who I am means. It is empowering to know yourself and to be yourself, no matter how that affects your life with others.

And that is something I have learned to appreciate this year. My first coming out was daunting because I was going into the closet. This time around, I gain the freedom of being *me*. When someone comes out as gay, it is a pinnacle moment in his or her life. It is the moment when the decision is made to be who he knows he is, and to let the chips fall as they may. Will he face persecution from the mainstream? Yes. Will he risk relationships, friendships, and his standing in the family? Probably. But what good are those things, if you cannot be honestly you?

It takes courage to declare that you know yourself, and that you do not care who else knows it because *you* know it—and I admire that courage. It also takes an incalculable strength to live in the closet, and that is part of the journey, too. I would not have been able to live in the closet longer than I did. I am weak. My heart goes out to all of those who are not able to be open and honest about who they are, for fear of what they will lose.

I long for the day this issue is obsolete, the day that my friends do not have to feel like their lives are political. I long for the day when equal rights isn't a campaign issue, when the news won't run front-page stories about celebrities and news anchors coming out of the closet. Then maybe, just maybe, our focus will be on something meaningful, something we can eradicate for the better, like the sex trade, or poverty, or AIDS, or homelessness.

The countdown starts in one minute, and I hold my necklace in my right hand and a glass of champagne in my left. Everyone is hunkered around the television watching the ball drop in Time Square, and I think fondly of my time walking through Manhattan. I think of Soulforce, of Memphis, of Revive Café, and of my softball team, P3. I think of Shawn and Phil, Lance, Scott, Jason, Will, and Angela. I think of Mel White and of Elizabeth and Nicole. I think of everyone, and I wonder what they are doing at this very moment. I also think of Patrick and his judgments, and of the Phelps family. One is probably open-air preaching right now, and the others are probably picketing some televised event, saying that God hates all of us. I think of Samantha and Matthew, and I think of Brent. I think of Jesus in drag, and I say a silent prayer of thanks for her. I think of all the people and the faces that have become so powerful and beautiful in my life, the mental collage of inspiration that has made me a better man.

Ten. Nine. Eight. Seven. Six. Five. Four. Three. Two. One. The seconds passed like hours last year at this time, but time passes normally this time around. And then the host shouts,

"Happy New Year!" and the camera pans to Time Square where billions of confetti pieces rain down upon the thousands gathered for the festivities.

Everyone in the room begins kissing, hugging, and wishing each other a Happy New Year—but I stay in the background by the kitchen. I silently take a sip of my champagne and reverently take off my necklace. I don't have a girl to kiss this New Year, but I do not need one. I kiss the pride flag on my dog tag and thank God for the things and people He has shown me.

I hear my brother next to me.

"Everyone, I'd like to raise a toast in this New Year's moment to my little brother, and to the fact that he's made it through a very interesting experiment. To Tim, straight once more!" Everyone laughs and raises their glass, toasting me. Anyone who hadn't heard about my experiment by this moment in the party did when my brother toasted me. But they aren't who I am worried about coming out to…Oh no, the ones that I am will know soon enough. I look over at the Pharisee and he raises his glass.

Happy New Year.

Happy New Year to you.

I take a minute and walk outside to smoke a cigarette. I need to be alone. I need to be alone because the biggest limitation of my journey just made itself evident. I think back to my brother's toast: "To Tim, straight once more!" and to the laughs and cheers I received. Everybody will automatically accept me back. I am straight Tim, and my orientation is no longer a social stigma. None of my other friends will be so lucky. No one else is afforded this luxury. My experiment lasted a year; their revelations relegate them to a much different fate. We aren't a country of equals.

I wonder where I would be right now if I hadn't gone through with my year. What would I be doing? What would I believe? Who would I be? I'll never know, and I am glad to never know. This year has been the most transformative of my young life.

I take a few moments to celebrate the passing of the old year into the new, but the excitement is quickly replaced by a solemn realization. Before I can truly celebrate, I have to come out again, and this time I have far more to lose.

35 the beginning

I like to think of my few days back out of the closet with the image of a space shuttle getting ready to re-enter orbit after a prolonged stint in space. The long mission was successful, and the shuttle is returning back to the place where it can be repaired and cleaned up, where the astronauts can rest. But that metaphor works best because re-entering the atmosphere is the most dangerous leg of the mission, after taking off. I will be re-entering through people, via the lie I have told them or allowed them to believe. I only hope they will understand.

January first is a different monster, this time around. Much like last year, I go first to a café on West End to meet up with Josh. I think of this time last year, when I was being driven to Josh's house as an emotional basket case. It was a first step into an alien world. I go to the café knowing I might even see a few people who I'll have to break the news to. It is a daunting thought, but I have to resist the urge to cower from it. The Bible says the truth shall set us free, and while I have been set free from who I was, I have to make that final descent in order to come to terms with the means by which I entered this experiment.

I have received positive responses during the first two days after coming out straight. Angela, my retired transgendered runway-model friend, told me that she felt I had done God's work; and in light of her being a mystic who does not believe in any particular god, her desire to speak in language that is important to me meant a lot. Several other friends from the bar were shocked but adjusted quickly, and after sharing my background with them a little bit more, they were happy that I did what I did. My LGBT friends in Memphis—especially Beth, who is still mostly in the closet—were so encouraged and overjoyed about my revelation that they could barely contain their excitement. When I asked them why they were so positive after I had lied to them, they told me that it was a beautiful thing to know an ally who actually attempted to understand. It was a humbling series of conversations. Samantha Hasty, Mel's assistant, was also more than accepting. Not only did she accept me, we have become even closer. "Now I know why you flirt with me!" She said with a laugh. I know she will be a life-long friend.

Steve, a friend from the bar whom I hung out with on Wednesday afternoons and in the coffee shop most days, was shocked. As I told him, I braced for my first real taste of anger from someone I never wanted to hurt.

"So are you going to be writing about me and about our conversations, or any of the times I tried to flirt with you?" he asked me.

"Steve, anything we talked about is between you and me. I am not writing an exposé, I promise." My response seemed to satisfy his concern, and after an hour on the phone, he made it clear that he still very much wants to be friends.

I would like to write about every conversation and moment I shared with people in the weeks after my re-entry, but that would be another book's worth of chapters. Needless to say, I learned a lot from my friends after the fact, too. And it was all worth it, in the end—every moment of discomfort and every moment of humility.

Not one of my gay friends rejected me for lying to them. The more skeptical of them just asked me questions, but by the end of those conversations they were content with everything they had heard. Some bought me drinks, and some made me buy them drinks. Some asked me if I would ever consider "switching teams" for a night, to give "*it*" a try (If you've read the preceding chapters, it probably won't be too hard to figure out who); and to them, well, I politely declined the offer. And in the end, there are only three people I have had a hard time finding the courage to tell. They are the three people whom I am the most worried will be hurt by my news. Until I talk to them, I still feel like I am in the closet.

Telling them is the only thing left to do before I start the next chapter of my life. But for some reason, I can't bring myself to tell Will or Phil…and I am especially afraid to tell Ben. These three guys, in addition to Shawn, have been my mainstay friends from the gayborhood. And all three of them have been seriously taken advantage of and wounded in the name of Christ. Hell, *I* was one of the Christians who hurt Will before all of this, harassing him after he came out. What would I do if I told these three friends, and they didn't want to be my friend anymore? How can I live with myself knowing that I might be just one more person who caused them harm? I simply cannot move forward with my life until they know.

~~~

The mirror in the bathroom at my dad's house reflects the image of a young man, well dressed for the night but as nervous as I have ever seen him. It has been a little over twelve months since I felt this nervous, and I still don't know how to cope with it. I guess all that is left to do is leave. My car's engine roars to life as I turn the key in the ignition, and before I can second-guess my decision I am already on the road to Tribe. The Pharisee sits in the passenger seat, eyeing me with curiosity.

I pull into the parking lot behind Tribe, shaking. I know everyone is inside. Except for two slow afternoons, this is the first time I have been here in a month. I have missed this place, missed the ambience and the crowd. It really did become a home while I adopted the label of gay. I walk to the smaller bar in the second room to order a beer from Will, who runs over and hugs me as soon as he sees me.

"How are you doing? It's been a while!" he says.

"I'm doing well. Trying to decide if I want to move in the next few months."

"Oh, my god! I'm so jealous! Let me get you that beer and we'll talk about it," he says, retreating to the taps where he fills a pint glass with my usual.

He places the beer in front of me, and I take a sip, nervously deciding how I am going to tell him. I'm so nervous, in fact, that my sip drains most of the glass.

"Whoa, there! You okay?" Will asks with a smile.

"Will, we need to talk about something." I take a deep breath.

"Are you okay?" he asks again.

"I'm okay." I try to compose myself. "You know how I was before I came out, how dogmatically I tried to get in touch with you when you came out?"

"Yeah."

"A few months after that, I felt convicted by how I acted toward you, and because of a situation I had with another friend who came out. I realized I needed to question what I have believed all my life. So I tried to figure out what would be the most effective way to understand what it was like to come out, and how the label of gay would impact my life... I'm not gay, Will. I came out to my friends, family—everyone—so that I could try to understand. I came here tonight to say I'm so sorry that I deceived you in the process."

"You're not really gay?" he says. I can tell he's processing what I've just told him.

"No. I'm not," I answer. Will makes a mixed drink for another guy at the bar, and I take deep breaths. "I was a bigot. I needed to change. I don't know why I decided to do what I've done, but it felt like the only way…"

"So you came out as gay, so you could understand how it changes your family life and social life and faith?" His tone is even, and calm.

I don't know if he is upset or angry, or okay with what I did. I feel a pang in my heart and a sense of sadness come over me. I look down at my hands before speaking. I can't look him in the eye.

"Will, I am so incredibly sorry for lying to you this whole year. I feel horrible."

"Why? Why would you feel horrible?" He waits for me to look up so I see him smiling. I feel a small measure of relief. "Did it change you? I mean, honestly change you?"

"Yes, it did. I never understood *who* I was condemning before...or why it was I was condemning them. I am a different person now. A better person, I think."

"Then why are you sorry? Why would you apologize for taking the steps necessary to question and overcome your prejudice?" he asks.

"Because I love you and don't want to lose you as a friend!"

"Give me more credit than that. Did you really think I wouldn't accept you because you aren't really gay?"

"Will, I lied to you."

"We are all liars here. Most of us spent years in the closet, saying we were straight to everyone we loved. How is your lie any different?" Will smiles and fills another pint glass with beer. "This one is on the house. You have just made my night, so your beer is on me."

"Thank you." I'm still nervous and shaking, but Will puts his hand on mine and speaks softly.

"Tim, what you've done means a lot to me—and it will mean a lot to a lot of people. Be confident of that. I love you, too."

"I hope so."

"I'm surprised I didn't see through it, though. I thought my straight-dar was better than that!" We laugh and I take a few more deep breaths.

"I've got to tell Phil and Ben, still. Know where they are?"

"They're outside, smoking and talking as usual," he says.

"Thank you, Will. Thank you, thank you, thank you!" I grab my beer and walk towards the other room.

"You have balls of steel, my friend…" he says, flipping a dish towel over his shoulder as I walk to the next room.

I walk outside, and Phil is where I was told he would be. "Tim!" he shouts. "The prodigal son has returned!"

"How are you?"

"I'm great! Ben is in the bathroom," he adds, seeing me looking around.

"Phil, I need to talk to you, and I need to do it now before I lose my nerve or am able to talk myself out of it."

"Okay, honey. What's wrong?"

"Nothing, technically…I'm just afraid you'll be angry at me."

"Why?"

"I'm not really gay." I let my words sink in for a minute before telling him everything I told Will. His face registers shock, and he takes a deep breath as he listens. "I just wanted to tell you that I'm so sorry for lying to you, and that I hope you will still be my friend."

"Tim…I don't know what to say. Of course I'm still your friend, but give me a second to wrap my head around what you just told me." He takes a few deep drags from his cigarette and gulps from his drink. Finally he says, "I'm not mad at you. I'm overwhelmed by what you just said."

"I know it's a lot to take in."

"Yes, it is, but Tim, thank you!" A grin spreads widely across his face and he laughs. "You just proved to me that what I have always thought about you is true! To think, you cared so much that you'd make such a mess of your life, just to understand…I can't imagine." He puts his drink down, ashes his cigarette, and then walks around the small patio table to me and wraps his arms around me. "I love you, Tim, and I'm not angry. Thank you for telling me, and for doing what you did. I couldn't be mad at you. Other people will be angry at you, to be sure, but I know you, and I know your heart is so big."

"You know, you, Will, and Ben are the only three I hadn't told yet, because I was so afraid you'd be angry. I was so scared you would feel betrayed."

"You were worried about losing me? Wow…That means a lot."

Hugging Phil feels like hugging a family member. I feel tears in my eyes and try to compose myself, but it's difficult.

"I need to tell Lance, and then we'll all catch up!" I say.

"He's at the bar. See?" He points through the glass window. "Good luck!"

I begin that short but fated walk to Lance as though I'm just a few short steps to complete freedom. The Pharisee looks over, putting his hand on my shoulder, and scowls. His nasty expression reminds me why I want to be rid of him, why I want to live the rest of my life without his voice lending itself as something more than what it is, the voice of a cruel and critical part of me.

I arrived here believing my fears would be justified, but so far they haven't been. The three people I was the most afraid of are here, and two of them have shown me grace. Ben is all that is left between me and the end of this part of the journey.

That's it. Go ahead. You can do it.

What do you want from me?

How does it feel to know that you haven't had to face any retribution for lying to these people? Ease the conscience any?

I know the time will come. I know I'll face judgment for this.

And you will deserve it. But worse than any you're going to face is God's judgment.

Why do you take so much joy from condemning people for their actions? Why can't you just love people?

By telling you the truth, I am showing you love.

I always used to say that, but I was blind. Now you can leave me alone.

I set the glass down on a table and walk towards the bar. Ben's back is to me. He seems to be in conversation with the bartender. I look over and see Will watching anxiously from the other room.

"Ben," I say, putting my hand on his shoulder. He turns around and smiles.

"Hello, there!" he says. "I was just telling a friend about you the other day!"

"That's sweet, if it was good stuff!" I laugh nervously.

"Of course it was all good. So how are you?"

"Well. We really need to talk."

"Sure, babe, the floor is yours," Ben says, grabbing his glass. He takes a sip from the tiny straw and waits for me to talk.

"Ben, I need to apologize to you and tell you about who I really am."

"That sounds interesting. What's going on?"

"You are the last person to find this out, but not because I care about you the least. I've been terrified of telling you because I respect you and love you, and haven't wanted to lose your friendship."

"Honey, you don't have to worry about me—"

There is a real possibility that he will be wrong.

"I'm not really gay." I slap my hand over my mouth like I did after telling Andrew and Maren that I was gay. After a few seconds I lower it. Ben stands with a blank expression on his face and waits. A few seconds pass and I force myself to speak. "I was raised a religious bigot, and I knew that something was desperately wrong with me. I came out as gay to everyone in my life so I could try to understand the pain and stigma that is attached to the label, and for the past year I've been living in the closet as straight."

Ben says nothing. His face betrays no emotion. As the seconds pass, I feel my heart begin to race.

"I spent twelve months immersing myself in the community, questioning everything the church taught me, so I could see for myself, and to the greatest extent I could, understand how the label makes life difficult for anyone who lives with it. I am so, so sorry for lying to you. I am so afraid of hurting you or angering you. I don't want you to hate me."

I feel so much fear, and so much apprehension, so much guilt. Why doesn't he say anything?

Everything inside me is twisting and knotting as I wait for him to give me some sign that he is either angry or upset.

Silence.

He puts his glass down on the bar and breathes. I fear the worst.

Ben begins to cry.

Tears roll down his cheeks like shiny beads, and his lips quiver. He breathes heavily, but still says nothing. And then, as if in a dream, Ben lightly touches my lips with his hand and begins to pray:

"Lord, be with your servant, Tim. Inspire the words that come out of his mouth as he shares the reality of this news with the masses, and as he shares your love and your grace with the masses."

He slides his hand to my eyes.

"Lord, protect his eyes and what he sees. Help him not to see any hatred, but only love, as he sets out on this journey of grace."

His hand once again moves, to my ears.

"Lord, block his ears from hearing the hateful words directed at him from people in the religious community and from this one. Protect his ears from the words of hate that they'll inevitably speak."

His hand moves to my heart.

"Lord, thank you for this heart! Thank you for the sacrifices he has made. Lord, bless this beautiful heart with every power you possess. Help him *never* to change, Lord, to be jaded, to be hurt. I love you, Lord, and Tim loves you. Thank you for letting us love each other. Amen."

Ben pulls me into a hug…not just a hug, but an embrace. He holds me so tightly I can feel his heartbeat through his chest. I feel the wetness of his tears on my shoulder as they soak through my shirt. I feel his breathing and the shivers rocking through his body. He pulls away for a moment and looks into my eyes, which have filled with tears, too.

"Timothy, I have never in my life felt so loved by a straight Christian. You have just given me the ultimate gift. You are going to be a force of love and grace for this community, for to any community you become a part of." He pulls me back into a hug.

I look around and I see a room of people staring. They are watching the exchange with interest. Then he lets go, we wipe our eyes and blow our noses on the small bar napkins, and we are silent. I look around the room again and something powerful happens, again. The Pharisee is nowhere to be found. He is gone. Something inside of me confirms that he's left for good.

"Who are you looking for?" Ben asks, his arm still around me.

"No one. Just taking it all in," I reply. I am free!

For the next three hours, Ben, Phil, and I talk. We talk about God, about our lives, about the experiences we have had that have taught us who we are, and about coming out. Lance prods me to tell my coming-out story as everyone in our circle has done. He tells me he feels it is every bit as valid as anyone else's coming-out story. For the first time in my life, I am standing in a gay bar, a straight and Christian man, and I am accepted as one of the group without a second thought. I have found a new home and a new family—one that I never imagined I would be part of. My cup runneth over.

Ben prayed over me, prayed for my safety and my calling; and when that happened, the Pharisee in me was overcome. I think the Pharisee left me because nothing is left to tie us together. For the first time in a long time, I feel whole. Not because my eyes have been opened to a "new way of life," because there is nothing new about this. *Love is the original way.* I also feel inspired because most of my fears were never realized. I was, in the end, accepted wholly and completely, as myself, by people who I have only this year learned to accept and affirm.

I leave the bar after tear-filled hugs and goodbyes, and I feel like a different person than I have been before...a better person. I think I am, for the first time, really following Jesus. The relationships I have formed along the way are a blessing. Nothing about life is easy, but walking in another person's shoes is essential, because only then can we live with and for each other the way we are meant to. *Ubuntu.* I am because you are.

I have learned something about labels this year. It is the journey that defines us, not the labels people try to associate with us. I am not gay Tim; I am not even straight Tim.

I am Tim, and in the end, that is all that really matters.

The Beginning

epilogue

My experiment ended, but it hasn't finished. I don't think it will ever finish because every day I am learning more about people and about myself.

I am sitting in a café in Southeast Portland, sipping a latte, and trying to decide what still needs to be said, and what is better left off the page. In the two years since coming out as straight, I am only now able to process everything that happened. Writing two drafts of this book has helped. As I wrote I was forced back into the memories of people and events that so radically changed me. I wrote about them and felt like I was back in Nashville listening to their stories and enjoying their company. Oddly enough I feel more capable of loving them now than ever, and I feel closer to them somehow, even with the distance.

Four months after my second coming out, I decided to leave the nest, once and for all. Nashville became too small, and leaving felt like the only tangible option. I packed up my Honda, and set out to Portland having never even visited the Pacific Northwest. It was the most therapeutic journey of my life, and my pilgrimage from the East to the West was a healing experience.

The friends that I made during my year have more than kept in touch. Shawn and I are closer than we ever have been. Weeks and months may pass in between conversations, yet somehow we know that the role we have played in one another's life has solidified into something beautiful, a life-long friendship. Likewise, my childhood friend, Will, has continued to be an endless source of encouragement, and seeing his face when I visit home is always something that warms my heart. I have been blessed by the honesty and trust we share. He has never held my experiment against me. If anything it has strengthened our bond, and I am honored to be a part of his life.

Lindsey Hawkins, aka Samantha Zander, is now married to her soul-mate, Jesse. She has become my mentor in non-violence activism, and every so often when we talk, I still facetiously try to convince her to have an affair with me. I know we will always be close, and that our paths will always run parallel. She has made me a better man and a better human, and no one has ever set a higher example of peacemaker for me to aspire to. And Elizabeth, my childhood pastor's daughter, has also become an unexpected sister. We met so randomly towards the end of my experiment, and I am thankful for that. She and Nicole married soon after my move to Portland, and both are flourishing in their faith and their marriage.

And then there's my best friend Josh. No one in my life has ever invested in me the way Josh has. Josh is my brother, and none of this would have happened if it hadn't been for his unyielding support, and endless encouragement.

My relationship with my family has also been reconciled. My mother, once an adamant conservative, is now an ally of the LGBT community. She and I have walked into this world of grace together, and her friendship is priceless. I love my mom. Her strength and passion for people is my North Star. It guides me and inspires me and I owe her so much more than I could ever hope to express.

Shortly after my move to Portland, my sister-in-law, Maren, gave birth to my first nephew, and I have never been as proud of my brother as I am seeing him as a dad. We have more than reconciled, we have bonded together as a family, and I still look to him as a hero and one of my closest friends. Our family has lived in a perpetual state of transition for the past eight years, but now, as things settle down, I am filled with gratitude. We have made it through so much, and I am thankful to God for his endless mercy.

In the past two years ve continued to immerse myself in the LGBT world. I've attended churches, both conservative and open and affirming, I have participated in Pride days and AIDS walks (where I still saw not one conservative, mainstream church presented), and my community of friends has never been more diverse. I am in tune with people, for the first time in my life. I feel the pulse them in the pulse of Portland, inside myself, and I am thankful that God has taught me how to love.

We live in a society that condones culture wars, and even proudly proclaims them, but as with any type of war there are casualties, and those casualties are not people we can afford to lose. The sanctity of human life that I have been taught about all of my life doesn't just apply to a fetus inside its mother's womb, it applies to all living and breathing men and women. It applies to me and to you. It applies to the murderer on death row, and the 5th grade school teacher that faithfully teaches children day in and day out. We don't get to choose who is made with the *Imago Dei*, the image of God, and we don't have the right to choose who we are called to love.

For years I have been living on a self-created mountain of moral absolutism, and thankfully my year taught me that that life is not what Christ has called me to. Since my year ended I have struggled daily with one question. *Where do I belong?* And now I feel I know the answer. As a Christ follower, I am called to live in the wounds that my mountain has created. It goes beyond living in the tension because it means living within the hearts of others, walking with them in the ever deepening of their pain, and if I am ever to fully emulate Jesus then I must live in the blood and gore that the church has created. That I created.

I have heard the question posed, at what point can one be an ally to the queer community? I think for me being an ally means that I must shift my focus off of my perceived moral imperative and live in community and relationship with all people. I must sacrifice and serve without the condition of labels, and without worrying how it will make me look. And while all of this may sound like the typical ranting of a now liberal Christian, I challenge you to see past those labels.

My mother said it best towards the end of my year. She looked at me and said in earnest, "I don't think Satan is just the father of lies, I think he's the father of labels." And I have to agree. I am Tim. After two decades of trying to define and categorize myself and everyone else around me, that is the only label that I choose to keep. It's funny how names are underrated. The world seems to be addicted to labels. Steve the lawyer, Josh the rapper, Renee the lesbian, Methodist minister...Every name has to be paired with something "greater", or more recognizable than itself. Before I started writing this book I always dreamed of being Tim the writer, and now that I have actually written a book, I think my name will do. Names are what this ended up being about. This has been my journey from Tim the writer, to just Tim. It's also how Steve the lawyer, Josh the rapper, and Renee the lesbian, Methodist minister became Steve, Josh, and Renee. I think that is all that matters.

As a Christian oftentimes people expect me to have the answers, and in my pride I'd like to think I do—I can't help it, I was raised Baptist—but there are certain things I'll never have an answer for.

I may never again be confident that my truth is absolute, and I doubt I will ever be able to take definitive stands on certain ideas that seem to divide everyone else. There are issues that conservatives rally behind, and those outside the church rally against, and I may never be one hundred percent either way. I will never understand how people that claim to love Christ can bully someone to death, nor will I understand why certain people among us allow their self-destructive natures to guide them towards a reckless abuse of alcohol, power, or sex. I will never understand hate and the many forms it takes. It is a cruel shapeshifter, and an evil master.

All said, there are a few things I am sure of, and in the context of my own life I feel blessed. I am sure of love, of the radical and unyielding power it holds, and I'm sure of the barriers it can overcome. I am sure of relationships, especially those fueled by love, and sure of the prejudices that relationships can overcome. I am sure of my God, who I believe more than ever sent his Son for me, and I am sure of the reconciliation he offers, whether that be between families split apart over divisive issues, or members of opposing political parties. I am sure of the beauty that all mankind has inherited—a beauty that can never be stripped away by bad words or deeds, or even other human beings—and I'm sure of arrogance, and its ability to poison anything that can be called good. Most of all I am sure of my teacher *empathy*, who taught me that if we take a moment to step into another person's shoes before we open our mouths, we can learn more about this life and our God, than by any other means. She is our greatest tool, operating hand in hand with love to create something dazzling, something that gives our breaths meaning.

Until this year I never quite understood why the LGBT community adopted the rainbow as a symbol for its existence. Diversity, unity and promise, a rainbow is said to express these ideals, but I believe it was chosen for an entirely different reason. I believe it was chosen because, above all else, a rainbow is beautiful, and everyone desires to be thought of as beautiful. For years I've lived color-blind in a world of rainbows, ignorant to the beauty all around me. And for the first real time, the words from my favorite hymn have meaning and are alive to me. "*I once was lost, but now I'm found, was blind but now I see.*" Maybe beauty really is in the eye of the beholder, and whether or not we see it is the choice. Maybe it is the only *choice* that matters, after all.

acknowledgements

Mom, I love you. For teaching me how to read and write and encouraging me when I felt unable to continue. For your strength and grace, and your example throughout my life. For your love of others. Thank you. To my wife, whoever you are, I cannot wait to know you. You've been with me all of my life and I yearn for the day *us* happens. To the rest of my immediate family, thank you for putting up with me. God owes you a good bottle of wine, or maybe a nice vacation. I know it hasn't been easy at times, but your love keeps me going. Andrew and Maren, thank you for giving me two little nephews to corrupt! I promise to teach both of them everything I know about beer, cigars, and the great subversives that are my heroes.

To Joshua, my "Jonathon," my beloved friend: You have never let me down, never let me feel alone, and never allowed me to give up. You not only pushed me into this mess, you also dove right into it with me. Now it's your turn. I dared ya.

To John Harrison, my dear brother and first reader when I had no publisher or tangible idea how this book might make it onto the shelves, your encouragement is the reason I kept writing. I love you, brother! To Connie, thank you for adopting me into your family. I never knew I could have a second family and I owe so much to you. Thank you for continually talking me off the proverbial ledge while I wrote this book, and thank you for encouraging me that my writing "isn't terrible." To my mentor, Chad Estes, I am so thankful for you. To Kari Sherwood, for being an ever vigilant friend and for taking me to Portland Zoo! I am so thankful for you. To Shawn, you are the most beautiful man on the planet. Your heart is pure gold, and your friendship is priceless to me. Thank you for loving me as much as you do.

To Will, Shawn, Samantha, Mel, Jay, Becky, and every other person who taught me just how much bigger God's grace really is. I dedicate this book to you.

To Dave, my dear friend at Bluehead Publishing, thank you for giving me my shot. You made a dream come true, and you fed positivity and peace into me all along the way. To my editors, Charity and Isaac, thank you for turning a mess into something readable, and for helping me name this book. To Burke and the team at Allen Media Strategies, thank you for the invaluable support you've given as publicists. And I would be remiss if I didn't thank the owners and baristas of my three favorite cafés: Anna Bannanas, First Cup Coffee House, and Satellite Coffee. I spent countless hours writing and editing my book in these three little shops. They caffeinated me and encouraged me while I wrote, and I would never be awake if it weren't for them.

In June of 2012, I launched an Indiegogo crowd-sourcing campaign to fund the cost of my publicists, and in eleven days I reached my $8,000 goal. Not only did I reach it, but in the days to follow I surpassed it by almost $3000. People from all over the world stepped up financially to help me make this dream a reality, and to all of you from the United States, Australia, Ireland, Canada, and my angel from Wales, know that without you this road ahead of me would be a lot rockier. Thank you for your support and friendship.

Thank you: Analiise Salo ~ Benjamin Ady ~ Bonnie ~ Cassandra Perry ~ Daniel Puneky ~ David Barford ~ Jeff Abarta ~ John Atkins ~ Justin Throneberry ~ Kaan Williams ~ Manuel Lara Bisch ~ Megan Elliott ~ Michael Kazarnowicz ~ Michael San Miguel ~ Perry Ross ~ Rick Koelz ~ Scott "Gringo" Blair ~ Zachary Nawar ~ Sally Conning ~ Adam Buckheit ~ Adrienne White ~ Alfred C. Schram ~ Alysn Ford ~ Antonio Michaelangelo D'souza ~ Aylynn Marsh ~ Bryce Anders ~ Buck ~ Bud Wilson ~ Candice Reich ~ Chad Estes ~ Colin ~ Cynthia Coe ~ Daniel West ~ Darryl Yong ~

Dave Thompson & Corrigan Gommenginger ~ David Calkins ~ Deirdre Milligan ~ Douglas C. Sloan ~ James Saliba ~ Jamye Swinford ~ Jason Heffernan ~ Jaymie Ford ~ Jeffrey Yasskin ~ Jenée Arthur ~ Jesus Segura ~ JoÌÇl Larose ~ Joanne Goldsmith ~ Joel Guenette ~ John Mink ~ Jonathon Sehon ~ Josef Ottosson ~ Josh Yochem ~ Julie Quinn ~ Kara Lien Roberts ~ Kurt O. Richards ~ Logan Carlton Marston ~ Luke Vierboom ~ Lynette Petkov ~ Maria Kettleson Anderson ~ Mario Raul Jara ~ Mark Savage ~ Marq Hwang ~ Martin Eldred ~ Mary Courtney Blake ~ Matthew Doran ~ Melisa Wilkes ~ Melita Caulfield ~ Michael Lawrence Schwartz ~ Mike Raven ~ Miss Sophie Hume ~ Morgan McColum ~ Nathan Scott ~ Nicole ~ Patrick Curtain ~ Paul Karlsen ~ Paul Kinney ~ Pete Cooper ~ Remco Douma ~ Renio Uittenbogaard ~ RF Conway ~ Rhiannon Michell ~ Rodney Vincent ~ Rowan Dax ~ Rowena Knill ~ Samuel E. Goodwin ~ Scott Johnson ~ Shawn Hurst ~ Shirley Ostrander ~ Sonja Lisk ~ Stephen Cruz ~ Suzanne Patt ~ Talayeh Saghatchian ~ Terry Clees ~ Thomas Bartels ~ Tom Jasinski ~ Tyson Gene Peveto ~ Roger Steven Smith ~ Sally Conning ~ Beth Kavanagh ~ Dan Bold ~ Deborah Perreau ~ Eric Brandt ~ Ian A. M. Robertson ~ Jeannette Aracri ~ Kevin Hudgins ~ Kirsti Reeve ~ Kristy McAllister ~ Leslie Johnson ~ Lisa M Campbell ~ Marie Linders ~ Matthew Billingsley ~ Natasha Roussel ~ Nathaniel Keifer-Wheals ~ Sally Conning ~ Suzanne M Wonder ~ Juliana Claro Mourisca ~ Conley & Kate Black ~ Peter Musser ~ Andrew Taylor ~ Brian T. Kelley ~ Elizabeth Chapin

about the author

Timothy Kurek, a Portland, Oregon based author and speaker is tackling some of the front burner issues of our day. His unrestrained style of immersion lends a uniquely empathetic perspective, engaging his audiences with empathy, humor, and refreshing candor.

contact info

For information about Timothy Kurek, or to book him for speaking engagements, please visit:

timothykurek.com

If your book club of ten or more would like to speak with Timothy free of charge, please contact:

info@timothykurek.com